Black Gauze, Prum
bs, Black Gauze, For

te hier und   Brau
un-curl tne   fair

William Forsythe, <u>Artifact</u> *Dieter Schwer*

Valerie Preston-Dunlop
Ana Sanchez-Colberg

with essays by
Frank Werner
Paula Salosaari
Sarah Rubidge

dance
and the
performative

a choreological

perspective ~

Laban

and beyond

**DANCE
BOOKS**

First published in 2002 by Verve Publishing, reprinted in 2010 by Dance Books Ltd.
The Old Bakery, 4 Lenten Street, Alton, Hampshire GU34 1HG

A catalogue record for this book is available from the British Library

ISBN 978-1-85273-142-7

Editor : Valerie Preston-Dunlop
Design : Glenn Hilling www.GlennHilling.co.uk

Typeset in Joanna and Trade Gothic

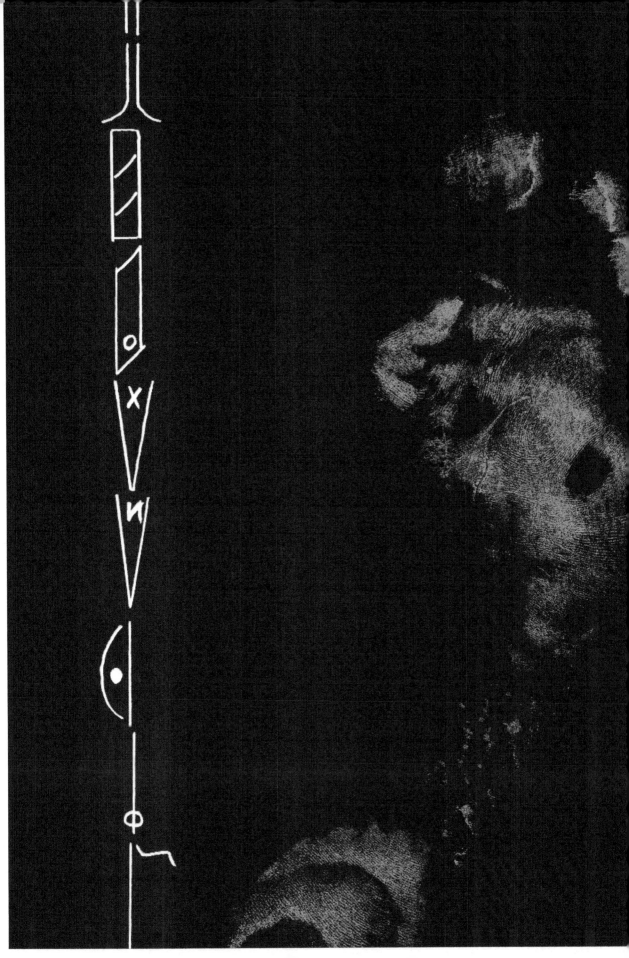

acknowledgements

Valerie Preston-Dunlop, as editor of the book as a whole, and
Ana Sanchez-Colberg, warmly acknowledge the support of the
following: Marion North, Principal of Laban Centre London,
for long term support and encouragement of dance practice
as research and of the application and development of Laban's
principles for dance as theatre; William Elmhirst, for support
for the project through a grant from the Dorothy Whitney
Elmhirst Trust; Glenn Hilling for his inspirational design
concepts for the book as a whole; William Forsythe for his
generosity is allowing an image of his company Ballett
Frankfurt as the cover of the book; Sarah Rubidge, Paula
Salosaari and Frank Werner for their generous collaboration;
All the choreographers, artistic directors, archivists and
photographers who have generously given images and
permissions for the visual design of this book without which
our endeavour to prioritise practice would have been frustrated;
Victoria and Albert/Theatre Museum Picture Library staff and
Phil Karg at the New York Public Library Dance Division
photographic services for assistance in locating and obtaining
permission to use illustrative materials from their collections;
Ralph Cox and the Laban Centre London Library staff for
generous assistance with search facilities; Diane Parker, assistant
editor of Dance Theatre Journal, for academic editing of the
text; Alex Beech for assistance with data on Transitions Dance
Company repertoire; Dorothy Madden for perceptive comments
on each reading of the text as it progressed and assistance with
the labour of indexing; Rona Sande for a dancerly eye on the
content; Anita Donaldson for assistance with the rigorous task
of proof reading; mutual acknowledgement by Valerie Preston-
Dunlop and Ana Sanchez-Colberg for years of stimulating
collaboration and studio work towards their proposals for a
choreological perspective on dance praxis in all its forms.

contents **part 1**
a choreological perspective
Valerie Preston-Dunlop and Ana Sanchez-Colberg

contents **part 2**
current modes of enquiry in choreological practice

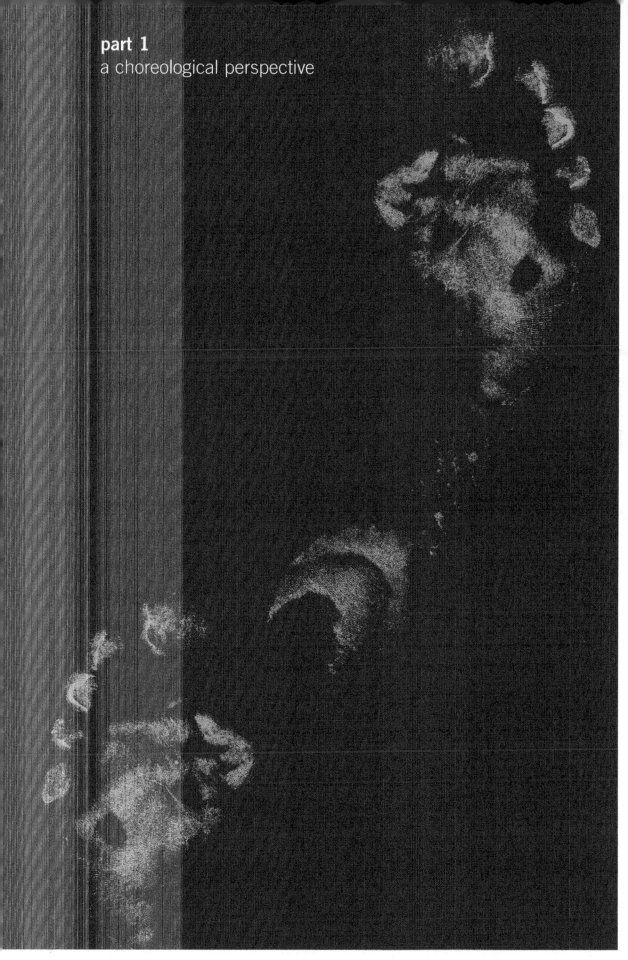

part 1
a choreological perspective

Kathleen
Ed Wubbe
Scapino Ballet Rotterdam
Hans Gerritsen

chapter 1
introduction

This book articulates the dynamic with which a practitioner-based research has grown, is growing, and is applied, integrating the three concepts in the book's title: the ontology of performative dance, discussed through a choreological perspective which has developed out of and beyond the seminal research of Laban.

Performative events are ones in which 'actors' and 'spectators' engage in an exchange of some sort. While 'performing' refers to the implementing, presenting and accomplishing aspects of an act of theatre, performative refers to "an expression that serves to effect a transaction" between the parties (Merriam-Webster, 1993). Performative events range from works of dance theatre to a speaker haranguing a crowd, to a silent anti-war demonstration, to a digital interactive installation, et al. The title given to this book embodies the thrust of its focus: an investigation into the nature of dance as it intersects with the concept of the performative. While all dances are potentially performative some performances address their spectators minimally laying emphasis on what is being presented and by whom. Others deliberately address their spectators, aim to and do arouse a response so that engagement and transaction take place. Some events go further so that the work itself is generated by both the artists and the spectators, who cease to be spectators and become interactors and co-authors.

In order to debate and articulate this focus a choreological perspective is used. Choreology, as a general term, is regarded as the scholarly study of dance. The term was first introduced by Rudolf Laban in 1926 in the curriculum of his newly opened Choreographisches Institut (Maletic, 1987). His purpose was to establish a culture in which dance scholarship, as theoretically sound practice, could develop alongside and intermingled with the making of dance theatre works. Laban regarded himself as 'an artist/researcher', not separately but concurrently, his outcomes being sometimes an advance in understanding dance and movement, expressed in a book, an article, a workshop or a lecture, and sometimes through the

the focus

choreology, Laban and beyond

creation of a choreographic work that embodied his understanding. Existing methodologies from associated areas, especially music, theatre, the visual arts, and anthropology were not forgotten, but the discovery of methods peculiar to dance was his focus. He introduced three divisions to his dance-specific choreological research: the search for adequate analysis of movement to create a notation of it (Tanzschrift), the interaction of the body with space, choreutics (Raumlehre) and the dynamically expressive body, eukinetics (Rhythmiklehre), his prime method being his obsessive observation of the moving person from which he developed an understanding of the hidden laws of human movement. Until his death in 1958 Laban continued to refine his theory/practice of the spatial forms in movement (Laban, 1966), referred to variously as choreutics, shape, space harmony and his theory/practice of rhythm and dynamics (Laban, 1971) referred to as eukinetics, expression, effort. Thereby he laid down the roots of dance specific theory/practice as well as dance documentation (Lange, 1985).

Since these seminal beginnings both methods of studying dance and dance practice have moved on. Dance has expanded through ballet, ausdruckstanz, modern dance, post-modern dance, physical theatre, tanztheater, performance art, et al. Choreology has developed and fragmented into specialist areas, notating and score reconstruction (Hutchinson, 1970; Knust, 1979; Benesh, 1969; Marion, 1990; et al), ethnochoreology for the study of dances and their particular ethnicity (Lange, 1980, 1984; Van Zile, 2001; et al), archeochoreology for the research into and recovery of lost dances (Liu, 1986; Hodson, 1996; et al) and choreological studies for the scholarly study of dance as a theatre practice. It is the latter that is the focus of this book.

The parameters of a choreological perspective on dance as theatre were first mooted in an internal paper in 1987 by Valerie Preston-Dunlop to facilitate the change of a study area at the Laban Centre London from Advanced Laban Studies to Choreological Studies. It had become clear that Laban Studies, advanced or not, could not account for current developments in dance as a theatre art, nor for the dance specific theories emanating from artists of a post-Laban era such as Merce Cunningham or Pina Bausch; and, that Laban's work included a range of applications, such as dance therapy and dance education, which were peripheral for the study of dance as theatre. The first doctoral research using 'a choreological method' for the study of dance theatre was awarded in 1992 to Ana Sanchez-Colberg. Since then, the honing work on core concepts has continued, as research at masters level and doctoral level, as well as choreographic research related to choreological thinking, has continued apace. Choreological study of dance as theatre has been introduced in conservatoire and universities through the international graduate body of Laban Centre London. The general mood in performing arts institutions towards the integration of theory and practice has strengthened in recent years so that a discussion of a choreological perspective is seen as timely.

Continuing in the tradition set up by Laban, both existing **practical scholars**
methodologies from culture studies and practice-derived
methods peculiar to dance are necessary since they interlock.
It is to the latter perspective that the articulation and debate in
this text contribute for it is the authors' experience as practical
scholars in the field of dance making and dance writing which
enables them to address the issues through the symbiotic
relationship of practice and concept.

The notion of studio-based research is well known to
choreographers. It is what choreographers engage in prior to
putting down a work. It is not necessarily understood by
academic scholars who have a particular concept of what 'research'
means and which some find hard to accomodate to practice.
Nor is it necessarily understood by those practitioners who are
not makers for whom the term 'research' refers to ways of
working not in their domain. However, practical people can and
do focus on a dance specific problem, and wrestle with it in
ways only available through practice to arrive at new movement,
new dance processes and new concepts. Time and again theories
researched in disciplines other than dance have to be interrogated
in the studio to discern their validity for dance practice,
resulting in confirmation, alteration, development or rejection.
Choreological methods aim to promote and enable practical
research by articulating and debating what is peculiar to dance:
its making, its performing, its spectating, its medium, its
choreographic treatments, its documenting methods, et al. The
organisation of this book details how these topics are addressed.

The choreological perspective accounted for here refers to dance **embodied**
as an embodied performative art[1], wherever and in whatever **performative art**
form that might occur, seen from the perspective of practising
professionals in that domain. Choreologists are scholarly, but
essentially practical, scholars in the sense of being practitioners
in one or more of the interlocking domains of dance.
Choreologists may be found practising as, and calling
themselves, choreographers, teachers, notators, reconstructors,
performers, historians; that is, in professions where corporeal
and verbal knowledge is integrated.

Choreological study locates dance within the field of theatrical **performative art**
performance; that is, performance that operates within a
theatrical framework organised by theatrical codes, in whatever
venue that happens to take place in a theatre, a cityspace or
cyberspace.[2] One form of dance manifestly operating within
this framework is tanztheater but it is by no means the only
one. Wherever engagement is set up between people (things)
performing and people spectating/listening/interacting in a
defined space, performative potential is in place. When the
spacetakes on the role of theatre space, a theatrical framework
and theatrical codes pervade production and perception.

---

[1] For a general discussion of performance and the performative, see Baumann (1989) and Kaye (1994).

[2] For a further discussion of 'performance', see Carlson, (1996); Kaye, (1994); and Schechner (1988). See also chapter 5
of this text on the plane of intersection of phenomenology and semiotics.

A theatrical framework sets out the physicality of a performance, in that people mount a work with the intention of it being watched and responded to. It also sets up that what is presented inhabits a world that is separated from the mundane. The space in which a theatrical performance takes place is liminal and ludic: liminal when it is no longer restricted by the rules of mundane behaviour but instead is open to one where another level of interaction takes place, one that is coloured by the virtual nature of what goes on in it. That change is palpable to the spectator. A space becomes ludic when the norms of imaginative play hold sway, where rules of action shift and alter, where participants 'play' according to rules of 'the game' they set up. Choreographers set the rules and in so doing provide the scenario for transformation of reality, and further, for a performative encounter.

Theatrical codes are entered into by artists and spectators alike. The expectation of being interested, moved, shocked, bored, or appalled, is present for an audience as soon as they enter the theatrical space. What distinguishes a performative event from a performing event is the level of and nature of the engagement of the artists with the spectators and, in response, the engagement of the spectators with them and with the work. Nigel Kennedy is able to transform a performance of a Bach sonata for violin and chamber orchestra into a performative event by the manner in which he behaves. He makes it clear that the customary 'rules' of Bach sonata playing are on hold by the manner in which he dresses, idiosyncratically, informally in boots; he speaks directly to his audience, and to his collaborative players; he lives the music, jumping and striding around the podium, lungeing at his cellist, eyeing his viola partner, turning his back on the spectators but engaging with his co-players. The audience sit up, pay attention, listen, feel, shout. They are not only performed to by the artists, they participate to make the event.

Lloyd Newson functions comparably, entirely in his own way. So do William Forsythe, Pina Bausch, Matthew Bourne… Through their own means they get the energy 'figure of eight' between audience and artists going. They turn a performance into a performative interactive event of dance theatre by making clear that the expected rules of dance performance are not in operation. Forsythe is known to start the performance before the audience is seated, Bausch is known to invade the auditorium with her performers, Bourne is known to shift the parameters of a classic, Newson is known to cast people not normally regarded as dance people. By no means all choreographers engage in those ways or want to do so. A choreological perspective starts from the position that the theatrical codes and framework which enable performative interaction to materialise may be in place, alongside a position in which performers perform and spectators spectate. The continuum between the two is appreciated, discussed and compared, and in choreological workshops is studied practically.

In trying to deal with the problems posed by embodiment, recent dance scholarship has adopted an inter/multi-disciplinary approach borrowing from methodologies in history, critical studies, feminism, linguistics and gender studies as a way to shed light on the issues of embodiment that relate to dance. Works such as Morris (1996), Desmond (1997) and Carter (1998) present a collection of the variety of writings which this inquiry has yielded. The focus in much of these writings has been to adapt, for the study of dance, methodologies and theoretical perspectives coming from fields outside dance. In so doing, an attempt is made to validate dance study as culturally significant and scholarly relevant. However, what most of these studies have revealed are the limits of this approach in its ability to solve the key problems of 'the body' in dance theory. The problem lies, for example, in the incompatability of movement with verbal systems, the inability of scholars to use movement's own symbol systems and notations, the non-transferability of a lived experience to the written word and the recognition of systems in operation in dance practice not accounted for, or ever accountable, by linguistic methods of signification.

Foster (1995) attempts to redress this imbalance by proposing that dance scholarship needs to reclaim the body of dance through the inversion of the usual glance. Rather than seeing dance through the established methodologies and perspectives, she proposes to see the methodologies and theoretical perspectives through dance. Similarly, Cooper-Albright (1997) proposes ways in which contemporary choreography and the dancing body 'confound' conventional assumptions about the body. Writers present the body 'as a passive surface' that is socially and politically inscribed or contrasted with the body as 'a natural phenomenon' essentially constituted and preceding cultural conditioning. Theirs is an attempt to go beyond a dance analysis which illustrates previously agreed theories outside of dance, and argue for a dance theory that comes from dance practice. Within this move, Desmond (1997) argues for the inclusion of an analysis of the 'textuality of the bodies in motion' (p.49). She proposes a re-evaluation of the special tools that will allow for the reading of 'visual, rhythmic and gestural forms'(ibid. p.50), traditionally referred to as a formalist perspective. For this she highlights the analytic systems stemming from Laban's theories of movement and space which have provided a first step towards a 'movement literature', a step which may help articulate aspects of the nature of embodiment in dance. Desmond in fact argues for a synthesis of what is normally defined as a 'formalist' description of the work's surface with perspectives on its cultural context. Jordan (in Morris 1996) supports this view, arguing that it will help 'contribute to the understanding of the broader picture' of what dance is (p.15). This is precisely where the authors of this text locate their enquiry. This is the springboard from which choreological study functions.

1980
Pina Bausch
Tanztheater Wuppertal
Gelt Weigeet

chapter 2
core concepts of a choreological perspective

2.1 embodiment and corporeality

Dance practice is one of embodiment. It will be shown that in dance scholarship in general, developments have located the specificity of embodiment to research in dance, and that these new perspectives have identified how scholarship that focuses on embodiment poses a challenge to other forms of critical analysis. Embodying is a practical process not necessarily compatible with verbal language.

Embodying is a process which gives tangible form to ideas. It is also a process by which the ideas dormant in practice emerge. In dance, it fuses the ideas with the movement and with the performer of the movement. Indeed, embodying a dance work fuses all the participants in the event in a multilayered tangible process. Tangible form emerges in sound and sight in a variety of media particular to each performance and each event. The embodiment of movement by performers is a more complex process than the word suggests. It is more than getting movement into the performers' bodies, more than their physical muscle, bone and skin. Embodiment of movement involves the whole person, a person concious of being a living body, living that experience, giving intention to the movement material. It involves perceiving oneself in the space and hearing one's sound, with kinaesthetic awareness of creating and controlling the movement.[1]

embodying as a process

Embodying a dance technique requires that the dancer identifies him/herself with the technique's culture. That culture is unique. A jazz culture is distinct from that of the Cunningham

embodying a technique

---

[1] Thomas Ots (1994) addresses the limits of the word 'body' as applied to embodiment. He discusses how in German there are two different terms for body: Körper, which refers to the structural aspects, and Leib, which refers to the living body 'with feelings, sensations, perceptions and emotions.' Unfortunately, there is no semantically translatable equivalent, although Merleau-Ponty's 'lived body' comes close. In utilising the term 'body', we will presume this double valence as a given. In fact, the dynamic tension between the body objectified by the view from outside (the Körper) and the body as 'experienced' (the Leib), that is, the view from inside, is particularly relevant to the study of dance and central to a choreological perspective.

Studio or of the Bolshoi. As Thea Nerissa Barnes discusses:

> *a frame of mind is needed which takes account of the historical flux of the*
> *technique in the culture/sub-culture/city in which it flourishes or is acquired.*[2]

This frame of mind takes account of the priorities that each technique requires, such as clothing, attitude to the teacher, personal investment in the movement, attitude to interpretation of the movement or exact acquisition of its form. Attitudes to sound, to sexuality, to the role of personality all matter in the embodiment of a technique. Then an understanding of the form's content, learned by living it and experiencing its layered potential, enables the embodying person to give the physicality required or the interpretation chosen. Learning motor patterns and transforming them through identifying with the feeling states that belong to them are further parts of the embodying process. Then the lived experience of the technique gradually seeps into long term memory, inscribed into the body and person, to be used as opportunity provides.

embodying a role Embodying a role requires a similar layered process of assimilation and investment in which the dancer's habitual inscription adapts to the choreographer's demands. Joseph Cipolla was cast as the figure of Death in Jooss' <u>The Green Table</u> (1932)

Kurt Jooss, <u>The Green Table</u> *Leslie E Spatt*

mounted by Anna Markard for the Birmingham Royal Ballet's 1992 season.[3] Over a six week period the sensate, intellectual, emotional embodiment took place; a gradual painstaking process in which minute detail of Jooss' style needed to become part of the lived experience of Cipolla. As a classical dancer, he had to learn what it felt like to shift weight on a horizontal line with no rise and fall, what it felt like to allow his torso and arms to work together in quite another way to his customary port de bras usage. He had to think of the image of Death, created in 1930s Germany, finding rhythmic qualities that stretched his balletic experience of dynamic range to embody the Death figure to Markard's criteria.

It is the current genres of tanztheater led by Pina Bausch, and physical theatre, that focus attention on corporeality. Corporeality sees the human body as a body that is personal, social, emotional, animal, mineral, vegetable, sexual, biological and psychological, as well as an agent of motion, and one that is given a context, a space, which is in itself socio-personal, political, domestic, abstract, conscious, unconscious, etc. Movement in tanztheater arises from the interplay of humans in these diverse and at times incongruent manifestations.

corporeality

It is suggested that concern with corporeality was a defining factor in the evolution of the German based 'dance theatre' and served to contextualise its main stylistic features (Sanchez-Colberg, 1996). Commencing with German Expressionism and the experimental dance theatre works of Laban and Mary Wigman in the 1920s, the notion of a dance theatre began to formulate to describe productions where

corporeality and dance theatre

> the dance form is not determined by dance (only)... On the contrary it is more of a compromise which has its origins in theatre, where the main accent is no longer on the dance itself but on the total stage event (Wigman, trans. Sorrell, 1966).

Productions of this sort saw the medium of dance as a way to deal with matters physical, physically. This corporeality can be seen to have its birth in the Gesamtkunstwerk of Wagner and later of Laban and Wigman which provide, as Wigman says, 'a final heightening of the opportunity for human expression' (ibid.) through its synthesis of theatrical means.

Gesamtkunstwerk brings into play a synthetic approach to the production as a whole including a concern with the dialectic between an individual's internal reality (their subjective life) and its external socio-cultural context. Where the dance's conceptual content has an effect on its material form, where there is an emphasis on emotion and, with it, a focus on the performer's presence as a central factor of the event, a corporeal work emerges. Such a work embodies an anti-mimetic attitude towards the performance event where narrative is subsumed in

---

[2] Thea Nerissa Barnes, former Artistic Director of Phoenix Dance Company, and soloist in The Martha Graham Company, in conversation, currently researching the documentation of dance techniques exemplified by Graham technique.

[3] Preston-Dunlop, V., while researching for Dance Words (1995), observed a series of rehearsals for the Birmingham Royal Ballet's 1992 season, among them The Green Table.

corporeal form and a polysemantism of the theatrical signs is employed. More importantly, corporeality links dance theatre to the radical developments within the avant-garde theatrical practice, to which German Expressionist dance belongs. It dealt directly with the polemic of the body on stage and the body's contentious relationship to a language structure and hierarchy which creates and defines the body's lived-social-political-theatrical and extra-theatrical reality.[4]

'here' and 'now'

A further facet of corporeality, again evident in the nascent genre of ausdruckstanz in the 1920s and furthered in German tanztheater and current forms of physical theatre, lies in the vision of dance based on the experience of the body in space, an experience capable of revealing to the perceiver the inexplicable and the unfathomable in nature. In this respect 'dance as a language', a phrase used by Laban, Wigman and Jooss, should not be taken as a methodological premise, but a mere metaphor which describes dance's ability to express (taken to mean bring out, make manifest) that which lies outside language - the 'unsayable things' which Bausch has so often referred to. The focus on space implies a concern with the body's engagement with the 'here' and 'now'. On entering this domain one has moved away from dance perceived as an art object to dance seen as a participatory human event. In Laban's works, this took the form of a vision where the participatory aspect of corporeality is crucial, its formulation promoting the richness of the experience of the participants (as in Laban's Song to the Sun (1917) while in those when the social aspect of corporeality is crucial, the body as social entity engages with political/cultural space (as in Laban's Gaukelei (1923).

reification

In contrast to the corporeality of tanztheater is the reification of the highly technically trained dancer, usually in a ballet environment, where the cultural agent aspects of the dancer are replaced by a negation of all things dialectic concerning the body as socio-political. The dancer may be disempowered creatively and objectified. In particular a ballerina denies her body's weight, her perspiration, her effort, even her breasts, while the corporeal dancer celebrates all these using them to the advantage of her art. The ballerina personifies stereotypical gender fantasies while the corporeal dancer disrupts stereotype and explores the complexities of gender. The ballerina operates in a hierarchic social structure while the corporeal dancer recognises and 'ensembles' with the equality of other 'corporealities.' The ballerina parades ethereal skill while the corporeal dancer parades her humanity. Salosaari's research[5] traces how classically trained dancers traditionally undergo years of reification in class and are then confronted by the need to function corporeally by post-modern choreographers. For many this is highly problematic both for the choreographer and the dancers. Ullysses Dove discusses his attempt at embodying 'the pain of love and loss' for Dancing on the Front Porch of Heaven (1992) with the Swedish Royal Ballet company members (Macrory et al., 1995). His passionate and corporeal style of choreographing and directing confronted their ability to create

beautifully sculpted forms. While he was not dissatisfied with
the result, the finished work was a compromise.

The process of embodying provides a perspective from within. **experiential knowledge**
The embodying person, from reified to corporeal, has a
perspective distinct from that of the observer. Embodying
material in dance is about presenting something (unutterable)
through a tangible person-based medium to be appreciated and
also living something (unutterable) as experience. The knowledge
from experience and the knowledge from observation are
distinct but essentially inter-related and ultimately inter-
dependent. Articulation of
this inter-relationship is
essentially choreological in
that it requires this multi-
level of complexity for its
knowing.

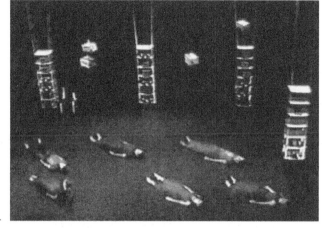

Ana Sanchez-Colberg, Futur/Perfekt
performance video still

Thus a choreological perspective commences from a position of **choreological**
embodiment and corporeality, aims to discuss, debate and **perspective**
arbitrate the lived body's own multiple constitution, namely, the
body as a cultural phenomenon and, most importantly, the
body that is not just a physical vehicle of meaning but an intersubjective identity-in-the-making. However, in recognising that
the notion of embodiment is one of locating the body in 'the
world', the discussion of embodiment in dance theatre is seen
not only as pertaining to the body as it is conventionalised and
represented in motion but, in fact, how it is constituted as
corporeality; that is, within the total world of theatrical
performance. Therefore, the body's relation to its spatiality, the
relation of spatiality (both personal and cultural) to motility, the
relevance of the elements of mise-en-scène to the way in which
the body is constituted in and via the stage space, are also relevant
to our inquiry as the earlier references to tanztheater testify.

Moreover, a choreological perspective moves beyond theories of
reading dance that place either the creator, the performer or the
audience in a privileged position. It proposes a triadic
perspective which examines the inter-relationship of these three
positions given the distinct fact that dance, like theatre and

---

[4] The complexities of the concept of corporeality cannot all be discussed here under Embodiment. In this text, the sections
Idea, Medium and Treatment, and the Nexus of the Strands of the Dance Medium include a fleshing out of the
manifestation of corporeality in dance art.

[5] See Paula Salosaari's essay in Part 2 on 'Multiple Embodiment of Ballet', a radical look at the ballet student as potentially
a cultural agent.

other forms of performance, is mediated by living, intending, feeling, thinking 'bodies'. At this point choreological study leaves behind the known territory of cultural and gender studies and the established methods in Laban-based movement analysis, and begins to forge its own methods, its own specialist modes of analysis and understanding.

theory / practice

The present inquiry focuses on proposing means for synthesising theory and practice. Embodiment and corporeality being the crux, it proposes a triadic perspective. This will offer an alternative to the current theories of dance derived from the reading/writing views of a dance event, often reduced to the choreographers' and the spectators' delineated functions. It proposes that the medium of dance is multi-stranded. This takes into account the complex way mise-en-scène operates in current border crossing dance processes and works. It proposes that these inevitably lead to fresh analytic methods that incorporate both extrinsic and intrinsic starting points to gain the 'broader picture' mentioned above. Finally, it locates choreological study at the plane of intersection of semiotics and phenomenology. These concepts are articulated in the following text.

2.2 a triadic perspective: creating, performing, appreciating processes

Choreological scholarship aims to establish a critical practice which seeks to debate / articulate the implications of embodiment within the complex web of inter-relationships in dance practice, which results from the inter-relatedness of the triadic perspective of creation, performance and reception. Choreological study promotes the view that these perspectives define different modes of engaging in dance and with dance. Traditionally each of these perspectives is associated with a role; namely, a choreographer, a performer, an audience member. This tradition encourages the problematic assumption that choreographers create (and do not perform and do not appreciate), that performers perform (and do not create and do not appreciate) and that audiences appreciate (and do not perform and do not create). The shifting nature of choreographic practice over decades/centuries shows that that is far too simple a position to take. In order to function historiographically, the manner in which the processes of making, performing and appreciating have overlapped, interwoven and sometimes become unified over time need to be known. The phenomenon of break-dancing is an example. Participants shift from one role to another as they admire each others' virtuosic and competitive expositions. Then they take their place on the performance spot, perform their own routines and elaborate as they go. Take an improvised work of the Israeli choreographer Ohad Naharin in which performers deliberately mingle with an ambulant audience. They spectate, deliberately slide into the work as performers and slide out again to become members of the public as the erstwhile audience find themselves performing. To engage in contemporaneous dance practice, the web of inter-relationships within the triadic perspective requires a more comprehensive articulation than the traditional point of view suggests.[6]

Dance practice itself explodes the traditional assumption in terms of the processes involved in making works today and in the created products themselves. Anyone familiar with the choreographic process will not need to be told that choreographers dance in the studio and perform in their own works.[7] Their choreographic process includes working with movement material on their own body. The range of performing involvement is large in that some choreographers complete their movement material on themselves as performers before coming into the studio; others generate the movement primarily from the dancers and only demonstrate occasionally and partially. Rui Horta was observed using both, coming into the studio with a 13-part phrase which he taught to the dancers, asking them to provide a 5 or 6-part phrase on the same topic. These he observed, chose or rejected. He then combined the two, his phrase, with each dancer's own material inserted at varying points along the 13-parts.[8]

The performers, in open/improvisational performative contexts, may be stated as the creators of the dance text in which the choreographer, like Prospero in his island, can only be a passive witness to the systems he or she has put into motion. Such a work was the site-specific performance event Sxedia Polis danced in the urban environment of Athens in 1996 and in London in 1998, improvised in profound slow motion, directed by Anastasia Lyra (Lyra, 1999) in which the public stopped to watch, walked through, and found themselves part of the event.

triadic making

Anastasia Lyra, Sxedia Polis *Takis Anagnostopoulos*

---

6 See Sarah Rubidge's essay in Part 2 on the role of the spectator in interactive computer installation works.

7 Martha Graham, Merce Cunningham and Mark Morris are well-known examples.

8 Rui Horta, Portuguese choreographer, artistic director of S.O.A.P. since 1991, in a workshop at Laban Centre London, 1993.

triadic performing

Choreographers are aware of the performing element as much as the creating element. Almost all have done or can do both. The editing process requires makers to stand back and look at what they have made and are making, at close quarters and at a distance. At certain points in the genesis of a work they have to become their own audience. For the choreographer, making, performing and appreciating overlap and inform each other. They are said to be triadic: three inter-dependent but concurrent ways of functioning.

Consideration shows that performers' processes are equally triadic in nature. Since dance is an embodied art, the performing process of embodying material is creative. Dancers have to make the corporeal image appear through intended, imaginative, lived action. Co-authorship or collaborative choreographing requires that the dancers share the making process as well as the embodying process. They are expected to find material, to offer ideas and to solve technical problems, to invest something of themselves in given material. They are both performers and makers. Christopher Bruce, making Waiting (1992) with London Contemporary Dance Theatre, gave instructions to the dancer to sit on a tyre, roll it, find ways of manipulating it, which Bruce accepted, adjusted, allowed to disappear, and moulded into a dramatically powerful solo.[9] Time and again dancers stand back to look at what is emerging. They offer comment, they learn each others' material by watching, they have to imagine what they look like by relating how they feel to how they look. They have to function appreciatively at close quarters and also, at a distance, as critics of what is emerging.[10] They function triadically.

triadic reception

During the making process the receptive role is usually taken by a trusted ally or an experienced artistic director of a company

Kenneth Tharp in Christopher Bruce's, Waiting Chris Nash

who feeds the other participants with a spectatorial perspective. Matthew Bourne relates how he asks friends to answer 'what did you see?' in last minute editing sessions of his works - Swan Lake (1995). This critical appreciation helps him to rid himself of his own knowledge of intended content, to see the work as others might see it. That helps him to decide how to sharpen an image, shift the balance of a scene, give stronger markers where a story line must come through.[11] These appreciating people may demonstrate, they may offer making and performing solutions, or suggest a change to the scenario or the mise-en-scène. Such a person functions triadically, less obviously than the choreographer and the performer, but nevertheless with skills that enable the products of their appreciative eye (and ear) to be translated into embodied dance.

In the presentation of a theatre work itself, particularly a traditional piece, the creator has normally completed his role by opening night. In a repertory company the choreographer may not be present for remountings of his work decades after its creation. Ashton's Symphonic Variations (1946), remounted from the score by Judith Maelor Thomas, with Michael Somes rehearsing the style, was just such a tradition in practice.[12] Ashton's part was not only complete but 'written in stone' in the score. The dancers were expected to dance his product with no variation, no addition. The audience were expected to watch, listen and appreciate. However, contemporary post-modern dance is unlikely to function like that.

In Pina Bausch's 1980, the performers invade the spectators'

Pina Bausch, 1980 *Gert Weigelt*

9 Rehearsal at the Place, London, 1993.

10 This process is visible everyday with Transitions Dance Company at Laban Centre London as the dancers participate in the creation of five new works each season, and reconstruct a sixth, rehearse two casts and prepare to tour the programme.

11 Related by Matthew Bourne to Valerie Preston-Dunlop for inclusion in Looking at Dances, (1998).

12 Birmingham Royal Ballet's 1992 season, quoted in Preston-Dunlop (1995).

space and require them to respond, to speak to the dancers, drink tea with them, so begging the question: are the spectators now part of the work? Dancers may stop dancing and critique what is going on. In Maguy Marin's Grossland (1988), they speak to the audience, so slipping out of their persona and taking on the role of commentator. Indeterminacy requires dancers to create 'on the hoof' during the performance, deciding on material, on exits and entrances, on interactions. Current dance practice shows that dances may be triadic not only during their rehearsal processes but also as part of the produced work itself.

intention

Within the triadic perspective, the relationship between notions of intention, impression and interpretation, as they relate to the embodied processes of making, performance and reception, is part of this inquiry. For the present purpose intention is defined at a fundamental level as a consciousness towards, through which we open ourselves through perception to the world, to others and to ourselves.[13] This definition goes beyond the commonly understood meaning of the word as something 'wanted' to be said, done, communicated, etc. Intention is not only located with the choreographer who wants to 'say' or communicate 'something'; intention is present in all participants. We, the participants, all draw our focus of attention to the dance event. Thus the event becomes 'our world' and we locate ourselves within it.

Intention is linked to the contractual interpersonal frames which operate in defining any performance event. Since a performative art is one in which negotiation takes place between creator/performers and spectators, it is imperative that all actively participate if a performative art experience is to be had. Indeed, coming as an audience member to an act of theatre is implicitly an intention to spectate. Audiences wish to engage with the work and the actors. Similarly the performers wish to reach the spectators. This willing is embodied in attending, paying attention, expectancy and, from time to time, interaction.

impression

Intention is linked to impression in the act of performing the work (Velasquez, 1986). Impression is not only the domain of the performer who has to execute movement in a particular way so that it may 'give an impression' and be perceived by an audience. Impression is also the constant dual channel of receiving and giving information through our senses (which Merleau-Ponty identified as the ground level of all knowledge), a duality which shapes and defines the identity of the dance event. Through the active intention of all participants, impression can be given and can be received. Dancers learn what it is to dance material and to find the intention required. Next, they learn to make the profound shift needed to become aware of themselves in space with a potential audience. Personal intention transforms into public impression.

interpretation

It is the inter-relationship between these two that leads to interpretation, not only understood as an arrival at signification (in the literal sense, although it could include that) but an arrival at the shared process of 'understanding'[14], of coming into knowledge of, in and through the experience of the dance. This is not limited to an audience who interpret a message hidden in a network of cryptic codes. Rather, interpretation is on-going: at the point of choreographing, of executing, of witnessing. Interpretation is transactional and intersubjective.

Interpreting is a process that performers are constantly engaged with as they learn and create a piece of repertory. They engage in a process of discovery to uncover the layers of the work so that they can truly be interpreters of the work. So too does anyone engaged in making, for as the work emerges, codes, signs and meanings formulate, are recognised, sharpened, softened, masked. Unthought of content arises, interpretations emerge unasked for.

Interpreting by spectators may be thought, erroneously, to be synonymous with understanding the narrative content of a work. What the work 'means' is what a spectator may hope to discover, but meaning is more complex than reading the referential signs successfully, although it may start there. In Cunningham's <u>Beach Birds</u> (1992), it is quite possible, gradually, to recognise the series of signs put in place by Cunningham and his collaborators which explain why the work has the title it has. Indeed the title leads one to look for and thence to recognise the white and black colour of birds that inhabit beaches. One can recognise the random rhythm that a group of standing birds might exhibit, their occasional cocking of head, fluttering of wing, changing of stance and other beach bird happenings for which words are inadequate. But that is only a beginning to interpretation.

Interpreting, being transactional, is a process in which the spectator constructs the meaning for himself, making use of what is presented to him, taking in whatever his roving attention alights upon, over time, and meshing it with his own memory, experience, knowledge, expectations and culture. (Indeed that is the identical process that a performer goes through in the interpretation of a role, and the maker of a work in recognising what he has made.) Interpreting is an active personal process. Interpreters transact meanings by engaging strongly with the work and engaging strongly with their own heritage, in some kind of ratio. The more they engage with the work the more likely it is that they recognise something of what has gone into it. The more they engage with their own heritage the more their imagination is stimulated to bounce off what they see and to enter their own world.

transaction

13 The issue of intention as a 'consciousness towards' is discussed in detail in Merleau-Ponty (1962). Garner (1994) discusses the relevance of Merleau-Ponty's thesis to the study of performance.

14 Merleau-Ponty defines 'to understand' as 'to experience the harmony between what we aim and what is given, between the intention and the performance' where the body is the anchorage in the world. See Merleau-Ponty (1962, p.145).

**aesthetic
appreciation**

In the case of <u>Beach Birds</u>, there is more to interpret than the fact that the dancers are portraying 'birdiness'. There is no narrative as such; the birds do not engage in any drama. They simply are. Also there to be seen are layers of Merce Cunningham's choreographic processes, these being Cunningham's birds, not anyone else's. Indeed, the birdiness may be seen as almost irrelevant, for the work is fundamentally a prime example of his and his collaborators' coexisting structuring treatment, in which the elements of the event inhabit the same space and time as each other as independent entities, requiring an aesthetic appreciation rather than a search for denotive signification. Cunningham enjoys seeing the same movement performed by different dancers who are in his company for reasons of their individuality of body build and motional quality: their 'awkwardness' as he puts it (Loader 1989). If the spectator is looking for the physique of a Balanchine dancer or a Royal Ballet principal, then that will colour not only his expectations but also his evaluation, all of which influence his interpretation. Cunningham's company is an ensemble of soloists, without stars. Here, the use of space is egalitarian, all spaces are of equal interest, all movements are equally valuable. If the spectator is expecting the exaggerated extensions required in a Forsythe work, or virtuosic turns and jumps, that will colour his appreciation. For Cunningham, men and women are dancers whose gender contributes kinetic possibilities rather than emotional possibilities. Duo work is mutual and may fragment into threes, fours, ones, or groups at any time, while the spectator may be looking for the big solo, the romantic duo, the corps de ballet scene. Cunningham requires his dancers to dance the dance material as it is, giving it only what it needs to be accomplished in the given duration. If a spectator were looking for the individual layers of dramatic interpretation expected in a narrative work then that would influence the nature of his engagement.

These elements embodied in the event carry meaning without being directly referential or narrative in content. They signify an attitude to art and to human existence. Engaging with <u>Beach Birds</u> performers' and creators' embodiment, intending with them, negotiating their coexistent structure, their ensemble, their egalitarian ethos, allows for another layer of interpretation to take place as those elements mesh with each spectator's personal attitudes. From Cunningham's perspective, the work is simply there as a phenomenon in its own right.

2.3 three constituents of a work: idea, medium and treatment

While the triadic perspective concerns three processes, a dance event itself comes about through a synthesis of three further constituents - idea, medium and treatment. To create a dance work or a technical tradition or a competitive dance routine, or any event of dance, the ideas of creative people interact with the dance medium through using treatments peculiar to the artists concerned. In this chapter ideas and treatments are discussed, the medium being explored in chapter 3.

Any art event is initiated by ideas which, to become realised as a work, are given a medium of some sort - a sound medium for music, a word medium for poetry. 'Given' is an inadequate term for it suggests that the medium is inert and merely receptive, while in any art the medium impacts back on the artist and her creative ideas through its unique properties. A piece of wood is not inert. It has grain, textures, colours, forms, all of which are capable of modulating the original concept or vision. Working with the medium is an arena in which ideas and medium interact with each other in the fashioning process. An emergent event of dance, triadic in nature, continues to impact back in workshop and rehearsal, so generating further ideas. These symbiotic exhanges continue through the procedures and processes of transforming an idea into an embodied choreographic work.

ideas

It is problematic to equate 'idea' with a surface narrative. A dance idea may narrate by referring to phenomena shared by all participants, or may not. Prokofiev's score Romeo and Juliet refers to the events in Shakespeare's well known play of the same name. So too does Bernstein's score for West Side Story (1957). The play refers to a forbidden love affair and the tragic events surrounding it. As soon as that is given place and time, a setting, a culture, an arena of discourse, then the simple idea of forbidden love begins to take on specific form. Ideas buzz. Many ballets have been made on this theme of which Kenneth Macmillan's for the Royal Ballet in London is one and Jerome Robbins' for the New York musical theatre is another. Currently hip-hop specialist Rennie Harris brings 'the complex energies of street culture onto the concert stage' (Hutera, 2001) in his retelling of the story from the perspective of black urban males in Rome and Jewels (2001).

narrative ideas

Robbins' idea was to challenge the very nature of the genre in which he was working, namely, the musical. Mary Clarke and David Vaughan (1977) describe the production as a landmark in which for the first time the tension of the dance dominated the pace of the entire action. At the time, 1957, it was dubbed a 'dansical'. Violence, restlessness and lack of glamour were more than an internal narrative to the work, they were a confrontation to the musical theatre of the period, and more, a suggestion that life as it is lived in New York's West Side should be addressed. Robbins' ideas concerned the codes of musical theatre; that is, the expected and agreed but usually unstated norms of how things should be. This confrontation of norms and codes is a frequent idea found in dance works. Just which code, in which bit of the medium, confronted by what treatment gives the work its flavour. Such ideas confront the

genre ideas

codes in 'the language' of dance theatre.[15]

cultural ideas   Macmillan's ideas for <u>Romeo and Juliet</u> (1965), according to Vaughan, centred on an interpretation of the Shakespeare text which promoted Juliet as the motive force of the interaction with a will to react against the conventions of her society. His catalyst, part of his medium, was Lynn Seymour, an artist of enormous dramatic sensibility. That accounts for his shift in the surface narrative of the work, but the fact that its creation took place in London in 1965 is not insignificant, for the emergent feminist movement was already apparent. The narrative element of the work has internal layers and wider cultural layers that are there to be shared.

medium ideas   Lucinda Childs[16] serves as an example of quite a different dance idea. Said by David Vaughan to have worked in the area of 'conceptual' dance, her 1970s work was

> concerned with sometimes infinitesimal variations within a rigorously controlled compositional structure (ibid. p.86).

The ideas are ideas about the medium, in this case the movement material. There is no narrative. The reference is to dance itself, promoting the concept that a story is unnecessary. So called 'abstract dances' have been in the canon before Childs. Alwin Nikolais[17] focused on abstracting the human body by fantastic costuming and multimedia works, succeeding throughout the 1950s into the 60s, while in Germany in the 1920s, Oskar Schlemmer[18] geometricised the body through (amongst other things) extending the skeleton with poles. Conceptual works have to engage the spectator through other means than a narrative, while remembering that, whether there or not, most audiences will search for a story line. Earlier choreographers have worked conceptually by forefronting virtuosity, fantasy or spectacular multimedia effects, that is, by performance ideas that impinge on the attention. The idea for Childs is none of these.

perception ideas   She confronts the perception of spectators, inviting them to engage with minutiae, to look, really *look*, to enjoy minute differences, to sharpen their awareness of differences, to shift their habitual form of attention. The ideas in her work are at least two-fold; the first about movement itself, the second about her spectators' mode of perception.

The dance idea may be one about the medium itself, as Childs' was. It is problematic to assume that culturally significant ideas in dance have to be narrative ideas. On the contrary, medium ideas and treatment ideas can signify and engage all participants to experience the work.

choreographic treatment   Choreographic treatments are the ways and means used to give shape to the original idea and emerging ideas and so create works with a particular identity - used by individuals, or by schools of artists, or (in the case of folk art) by communities, or over decades in genres. Choreographic treatments arise through the symbiotic relationship between creative individuals and a culture that is itself in flux.

Treatments of the codes of dance as a performance and performative art are ways discussed below by which major artists have effected their innovative practice. Such treatments take various forms according to the codes, rules and norms addressed. Dance is built on a network of codes, that is, agreed and observed ways of doing things 'right'.[19] Codes manifest themselves as established ways of training, as particular company structures, as making and rehearsing processes, as the rituals of performance, as behaviour imposed by theatre architecture, as regulated audience behaviour and so on.

codes, rules and norms

Codes are an essential part of any cultural exchange. Their observance facilitates interaction. All the arts operate through codes and their use, particularly through their celebration in traditional art works and art making processes and through their rupture by the avant-garde and all forms of newness. Newness is only created, performed and recognised because there exists something to be newer than, something to interrogate or to leave behind as history.

The tension that exists in the use of codes in dance has a tendency to divide the dance theatre community into two. The world of ballet tends to hold to its traditional codes while the world of modern/contemporary dance creates new codes with each major choreographer. These the next generation immediately flout in order to develop and establish their own codes. It is an endless becoming.

Major dance artists of this century have developed what are regarded as personal treatment methods, or personal choreographic processes and devices. George Balanchine, Martha Graham, Merce Cunningham, Pina Bausch and William Forsythe are well known examples from the 20th century. Each responded to the dance culture they entered and the societal culture that they found themselves in or which they sought out. Each embodied a response through a unique mix of collaborative transactional and symbiotic relationships of performing, making and appreciating which they embodied through their choice of and treatment of ideas. Each in turn influenced the dance culture through their work and also the society in which their

idiosyncratic treatment

---

[15] See Pierre Guiraud's account (1975) of Jacobson's communicative functions, especially the metalinguistic function concerning codes.

[16] Lucinda Childs, participant in the Judson Church experimentations of the 1970s; see Banes (1980).

[17] Alwin Nikolais - American choreographer and theatrical innovator; see Marcia Siegel in Dance Perspectives (No. 48, 1971).

[18] Oskar Schlemmer, German stage designer and kinetic artist; see Schlemmer (ed.) (1972).

[19] Here, codes are taken as systems of principles such as codes of dress for a ballet class; principles on which movement systems such as release technique is based; closed codes of movement behaviour through which classical mime or Bharatanatyam communicate meanings. Rules are taken here as (usually) written orders or regulations, possibly binding. Norms, usually unwritten, are taken here as "principles of right action binding upon numbers of a group and serving to guide, contrive, regulate proper and acceptable behaviour" (Merriam-Webster 1993).

iconoclastic methods were negotiated. Here, brief pointers are discussed since fuller choreological study of an artist's treatment methods can only be undertaken in the studio.

Balanchine   Balanchine's way of working is understood as a mix of deep respect and confrontation of the codes of ballet, codes that he had received through his training and his apprenticeship in Russia. He retained the pointe work, the pas de deux, the music-based choreography, to mention only three issues. As Nancy Reynolds writes, he worked from a 'creed of classicism'. Alongside that he subjected the classical vocabulary to 'various inversions, distortions, reaccentuations and unexpected sequences of steps' (Clarke and Vaughan, 1977, p.40). His revolution, against Fokine (himself a ballet revolutionary)

> was not through idolatry and archeology but through constant innovation, experiment and discovery (Taper, 1974, p.261).

He is known to have prioritised the movement material over everything else. To achieve that, he shifted from lavish and referential costuming, which attracted the eye to the wearer and to a narrative, preferring simple body coverings reminiscent of classwork which forefronted what the body was doing. The original costumes for Apollo (1928) in Paris were decidedly hellenic, but when Jacques d'Amboise danced it in New York, he was dressed in black tights and white off-shoulder top. In Agon (1957) the men wore T-shirts over black tights, the women white tights and black leotard, which visiting Bolshoi dancers witnessed with astonishment, expecting the story of Agon to be interpreted with drama and supporting designs (ibid. p.286). Emotional interpretation of a role by the dancers expected in ballet, he replaced with a focus on the motional qualities unique to valued ballerinas, Tanaquil Le Clercq for example. For her he created specific 'pure dance' roles and cast her in the Adagio in Symphony in C (1948) that maximised her way of performing with her personal physique, 'her elegance and her musicality' (ibid. p.245). He respected the traditional norm that music for ballets is essential, but in place of a romantic sound he worked, over a 50 year span, with a musical iconoclast, Igor Stravinsky, bringing to American ballet the modernity started by Diaghilev and his colleagues in the Ballets Russes in Paris. His renowned musicality went far beyond the rules of musical visualisation of his predecessors, to use counterpoint between movement and music, anticipation of one by the other, contrast, complement and echo.

Arlene Croce, discussing Balanchine's choreographic treatment of his dancers' talents, writes of his and their 'effect' on the audience, implying that Balanchine's works are primarily performances. The spectator is there to receive. For Merrill Ashley in Ballade (1980).

> he has left the ballerina to decide what emotion - poignant, sentimental, tragic, grandly impersonal - the experience of the ballet will convey to the audience (Croce, 1982, p.278).

She describes Balanchine's customary use of his dancers

> to focus and control the mind of the audience (ibid. p.277)

To Croce his works are not transactional, by intent.

Martha Graham, the monumental pioneer in the American modern dance revolution of the first half of the 20th century, worked at much the same period and in the same city as Balanchine, but she did not start from a base of ballet. She had no movement code to celebrate as Balanchine had. Although her treatment resulted in a new movement vocabulary and technique, her work arose from the exploration of deep human emotion in a culture of the American pioneer for which new expressive means, and hence new movement, had to be found.

Graham

Martha Graham, Errand into the Maze. Set designer Isamu Noguchi *Anon*

She immersed herself in profound narrative ideas as her notebooks show; in myths and themes that explore man's relationship with the cosmos. Some of her titles suggest her arena: <u>Primitive Mysteries</u> (1935), <u>Errand into the Maze</u> (1947), <u>Diversion of Angels</u> (1948), <u>Night Journey</u> (1947), <u>Clytemnestra</u> (1958). Peter Williams described her themes:

> Hereditary carnal lust is the motivating force in 'Phaedra'... Jocasta's incestuous marriage is the main theme in 'Night Journey'; the seduction and beheading of Holofernes in 'Legend of Judith'; the ferocious and sinister story of Troy and Mycenae leading to the murder of Agamemnon and Cassandra in 'Clytemnestra' (1962/3) (in Preston-Dunlop 1964 p.27).

She offers roles - Oedipus, Teresias, Jocasta, Medea - and archetypes - One who Seeks in <u>Primitive Mysteries</u>, the Bride in <u>Appalachian Spring</u>, the Leader of the Chorus in <u>Night Journey</u>, the Red Girl in <u>Diversion of Angels</u>. She developed a consistent treatment of the medium, by which she, her dancers, her musicians, her designers promoted a world of passionate, ecstatic, agonised dreams and illusion (Grimm, 1984).

Graham's treatment of the notion of 'steps' was radical. As all who have taken Graham-based technique classes know, the floor is an essential part of the dancer's space, the pelvis is prioritised as the initiating centre of movement, contraction and release are the rhythmic polarities which propel dynamic action forward. Spirals, tilts and falls became basic moves and, as Bonnie Bird, an original Graham company dancer describes:

> (the technique) *reflected how the body shaped itself in states of emotion: the cry, the laugh, the pleading, the revolutionary call* (in Preston-Dunlop, 1995, p.180).

Thus Graham established not only movement codes through which to communicate her vision, but the Graham dancers developed behaviour and dress norms through which they might be distinguished from their pioneering rivals, the Doris Humphrey dancers.

Graham did not set out to make a technique but to make theatre works. The technique became a necessity, a way of training dancers to enable them to perform her ideas. It arose from her need to embody highly charged ideas in a 'modern' way and an American way.

Starting her career in Ruth St Denis' company, Graham rejected St Denis' treatment of dance as subordinate to music through exact visualisation in the dance material of its phrasing, melodic line and dynamic flux. Instead, Graham forefronted the dance. The music had to reflect the dance, not the other way round. Specifically composed music was a support, not a starting point.

Graham's mentor was the musician Louis Horst. It was he who helped her to develop her powers of self-criticism and her knowledge of the world of art. Horst introduced the early dance pioneers to the atonal music of Arnold Schoenberg, the bitonal sounds of the Parisian composers Francis Poulenc and Erik Satie, the expressionist paintings of Emil Nolde, the exotic figures of Gustav Klimt and naïve figures of Paul Klee, the geometric architecture of Gropius and his Bauhaus colleagues (Soares, 1992, Madden, 1996). These and the current cultural energies abraded against her own passionate and visionary nature resulting in her unique choice of, and treatment of, ideas.

Unlike Balanchine, Graham was a soloist in her own company. She paid attention to the interpretation of the dancer from that perspective. In many of her works, emotional imagination was required to add the performer's layer of drama to the already symbolic material. <u>Errand into the Maze</u> is the work she mentions where she used the fear she experienced in a near flying disaster to imbue her traumatic solo on entry into the maze (Grimm, 1984).

Are Graham's works performative? Do they engender engagement with an audience and demand a transactional appreciation? In 1964 as a young dancer Preston-Dunlop wrote:

> When Graham brought her company to London in 1954 the theatre was half empty and the audience openly hostile. Many dancers were not even prepared to come and see what she had to offer. For the few whom she conquered her success was intense but in the main people were sceptical of the woman and her work (1964, p.28).

What was the intensity that she evoked for the few, but that would become the intensity of the many? The review continues:

> It has been said that ballet is popular because it can be a form of escapism. One can forget the daily round by submerging oneself in the dream world of 'The Sleeping Princess' or 'Swan Lake'. Graham also gives her audience a dream world but submersion is impossible; one is not transported away from living but plunged right into the glories and disasters of it... She manages to transcend the limits of the specific situation to speak about human relationships in general. This is what makes her work far more disturbing... She jettisons her audience right into the centre of things by her startling integrity; one is in it with her and therefore disturbed (ibid.).

That is the point: the spectators are not witnessing characters embodying a disturbed theme, but transacting what is projected with their own experience of relationships to become disturbed themselves. It is quite another transaction than the one Merce Cunningham was about to demand by his work.

Cunningham

Merce Cunningham, having started his career with Graham, had her dominant theatrical codes to address and shift. He had to find treatments of the dance medium to embody his vision that art and life are not separate worlds but one and the same. To get away from the illusory human feelings that dominated Graham, he chose to remove the base of rhythm in dance from that associated with human behaviour and the organic balance of opposites. To find new movement and new structuring methods he put together actions, spatial directions, limbs and torso, timings et al., selected not by choice but by deliberate chance methods. For Cunningham, the arbitrary way in which simultaneous events in life coexist with no reference to each other, provided him with an overarching treatment. With his long time collaborators, composer John Cage and designer Robert Rauschenberg, he presented movement, sound and decor as co-existing elements. His dancers learn material derived by chance, to give it the rhythm and phrasing demanded by the actions themselves, uncoloured by any additional feeling states. He structures the work according to plans derived by chance.[20]

---

[20] See Preston-Dunlop's essay "Looking at Dances" in Part 2 for further discussion of Cunningham.

Cunningham's way of working created not only a new form of making, new demands for performing, but also new norms of appreciating. Interpretation of Cunningham's work lay firmly in the lap of the spectator. Quoted in 1968 he said:

> We don't aim at producing a specific, emotional result. We present the event and leave it up to the audience to decide what is and what is not expressed. I have a feeling it produces some kind of atmosphere (in Denby, 1968, p.11.).

By giving no message and by offering no narrative signs, he offered instead the work, to be looked at for itself, to be appreciated for its coexisting differences, inviting a phenomenal negotiation between event and appreciating self: 'It asks you to observe what is happening now' (ibid. p.24).

tanztheater treatment
Laban and Bausch

The treatment of Pina Bausch is discussed here in terms of her placement in the genre of 20th century tanztheater through the shared priorities of Rudolf Laban, Kurt Jooss and Bausch herself. Her treatment has its roots in German Expressionism and the works of Laban through a shared focus on corporeality and the experience of being 'here', 'now', living in the moment of making. The contextualisation of corporeality was achieved through the use of features from other art forms. For Prometheus (1923), Laban envisioned dance theatre as a form of 'dance oratorio' fusing together the aesthetic, plastic and religious aspects of a work. This oratorio was seen as 'the summit of human artistic performance' through the 'simultaneous employment of dance, sound and speech' (Laban in Szeeman, 1980, p.340).

Not only were elements of various art forms synthesised but also different kinds of dancing bodies, including professional and amateur dancers, singers and actors who were fused in the form of Neue Tanz (New Dance). A similar concern can be found in Bausch's work:

> Je cherche de parler de la vie, des êtres, des nous, de ce qui bouge. Et ce sont des choses dont il n'est pas possible de parler en respectant une certain tradition de la danse. La realité n'est pas être toujour dansée. On ne serait ni efficace ni credible (Bausch in Gubernatis and Bentivoglio, 1986, p.10).[21]

The synthesis of various art forms, a central treatment of the dance medium, goes hand in hand with the idea of bringing together and making manifest 'other' aspects of our human condition which can only be accounted for in bodily performance, and not through language structures. Laban believed in the existence of two worlds - the world of everyday appearance (the space of action) and the world of an unseen higher order (the space of silence). Dance was the dynamic flux between these two. It was not a 'message' to be told, but an expression of that oscillation:

> Dancing can induce an enhanced, or at least a different kind of consciousness from our normal practical everyday awareness of the world... Behind

*external events the dancer perceives another, entirely different, world... a
hidden forgotten landscape lies there, the land of silence, the realm of the
soul... The sound of the human voice and the movement of the human body
if rightly used can alone bring us near to glimpse these worlds (Laban,
trans. Ullmann, 1975, pp. 89-90).*

Laban's sentiment is not far from that expressed by Bausch
when she states:

*Somehow we are very transparent, if we see each other like this. The way
somebody walks or the way people carry their neck tells you something
about the way they live or about the things that have happened to them...
Somehow everything is visible (through movement) even when we cling to
certain things (in Loney, 1984).*

Moreover, the interplay between internal/external reality which
gives impetus to their work determines the treatment of the
medium. Inasmuch as dance springs, as Laban writes, from an
'inner necessity' which satisfies a 'human need', the body in
motion/on stage will 'create its own patterns of style'. Speaking
of her process Bausch states:

*I never start from the beginning. I have a lot of things... I don't yet know
what they will become... Then gradually I begin to see where a work should
start... What we have been working on is usually a big mess of things... a
big chaos of materials, in relation to the finished piece... there isn't a
design... it all comes from the work (ibid. p.32).*

Pina Bausch, *Cafe Müller Gert Weigelt*

---

21 Trans: "I aim to speak of life, of being, of us and we, of what moves us. And those are things which are impossible to
speak of within a single dance tradition. Reality cannot always be danced. It will be neither efficient nor credible". AS-C

At the centre of the work is the performer on whose personal histories - inscribed in the body - rests the development of the content of the work. The relationship between the subject's motion and emotion is central to the work. In Kurt Jooss' treatment the individual performer needs to 'find the movement it should be making' and why 'it should be that specific movement'. Furthermore he states:

> Behind every movement there is an inner state, an emotion, an idea so that the movement speaks of that experience... In an uninhibited body with free flow of emotional, physical movement, there is a continuous interrelationship between the physical and the psychological. There is no movement, or there should be no movement, without a psychological background, and no psychological tension without resulting movement, so that it works both ways (in Gruen, 1976).

Similarly, in Bausch's work 'the human being is the model' (Hoghe, 1980, p.73). Repeatedly she has mentioned her concern with 'what makes us move... not how'. Given the focus on the performer's presence made visible performance after performance, the treatment in dance theatre mitigates against the notion of mimesis. The aim is not to represent but to present, to regard the events on stage as fragments of actual reality which become tangible through the act of repetition. Thus the 'reliving' becomes the 'lived' (Melrose, 1994, p.204). The moment of actuality is arrived at through various methods - improvisation, manipulations and encounters with the grand scale environments in which the pieces take place, the manner in which the movement is repeated over and over again until the 'represented' becomes actually present. Bausch's works, such as 1980, do not aim to transmit a 'single message', a particular narration of the events on stage. Rather, the work aims for an openness of the signs on stage to allow the audience participation in the creative act. Laban advocates that the spectator should

> ...distil in his own way the material presented... the form suggests certain directions in which the spectators' distilling process can operate, but without being able to totally determine it (1950, p.98).

Similarly Bausch states that:

> chaque chose acquiert une signification différente de l'instant ou on la place en regardes les autres (in Gubernatis and Bentivoglio, 1986, p.11).[22]

Moreover she denies a single authorial vision:

> I just can't say this is how it goes... I am watching myself...You can see it like this or like that. It just depends on the way you watch. But the single stranded thinking that they interpret into it simply isn't right...You can always watch the other way (in Hoghe, 1980, pp.71-72).

All these features point towards a crucial treatment operative in the genre, its view of dance as an art form which shapes experience as an event participated in, not as an art object aesthetically perceived. Whether it be Laban's <u>Sang an die Sonne</u>, a three day festival in 1917, or Bausch's assault on the senses through the use of leaves, grass, water, dirt, or cakes which are offered to the public, the aim is to explore not just the changing content of the work but also the 'how' with which the work communicates. In doing so, the genre continues to challenge conventional notions of the way in which dance is made, performed and received - the connection between intention, impression and interpretation as processes common to all those engaged in the dance event.

As we have seen, the treatments prioritised by iconoclastic artists arise from their confrontation of the traditions of dance in which they find themselves. In the case of William Forsythe, it is the codes of ballet that he both celebrates, ruptures and expands, and the choreutic theories of Laban that he embraces and explodes to provide himself with a personal way, and a company way, of finding a new movement vocabulary. He returns to the earlier interpretation of the word 'choreography', which has become generalised into the making of dances by any means (not to say its use as choreographing a dinner party or a political meeting) to that of writing dances in space. Developing the concepts of the deconstructivist architect Daniel Libeskind 'who exposes the possibilities of spatial inscription', Forsythe investigates the manifold options that Laban's theories (particularly of choreutics) suggest.

Forsythe

For both men:

> Movement is, so to speak,
> living architecture -
> living in the sense of
> changing replacements as
> well as changing cohesion.
> The architecture is created
> by human movements and is
> made up of pathways tracing
> shapes in space (Laban in
> Baudoin and Gilpin, 1989)

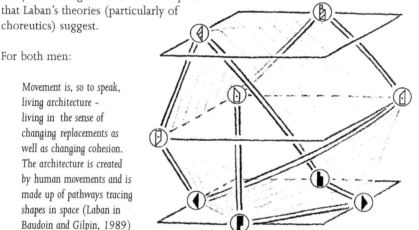

Rudolf Laban, lemniscate drawing in <u>Choreutics</u>

Forsythe problematises Laban's concept of a kinesphere with a constant centre that coincides with the central point of the human body, a model that sits well in classical ballet and in the expressionism of the whole-bodied movement of Ausdruckstanz:

> But what if movement does not emanate from the body's centre? What if there were more than one centre? What if the source of a movement were an entire line or plane and not simply a point? Choreutics inspires such questions.[23]

---

[22] Trans: "Everything acquires a different meaning the moment one looks at it from another situation".

[23] Baudoin's and Gilpin's programme notes for the William Forsythe Reggio Emilia Festival Danza (1989. Book 2, pp.73-78).

Laban postulates

> Dream architectures can neglect the laws of balance… yet a fundamental
> sense of balance will always remain with us even in the most fantastic
> aberrations from reality (Laban, 1966).

but Forsythe departs from him again

> Forsythe searches precisely for those superkinespheric moments when the
> limits are transgressed, when falling is imminent (Baudoin and Gilpin, ibid.).

Failure to maintain balance becomes one essential Forsythian
project. Forsythe's treatment of his ideas encompasses a
multitude of means. He shares Libeskind's interest in
'disappearance' and Michel Foucault's concept of historical
ruption. The spatial inscriptions that Forsythe wants to be seen
are replaced again and again by different movement, while
other moves that ergonomically must occur are made 'invisible'.
His eye is on his virtual inscriptions, unlike Laban analysts who
identify every detail of actual change. While Laban's inscriptions
around the centre are peripheral, transversal and central, axes
and equators, rings and scales, Forsythe uses an array of

William Forsythe, _Steptext_: Deborah Bull and Adam Cooper _Leslie E. Spatt_

operations: arc and axis, cross and pass, bridge, extrude, replace, collapse, and so on.[24]

Forsythe's treatment of his dancers as 'agents' requires a particular way of rehearsing. He structures the movement material and passes it over to the dancers as a 'sketch' for them to work with and transform into material (Figgis, 1996). As an ensemble they co-author the movement of the work. His treatment of theatrical space emerges out of his 'agents' engaging with it, and what Forsythe puts in it as motion, light, object, environment, on equal terms. They may push round a powerful mobile floodlight, so generating disappearance and spatial rupture. They may engage actively with a theatrical snowstorm, or with falling scenery. Centre stage as a prestigious place for a soloist may be replaced by a spot in shadow on the perimeter, as in <u>Steptext</u> (1999) or <u>In the Middle Somewhat Elevated</u> (1988).

Choreological study articulates the interconnections between ideas, medium and treatments through both a verbal and a visceral practice. Coming to know how these interconnections work in the studio, what embodying them feels like, what intentions and impressions they require and produce, and what interpretations they offer, and give rise to, are part of choreological practice.

choreological perspective

2.4 process and product

The choreological perspective so far detailed and its concern with the tripartite relationship between the activities of making, performing and reception, and the three inter-relating processes of impression, intention and interpretation, has as a direct consequence, the need to reconsider the relationship between notions of process and product as it pertains to dance. A choreological perspective does not aim to arrive at a singular definition of these terms. Rather, it brings divergent applications of these concepts into a comparative dialogue, and demonstrates how these terms have been used differently by various artists, giving dynamic contrast to dance making. These fluctuating applications embody particular opinions on the nature of dance and its relevance as an art form.

Conventionally, process has been understood as that which happens before the production. It is the 'invisible' activity which includes the formulation of a concept and the concept's research through hours of rehearsals, to arrive at a bulk of material. This 'raw' material is then subjected through repetition to a process of selection and refining, which then

conventional process / product

---

[24] CD Rom by Forsythe (1999).

leads to the 'right' performance, as well as to the refining of the ideas. Some things will be excluded whilst others will begin to be shaped into a 'form' which will result in the 'work'. The identity of the dance - the work - is seen as a product of that process. This is in many ways coloured by our notions of how particular processes produce particular things. This is especially relevant to what has been defined as 'formal' or 'theatrical' dance, whose identity is fixed in a particular relationship between the ideas and emergent form.

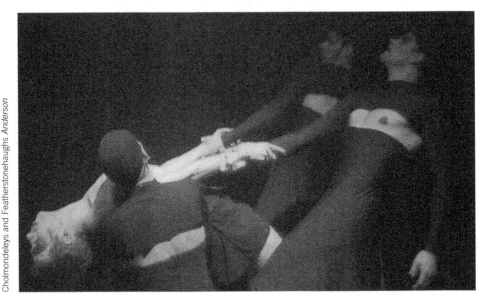

**post-modern
process / product**

For example, for the creation of <u>Smithereens</u> (1999) with the Cholmondeleys, Featherstonehaughs and the Victims of Death, choreographer Lea Anderson collected innumerable visual images from the 1920s Weimar Republic which she submitted to a postmodern cut-and-paste process. She reassembled a whole host of visual references with consummate skill, which the company danced with virtuosic dexterity. But Anderson confounds this traditional process / product divide by her presentation of it. The spectator has access to the myriad of costume and character changes that take place during the performance. By manipulating the height of the backdrop to leave a gap at floor level, access is given, from the knee down, to the performers' process of preparing / transforming themselves for the next episode. Their process becomes part of the presented product. Anderson both uses the traditional process / product relationship in her making strategies but confounds it in her manner of presentation.

identity

Within the history of dance analysis, the traditional relationship between concept and form and its links to notions of identity has been articulated in the arguments between, amongst others, Margolis (1984), Armelagos & Sirridge (1978) and Goodman (1976). Issues pertaining to that debate remain open and have been discussed further at conferences on reconstruction politics, and rigorously addressed in the research of Rubidge (2000) on the identity of the open work of dance.[25] It is a debate that finds a particular forum in instances of re-creations and reconstructions of works, where questions of validity of a new version or a variation of an original are raised.[26] As an example are productions of <u>Swan Lake</u>. Within the context of classical tradition <u>Swan Lake</u> is perceived to be stable on the basis of a) a musical score, b) its general libretto, c) aspects of characterisation, d) code of movement (although syntactical and morphological variations are possible, i.e. Baryshnikov's <u>Swan Lake</u> versus Peter Wright's), e) general maintenance of

Lea Anderson, <u>Smithereens</u>.
Cholmondeleys and Featherstonehaughs *Anderson*

Romantic themes (male hero, female swan). However we are also struck by more recent reconsiderations of <u>Swan Lake</u>. Mats Ek (1987) gave us the first gender bending exploration of the ideal Romantic version, where a bald chorus of swans, male and female, wore the classical tutu but were barefoot and amongst them were skin colours of all sorts. Ek did away with the musical score as a stable feature by altering its order, as Matthew Bourne did for his version of the work (1995). Bourne expanded further the gender shift to an all male corps of swans, not in female dress but barechested in feathered trousers.

Within this consideration of process and product, words such as idea / structure, content / form, idea and its representation, 'reality' and the mimetic 'other' of performance, individual style / group style, are discussed as dichotomies in between which the 'work' balances and exists. This is the language of aesthetics where the object acquires an independent form after the process of creation, but, consequentially, loses its materiality at the moment it becomes that object. The work is found in the virtual 'other' of the gaps between the dimensions of creation / performance and reception. It is also the language of manufacturing in which the success of the product is based on

[25] See Rubidge's essay 'Identity in Flux' in Part 2.

[26] See Preston-Dunlop's essay on Issues in Revivals and Re-creations in Part 2.

its success at matching the consumers' expectations of what is, should or shouldn't be. Both are ideologies that have dominated our reflection on dance practice.

fluid process / product

However, with the advent of a dance avant-garde as far back as 1916 which has questioned the perspective of dance as an aesthetic object to a view of dance as an event, a choreological perspective needs to be able to debate the resulting significant shift in the usage and relationship of these two terms. Within this context - associated to the anti-art events of the Cabaret Voltaire in 1916 (Richter, 1965), to the dance fests of Laban in 1917,[27] to the site-specific experiments of the Judson Church (Banes, 1980), to the marathon events of Pina Bausch and Robert Wilson - the previously stable definitions of process and product have undergone not only a fluidity but also a multiplication of meaning. A choreological perspective suggests that the terms process and product refer to different things at different moments of the 'dance making', both before the performance and at the moment of performance.

dance as event

A consideration of dance as an event includes the notion of process - of rehearsal, research, thinking, etc, which leads to the selection of what is relevant / essential to any work to be the work, as discussed.[28] However, process not only precedes, but it is not excluded from the moment of performance. The view of dance as an event questions the dividing line between these concepts in such a way that process and its features permeate 'the work' in a variety of ways. Amongst the best documented are the improvisational experiments of the Judson Church, in particular Steve Paxton's contact-improvisation works where the 'work' only exists at the moment of performance (Banes, 1980), without the convention of the poietic as proposed by Nattiez.[29] Moreover, in Yvonne Rainer's Trio A (1963), the subjective elements of the performer's physicality and personal features which, traditionally, are objectified as a way to give stability to the dance object, are brought into the performance. This destabilises the 'work's' identity and raises questions about the validity of the notion that there is a single, representative, 'true' version of any work.

process in performance

However, process/performance practices not only allow for 'features' of the 'rehearsal' process to become a feature of the work. Process at the moment of performance includes the manner in which the event 'reveals itself' as a world to enter and be perceived. It is as proposed by States (1985) and Garner (1994) that ultimately it is the process of performance that gives the work its 'shape' in that

> it is through the audience, and its efforts of comprehension that order (or
> fail to order) what takes place on stage, that a play's events receive
> perceptual and cognitive shape (Garner 1994).

It is the manner in which the choreographer, the performers and the spectators enter into negotiations / economies / tactical interactivity / transactions which give 'identity' to the dance event. The work is not an invisible conceptual other, it is the interaction at the moment of performance. It is the way in which the materiality of the event takes place (its coming into being) but this coming into being is a negotiation, unstable and flexible between the combined intentions / impressions / interpretations of all involved in the event. In many cases artists, and indeed theorists, dispense with any notion of product and speak of the instantiation of performance, of the evolving temporality / spatiality of the event. Those involved in the event face a stage that

> exists in its own terms, and must build an understanding of events out of the immediacy with which it is confronted and in which it participates (Garner, 1994, pp.xiv-xv).

Although Garner was referring to audiences in particular, a choreological perspective adapts this statement for current dance practice to include a discussion of the moment of performance as a process which is tripartite, one which involves the making of sense, the performance of an understanding and a reception / comprehension / appreciation of that making and performing.

Within the context of the making, the relationship between process and product from the choreographer's perspective includes the setting of performance strategies and contexts which begin to locate the performance in time and space. Traditionally, this has been understood as the way in which narrative strategies are created. A ballet and modern work tend to follow the Aristotelian structure, with the dramatic arc comprising preface, introduction, development, conflict, climax and denouement. Ritual dances opt for a cyclical line, the return to the beginning reinforcing the notion of infinite, spiral evolution. Postmodern dance has opted for structures of juxtaposition and contra-contextuality, and aleatorical methods which force the spectators to enter into a different perceptual relationship with the materiality of the dance.

process / product and narrative

These kinds of narrative structures affect the performer. Performing a dance whose success lies in the exactability of its repetition, such as the staging of Kurt Jooss' The Green Table, is very different from the challenges described by former Cunningham dancer Carolyn Brown of performing a non-narrative work such as Rainforest (1968), subject to the effect of floating pillows, and with no fixed musical score with which to 'ground' the performance. Likewise, the dancers, to perform well in Wim Vandekeybus' What the Body Does Not Remember (1990), must keep the complicated system of movement,

27 Szeeman (1980), in which Laban's Sang an der Sonne, improvised on the mountain side is described.

28 This will be debated in Rubidge's discussion of Passing Phases and Halo, and explored choreographically by Sanchez-Colberg in the case study of Theatre enCorps' Futur/Perfekt in Part 2 of this text.

29 See Preston-Dunlop's essay 'Looking at Dances' in Part 2 of this text for discussion of Nattiez's perspective.

partnering and flying bricks going. For the spectator the process of performance is, for example, surviving three hours of a Bauschian work in which you are supposed to get bored (!!!) so that you can enjoy the rest, or, to feel saturated with the chaos on stage, to then be able to 'enjoy' the moments of rest.

process and meaning

States argues that narrative in performance is not linguistic but cognitive / phenomenal. The relationship between process of performance and meaning may be about making sense rather than receiving a sense. Interest lies in how the 'here and now' of performance, located in its own space and time, relates to other spaces and to other times, to remembering and projecting through what is occurring in the event, now. The relationship between the actuality of the performance and its references, connotations and accidents has to be accomodated by very different kinds of narrative structures when one considers the idea of narrative form in its theatrical perspective. Narrative means much more than story telling, although many ballets of the 19th century do just that. Narrative structures offer a play of time / space - juxtaposition / contradiction / simultaneity of events as the following instances show.

process and reality

In Mats Ek's duo <u>Smoke</u> (1995), the table and how it is touched exemplifies how Ek links to past and future events in the work through an attention to the poetics of sensations and impressions. Here it is no longer in the Aristotelian mode but nevertheless narrative. Lloyd Newson's strategies shift the event's here and now from the real to the unreal. In <u>Strange Fish</u> (1992) Newson shifts in one scene from the reality of a mimetic party, of mixing and not mixing with 'friends', to the imagined dream-like dance-like nightmare of one performer's gauche attempts at fraternisation. He offers a game of perception between the reality of the world on stage and and the world outside of it. Pina Bausch provides her spectators with actual sensatory stimulation, cutting through the sensory gap between performer and appreciator. In one work she offers them the smell of grass, in another the wetness of water. In <u>Iphigenia in Taurus</u> (1991) after a particularly chaotic scene on stage, Dominique Mercy / Orestes, lies on a table, resting/sleeping. The programme tells us it is now the 'nightmare' scene when the Furies visit Orestes in a dream. From the cavernous emptiness of the opera stage the audience begins to perceive that the whole of the lighting bridge is descending upon the performer / character. One notices that the lamps are still on, hot, burning. We begin to get uncomfortable in our seats. Suddenly the silence is broken by the metallic din of the lighting apparatus as it begins to rotate menacingly on top of the vulnerable body. The figure remains motionless as the stage world dances chaotically around and on top of him in a vision of hell.

In Theatre enCorps' <u>Now We Are No Longer</u> (2000) Sanchez-Colberg collaborates with her designer so that video footage of the performers presents images of them as other selves simultaneously with the performance. Past and present events link. Wim Wandekeybus, in <u>Roseland</u> (1990), has his performers pass bricks to each other, throw them and catch them, a process in which the audience may be invited to participate.

These works each address the issue of how an event establishes its particular 'here' and 'there' and proceeds to transform them. Such questions ask us to relook at traditional definitions of the 'who' and 'what' of performance and at what makes a performance 'work'. A clear divide no longer exists between what is intrinsic to a performance and what is extrinsic. Referential frames which delineate the boundaries between dance and not-dance, between the dance and the dancer, between dancerly movement and mundane movement, between then and now, between process and product, and so on, are no longer, or not necessarily, adhered to. Because dance theatre operates in what Turner terms a 'liminoid space' (Turner, 1982, pp.25-27), that is a space of ambiguities and subversion, the frames of normality cease to operate there. Instead liminal frames operate in which the 'anti-structure' of play (Sutton-Smith, 2001) takes over from the structured norms of reality.

**choreological
perspective**

Factor 6
Lea Anderson
Transitions Dance Company
Fred Whisker

chapter 3
the strands of the dance medium and their nexus

The nature of the dance medium is a topic of articulation in choreological study where the medium is regarded as multi-stranded, each strand being interrelated with the others. The term 'strand' conjures the image of material capable of being interconnected, such as plaited hair, rope, wool, sand. The strands of the dance medium are stated in the first place as the performer, the movement, the sound and the space, while their inter-relatedness is their nexus.[1]

Since we are dealing in this text with the performative in dance as a theatre art, the phrase "collective art of the theatre production" used by J. M. Burian to discuss the multi-stranded nature of the scenographic work of Josef Svoboda (Burian, 1993), resonates with the concept of the strands for dance theatre. So does the much used term 'mise-en scène'. All three terms embrace the concept of multistrandedness and polysemanticism as it manifests itself in various theatrical practices.

strands of the dance medium

The term 'strands' is preferred to 'components' (Adshead, 1988, p.21 et seq.) which suggests irreducible separate essentials. The latter term suggests a failure to take account of the fact that it is the flux of inter-relationships within the medium's parts that binds the work together and provides it with its complex polysemanticism[2]. The interlock of the strands, rather than the sum of the components, is the preferred concept of what constitutes the form of the work.

---

[1] The general concept of the strands proposed by Preston-Dunlop (1986), after lengthy work in response to the 'identity crisis in dance', debated by Adina Armelagos and Mary Sirridge in 1978 (JAAC Vol 37, No 2), was further developed by Sanchez-Colberg into a systematic methodology first published as 'Style and the dance: A clarification of the concept of style as applied to dance and a methodology for its research' in CORD Conference Proceedings, Dance and Culture Conference, Toronto, (1988).

It appears in Fernando Crespo's unpublished MA dissertation (1988), A justification for the inclusion of the strands of the dance medium in dance analysis. It was the research method in Sanchez-Colberg's doctoral research in 1992. It is illustrated by dance works in Preston-Dunlop's Looking at Dances (1998).

[2] Polysemanticism: See Aston and Savona (1995) and also Pavis (1982) and Eco (1980).

movement

The assumption that dances are made primarily of movement[3] is highly problematic since that position fails to take into account not only that movement is always mediated[4], but that present choreographic practice patently exhibits that assumption as untenable through its border crossing modes. The received position, formulated in the first decades of the 20th century, prioritised movement in an attempt to extricate dance from reliance on music[5], a position firmly in place at that time and indeed still to be found in place to-day co-existing with other ways of working. The use of notated scores underlines that position, for the score suggests that it is possible to isolate movement from the mover. Choreologists concerned with reconstructions from the score have recognised the problem, as the literature shows.[6]

movement styles

Armelagos and Sirridge discuss the concerns of dance reconstruction from the score identifying those ingredients that are customarily regarded as incidental but which are in reality essential. They name as essential the personal style of the dancers as well as the style of the movement written in the score. It is necessary to consider both in order to recapture the overall style of the work. An example might be given of the remounting of Martha Graham's <u>Primitive Mysteries</u> decades after its premiere. The lighter physique and increased technical facility of the later Graham company dancers lacked the elemental qualities of the original pioneering young women. The work could not be refound with them. Armelagos and Sirridge discuss the role of the aural elements of a work and its spatial setting. It is, they suggest, crucial to consider the interrelationship of all the parts in order to discover the identity of a work.

multistranded works

Today, contemporary choreographers such as William Forsythe present problems for the notating of their works because their creative position is one of co-authorship in a multi-stranded embodied medium. Isolating the movement of their works from the performers' mediation of it is almost impossible. Pina Bausch's tanztheater works are not movement pieces but theatre pieces in which highly individual improvisation, vocal utterances, interaction with props and set take place. A movement score would not constitute the work. Lloyd Newson's physical theatre works such as <u>Strange Fish</u> (1992), or Wim Vandekeybus' event for film <u>La Mentira</u> (1995) are so multistranded that any attempt to prioritise the movement would be farcical. William Forsythe's <u>Loss of Fine Detail</u> (1992) involves movement, nudity and costume issues, snow shovelling, distorted speech, et al. Considering the movement alone loses the dance.

3.1 the four strands

Entitling the four strands of the dance medium as 'performer, movement, sound and space' is a generalisation. It is recognised that, as such, the terms are inevitably inadequate. All words are culture bound and the dance world consists of several cultures each with their own language for their domain and for their medium.

Naming the strands used in a traditional classical piece requires particularisation. At a Birmingham Royal Ballet rehearsal, performers were referred to as 'ballerinas' or 'corps members' or 'soloists'. The movement material was referred to as the 'steps', or the 'pas', referring not only to what the legs were to do but to the movements of the whole body. The aural element was referred to as the music, the rehearsal pianist or the orchestra. The space was referred to as the stage. This particularisation would be inappropriate for a site-specific contemporary work. Here 'performer, material, sound score, on site' might be the terms used by the participants in such an event.

'Performer' is problematic in light of the overlapping nature of the performer / creator / spectator triad in a work of co-authorship. Forsythe's Ballett Frankfurt dancers, whom he terms his agents, do more than perform given movement; they turn his sketched phrases into dance material through resolving technical difficulties, finding the timing and flow of the material and investing it with their technique and intention. 'Body' in place of 'Performer' is used in many books on dance but is immediately problematic by suggesting the impossible; namely, an impersonal physicality when works require dancers to be highly personal, creative, individual, thoughtful people. On the other hand, the supreme importance in dance performance of its 'bodiedness' favours the term 'body' over 'performer'[6]. The problem recedes when it is recognised that each dance sub-culture has a particular point of view and practice and therefrom particular naming of the constituents of their art form. Any generalisation has to be regarded as establishing technical terms for choreological discourse; in this case, for categories within the medium.

performer

'Moves', 'material', 'action', 'physical language', 'gestures', 'steps', 'motion', 'the technique', are some of the terms found in dance practice for the movement category of the dance medium. 'Motion' was the term coined by Alwin Nikolais and used in the Murray Louis company's practice to distinguish

movement

---

[3] See statements on the medium of dance in Preston-Dunlop (1995, p.530 et seq).

[4] Mediated: through the existence of an intervening agency; in dance, the agency is not one easily identified agent but several interconnected agents that arise because dance is an embodied art and a triadic art.

[5] Laban's and Wigman's efforts to establish Absolute Dance, autonomy for dance, in the 1910s and 1920s in Preston-Dunlop (1998); Humphrey's rejection of St. Denis' music visualisation methods in Jordan (1996).

[6] Armelagos and Sirridge (1978); Anderson (1983); Marion, (1990), et al.

disembodied movement from movement mediated by an intending and committed dancer. 'The technique' is how prescribed movements are referred to in Competitive Ballroom and Latin dancing - the technique of the rumba or of the cha cha cha being the steps, body positions and partner holds that must be present in any created routine for competition.

sound 'Music' is how some dance people refer to their aural element whether it be music per se or not. The 'sound score', the 'sound track', the 'aural line', 'accompaniment', are terms used. Sound is the general term adopted for choreological discussion of any manifestation of an aural part of a work.

space The 'stage', the 'studio', the 'dance floor', the 'dance space', the 'venue', the 'site', the 'set', the 'space', are all names used for what is called 'space' in this text. What is in the space is subsumed in that category: the set, objects, lighting, smoke screen, dance floor, backdrop.

Isamu Noguchi designed for Martha Graham's works consistently over thirty years:

> *The relationship of dance to its ambience is important, which is why I do sets. To me, dance is an extension of a sculptural air - the air we happen to sit around in. Merely to say dance is another form of art is not enough. Art is more than what one happens to be looking at (in Tracy, 2000).*

The set designer creates his facades and objects to turn a mundane space into a liminal space, perhaps a liminal place. For Graham's <u>Appalachian Spring</u> (1944), Noguchi

> *attempted through the elimination of all non-essentials to arrive at an essence of the stark pioneer spirit, that essence which flows out to permeate the stage. It is empty but full at the same time. It is like Shaker furniture (ibid. p.44).*

The space is empty enough for the Graham dancers to dance but filled, transformed into the ambience that Noguchi, together with Graham, creates. The relationship is symbiotic.

3.2 the nexus and sub-strands

nexus The various ways in which the strands interweave and signify in practice gave rise to the concept of the Nexus of the Strands of the Dance Medium, which is a central methodological position in a choreological perspective within the wider concept of the triadic perspective of the art of dance itself. Nexus is best conceived of as a web of interelationships between those instances of each strand of the dance medium that particularly interest a choreographer in a work.

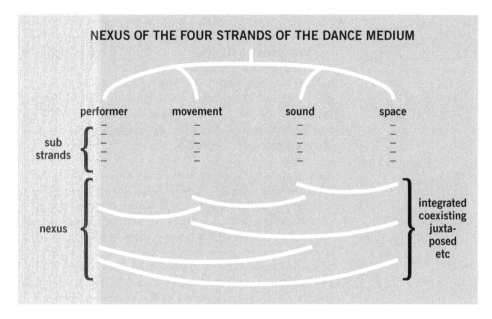

NEXUS OF THE FOUR STRANDS OF THE DANCE MEDIUM

performer   movement   sound   space

sub strands

nexus

integrated
coexisting
juxta-
posed
etc

Practice suggests that six fundamental nexial connections are used:

> the performer-movement connection,
> the performer-sound connection,
> the performer-space connection,
> the movement-sound connection,
> the movement-space connection, and
> the sound-space connection.

In Rosemary Butcher's visual performance work <u>Scan</u> (2000),
she prioritises the connection between the space and everything
else, as she has done in her earlier works, <u>The Site</u> (1983) for
example. In <u>Scan</u> she requires that the spectators are on all four
sides of a constricted square dance floor installation, seated so
close to the dancers that they may not always be able to see

nexial connections

Rosemary Butcher, <u>The Site</u> *Chris Ha*

complete bodies. The dance floor is lit from above by lines and stripes of warm light which emerge and change, restricted to one basic direction at a time, no diagonals or curves. Her movement material for her four dancers integrates with the light by its prime limitation of also not crossing the space diagonally nor passing through it in curving pathways. The work concludes with dancers corporeally absent, but visible as fragments of themselves in a film projected onto a deeper layer of the central square of the dance floor.

She has made decisions about nexial connection between the sound and the space. The score is digitally pre-recorded stereophonically and is heard through several speakers placed behind and around the spectators as a moving aural ambience. The nexial connection of performer/sound is played down. The spectator could be given stronger access to the dynamic energy of the performers if they had been asked to allow their footfall and breathing to be heard. However, Butcher does not forefront that but rather the spatial forms of the dancers' intertwining bodies. The connection of the four dancers with their material is given through their virtuosic articulation and dexterity of it. They perform consistently intricate and fast gestural movement whose form and dynamic is reflected throughout their being, interspersed with tensioned stillnesses. Dominant structures are touches, grasps, lifts, leans, woman to woman, man to man, woman to man, punctuated by fast falls and immediate rises. No dramatic intent is required but rather a concentration on the placement and timing and technical strength, presenting an apparent ease with which the near impossible is achieved.

nexus as treatment

Through her aesthetic choices Butcher shows how the nexus between strands is a crucial aspect of choreographic treatment of idea. It also shows how comprehensive knowledge and experience of what possibilities are contained within each strand enables all participants in the making and presenting and appreciating of a work to make highly sophisticated choices. These possibilities are termed sub-strands in choreological discourse; that is, those visual, aural or kinetic items which broadly, are contained under the general heading of each of the main strands. It is choice of these 'items' or 'means' within one strand, connected nexially to 'items' and 'means' in other strands, that sets up the cohesion of making.

mise en scène

In discussion, it has been suggested that mise en scène is an established and sufficent term for what is proposed by the concepts of the strands of the dance medium. That is disputed here. Mise en scène presumes that there is a text to be 'put on stage' (Aston & Savona, 1991 p.121). That might be the case for dances in opera (see Stuart Hopps choreography for Mark Anthony Turnage's Silver Tassie) and musical theatre (see the singing/dancing roles in the 2001 London production of Kiss me Kate). But it is not the case in all dances in that the movement material is only regarded as 'the text' when it is a fixed form or notated. Lighting, costuming, props might be integrated from the beginning of rehearsels, and frequently are, in postmodern performative works. Forsythe is his own scenographer. But mise en scène practice does share polysemanticism with the nexus of the strands practice in that it is the mix of the elements of staging (with the text) or the mix of the substrands of the dance medium that provide the compex signs in a theatre piece and in a work of dance.

We continue with some examples from Butcher's practice in Scan, in the first instance those under the umbrella concept of 'the performer' . Her four dancers are mature experienced artists. Their look suggests that gender matters, albeit played down but present (in contrast to a piece in which androgyny, youth and inexperience are forefronted). Gender difference is embodied through costuming but played down through similarity of movement material and lifts, while individual personality is enhanced through avoiding a standard dancerly look, retaining individual hair styling. Individuality is played down by common movement material, albeit never in unison. The physicality of the dancers is forefronted by placing them so close to the spectators that even their body heat is felt. It is played down by the legs being covered in trousers (unlike the exposure of legs and arms of Deborah Bull in Forsythe's Steptext, in which every sinew of her body is visible, but in her case played down by maintaining the physical distance offered by a procenium theatre.)

Important in a choreological perspective of nexus connections through substrands is the original concept of the tripartition. Engaging with Butcher's work requires that one look at it from the three perspectives: the making of the work centred on Butcher herself with her dancers and her lighting and sound directors, the performing centred on the lived experience of the dancers and technicians, and the reception centred on the spectators' perception. The experience of the dancers of their close proximity to the spectators and each other is as significant as the other way round, as is Butcher's decision that this extreme proximity should happen.

It is choreographic practice that constantly enlarges the possibilities within each strand as well as ways of connecting them. It would be unhelpful to 'list' possibilities since they shift, change and increase with each generation and each artist. It is however helpful for broad categories to be known. Under 'performer', the following can serve as a starting point:

- Physique
- Ethnicity
- Technical ability
- Personal style
- Costume
- Hair
- Shoes/feet
- Reification
- Gender
- Age

Differences of physique may be sought by Lea Anderson in her selection of the members for her two companies - the Featherstonehaughs for men and Cholmondeleys for women - while uniformity of physique will be preferred for the corps de ballet in a production of <u>Giselle</u> (1841).

gender

The substrand 'gender' may be significant for Jerome Robbins' choreography in Bernstein's <u>West Side Story</u> (1957), based as it is on Shakespeare's Romeo and Juliet love story, while it is fluid for Twyla Tharp's <u>The Fugue</u> (1970), which she created first for one sex and remade for the other.

ethnicity

Ethnicity of narrative, and therefore of casting, is also significant for <u>West Side Story</u> since the two families are caught up in Puerto Rican/white American antagonism. Cast changes which involve a change in the ethnic characteristics of a dancer can confuse and may ruin the impact of a work. One scene in Dorothy Madden's <u>Zero Six</u> (1974) refers to war. The original female soloist in that scene had an oriental physique which immediately resonated with the American public to the traumatic Vietnam war. When mounted in London in the 1980s, without an oriental soloist, the scene was impoverished, but in any case it would not have resonated so powerfully in Great Britain. To retain the work's strong message, Madden had to shift the reference to European war with an occidental cast.

dance and the performative

Dorothy Madden, <u>Zero Six</u> *Anon*

costume and make-up

In <u>Smithereens</u>, Lea Anderson, as always, paid attention to both the aesthetic and the semiotic in her choice of costume design. Selecting from her research into dance in the Weimar Republic, she picked up on the exotic look of the Berlin cabaret for the 'lit up' dress for Teresa Barker. Josephine Baker? Valeska Gert? She cross-dresses her dancers; the female Cholmondeleys and the male Featherstonehaughs all being comfortable in fishnet tights one moment and a suit the next.

shoes

A constituent considered of interest in a work within the strand 'performer' might be the shoes that are worn. Choreographically they are chosen for a purpose; design-wise they have to be bought or capable of being made, from the spectators' perspective they give off style. Possibly shoes are put on or taken off during the performance. That act will have a function in the work, prosaic or symbolic. Lack of shoes may stand as a metaphor, and as it did for Martha Graham as she connected deeply with the ground rather than pushing against it as does the blocked shoe of ballet. The kind of shoe may be at variance with the rest of the costume as it is in Edouard Locke's <u>Duo One</u> (1993), where running shoes and a black tutu are juxtaposed on the same female dancer's body. The two cultures represented confuse, pose questions, they require interpretation.

Shoe/music nexus may offer a solution for the creator as it does in Christopher Bruce's <u>Swan Song</u> (1987), where the unison tap dancing of the two tormentors of the prisoner is one of Bruce's means of embodying threat (taking into account that the embodiment is not the sole province of Bruce or his dancers, but equally his spectators). Blocked ballet shoes worn by men confront gender norms in ballet culture. The flippers on the feet of the landlocked dancers in Decouflé's <u>Codex</u> (1993) clearly juxtapose two incompatible elements. Together with Turkish folk dance music and formal counterpoint choreography, the confusion of image makes classic comedy.

flesh

The bare feet and body of a young woman treading on, then writhing on pebbles in Lloyd Newson's <u>Strange Fish</u> appear in a complex work of physical theatre exploring the connection, and the agony of disconnection, between people and their worlds. The gross physical discomfort in the scene suggests all manner of tortuous avenues as the contradiction of the two elements - soft flesh and hard stone - and their cultural associations, impinge on the spectators' interpretative attention.

sound, its substrands and examples of nexus

What kinds of noise might become a sound score for a dance? At the beginning of the 20th century Ruth St Denis, Emile Jacques Dalcroze and Mary Wigman each had a decisive point of view about sound in dance.

music domination

Dalcroze, in Geneva and Dresden, started with music, and used it to educate young people by teaching them to 'experience music through the rhythmic expression of the body' (Sorrell, 1986). As the dancers embodied the structures of the music in bodily movement, complex counted and felt counterpoint in the body's co-ordination emerged. The music was played live (there being no such thing as recorded music in 1910), on piano or percussion instruments, mostly metrical. It dominated the movement and the mover.

music visualisation

Ruth St Denis, in New York, started with music also, both piano and orchestral, which she visualised in her choreographies. Her music visualisation method, codified and thorough, required that the dancer listen to the rhythm, the melodic line, the pitch, the timbre, the instrumentation, the tempo, the phrasing, and from that listening create movements which embodied, and made visible for the spectator, the music's content. For St Denis, the music dominated but her wide choice of music, exotic and classical, and her acute ear for music's content as well as its structure, enabled her to create improvised movement for herself and her company which was received with acclaim.

Vaslav Nijinsky choreographed <u>The Rite of Spring</u> to Stravinsky's score in 1912. As was customary, the score came first, and the dance was designed to follow it, closely. Stravinsky's innovations were striking in the rhythmic aspect of his music. Looking at the frequent changes of time signatures in the score it is clear that for dancers used to Tchaikovsky and Chopin, making, performing and appreciating with this music was a new and difficult challenge, as Bronislava Nijinska's memoirs inform us. For <u>The Rite of Spring</u> Nijinsky did not depart from the usual music / movement nexus of the time; he followed the music closely while his innovation lay in the choice of radically different movements. The rhythm was metric; it had a discernible pulse that did not remain even but changed rapidly. In the Sacrificial Dance the opening bars are + 3/16 2/16 3/16 3/26 2/8 2/16 3/16 3/16 2/8. <u>Les Noces</u> has similar changes.[7] Since the music was in this irregular metric rhythm, so too is the dance.

dance and the performative

Mary Wigman, abandoning her studentship with Dalcroze, associated herself with Laban and his massive experiments to revitalise dance. These included removing the dominance of music and with it the dominance of metred time. She became known as the presenter of Absolute Dance - the dance which stood on its own, musicless, without narrative, the dancer and the dance empowered to present themselves as the message, the moving body creating the sound through breath and footfall. She and Laban experimented with the mover dominating the musician, vice versa to the norm. In <u>Hexentanz</u> (1914), her percussionist watched acutely her every move, her pauses, her non-metric movement rhythms, her intense dynamic range, and integrated his beating of the gong and drum with her bodily actions (Deutsche Rundfunk, 1985).

Mary Wigman, <u>Hexentanz</u> Anon

These early practices point to sound substrands of dance music and also to the nexial connections of sound - movement, sound - performer. The basic connections at this point were total integration, total absence of connection, total derivation of movement from music or music from movement. Understanding nexus is crucial because the web underlying the surface embodiment of a dance is as essential to the dance's identity as the surface form. In a casual look at a work, such as the film of Wigman's <u>Hexentanz</u>, the spectator can see the figure, the movement and hear the sound, but may well miss the point that this dance is a watershed in the history of the relationship between music and movement.

**movement / sound
nexus**

[7] Score published by Chester Music Publishers.

St Denis' analysis of music provides possible categories of the aural content of music that choreographers might and do forefront, or address, in their making. What Wigman and Laban introduced was the basis of rhythm and dynamic phrasing contained in movement itself; the possibilities of 'time, strength, and space'(Wigman, 1966, p.11), which later became Laban's study of human effort. It was Doris Humphrey, graduating from company membership with Ruth St Denis, who articulated the sources of bodily rhythm as motor rhythm, breath rhythm, emotional rhythm, and the basis of motion as suspension, fall and recovery, the giving in to and rebound from gravity (Humphrey, 1959, p.106). The nexial connections between sound and movement, sound and performer develop with Humphrey's emancipation from St Denis so that counterpoint and polyrhythmic connections emerge (Jordan, 1996).

music for dance

Louis Horst emphasised a requirement for the sparsity of music for dance so that the qualities of the movement might be more visible and the writing of musical works specifically for dances. Horst's scores were not intended to be played in concert, as Stravinsky's are:

> [Horst's] music would become an integral part of the dance, and as he himself said, not to be played, or judged, apart from the dance 'because it would be dull' (Madden, 1996 p.55).

The nexial connection had moved on by these practices to begin all manner of interrelatedness and interdependence which would gradually appear in practice.

Balanchine's music illumination

George Balanchine, working with Igor Stravinsky, created a masterly form of integration between the music and the dancers. Apollo (1929) is a prime example. While his works are always described as intensely musical, they are not visualisation, but music illumination:

> I had to try to paint or design time with bodies in order to create a resemblance between the dance and what was going on in sound (Denby, 1968).

Stravinsky's idea for the work was

> to compose a ballet founded on moments or episodes in Greek mythology plastically interpreted by dancing of the so-called classical school (White, 1966, p.340).

As White continues, Stravinsky, fortified by his admiration of classical ballet, envisaged the work as a ballet blanc, emphasising the similarity of aural images to such a ballet, not their contrasts. He wrote his score with this purity in mind:

> The absence of many-coloured effects and of all superfluities produced a wonderful freshness (ibid.).

Balanchine regarded this score of Stravinsky's as leading him to a turning point in his choreographic aesthetic. He found it restrained 'like a white on white canvas', disciplined, yet lyrical. It encouraged him to emulate the restraint, to give up his practice of using many possibilities in each work to find 'the one possibility that was inevitable.'

Looking for that inevitability he realised that

> like tones in music and shades in painting, gestures have certain family relations which, as groups, impose their own laws (Taper, 1974, p.104).

He had found what Laban had called the choreological order, the inevitable preparation and recovering for each gesture. Being educated as a musician and well aware of painting, he was able to make use of the kinship of tonal and colour harmonic structures to find those in dance. The music / movement nexus of Balanchine and Stravinsky has little to do with integration at surface form level but much more to each artist innovating a new grammar with a shared aesthetic.

Jane Dudley was moved by a performance she witnessed by the blind harmonica player Sonny Terry. It was not only his music but his playing and his 'great loneliness and greater weirdness' that set her going on Harmonica Breakdown (1940). He drew all manner of animal wailing sounds from his harmonica and his singing, with Brownie McGhee strumming his washboard with a spoon. Dudley catches her feeling for Sonny's person and condition when, as she said:

choreographer / musician

> I scratch my leg like a skinny old bony hound dog.[8]

This is not music visualisation but a response by a choreographer to a musician.

Not only the elements of music put in place by St Denis' method but the words of Brahms' Liebeslieder were a source for Mark Morris' Love Song Waltzes (1989). He integrates and counterpoints with Brahms' rhythmic structure and extracts images from the words, usually sung live in the orchestra pit. These he embodies in the gestural part of his movement vocabulary, adding a piquancy to what might otherwise be bland music visualisation. The nexial connections here are between specific substrands of music with substrands of movement - words (not melodies or body sounds or instrumentation) with sign carrying gestures (not abstractions or received vocabularies).

words and movement

Morris pays no attention to the co-existing nexus introduced by Cunningham and Cage. To audiences familiar with a way of engaging with works with co-existing strands, Morris' works can seem obvious through their reiteration in motion of things sonorous. His works contain so much redundant information as to inhibit engagement with any real curiosity. For others his

co-existing strands

---

8 Interview with Jane Dudley, 2001.

accessibility is a joy, and his humour thoroughly provoking.

The Merce Cunningham / John Cage development in practice, involving separate choreographing and composing for the same work, revolutionised the way sound and movement connected. The tripartite perspective offers three experiences of a work with co-existing strands:

- during the making processes, in which the place of performance and the duration of the performance are the only two limitations shared between the artists, each will make what he will for the agreed length of time and not share the outcome until the performance;
- the performing experience, in which the dancers hear the sound for the first time at opening night, and dance their dance with a sound score that shares their space, and with which they do not interact;
- the spectators' interpretation of the two co-existing strands, which neither integrate with each other nor are deliberately different from each other, is dependent on their listening and looking without searching for a non-existent narrative. Rather, they should look and listen in the same way that they are used to looking at and listening to the co-existing strands of activity in daily life, or possibly make their own reality (Caplan and Cunningham,1986).

juxtaposing strands

Juxtaposing strands that do not belong together has become a norm in postmodern performance. This treatment brings side by side cultures that embody opposing perspectives, or at any rate ones that are distinctly other. In Forsythe's <u>Artifact</u> (1985),

a dancer / actor intones through a megaphone. In contrast a phalanx of classical dancers bordering the stage create a soundtrack by the concerted swish of their feet on the dance floor in their phrases of ronds de jambe à terre, and their tendus. The unexpected positioning in the same scene of verbal and non-verbal sound and their distinctly different sources beg all sorts of questions.

Edouard Locke's <u>Duo One</u>, where his juxtapositioning goes across all the strands, has already been referred to. The dance starts with his hand full of little fish who are decidedly in the wrong place, out of water and struggling. The duo goes on to juxtapose heavy beat music with movement that draws on ballet, behaviour and tumbling, all of which juxtapose with each other. It is danced by a woman whose clothing contrasts with her frizzy hair, her tutu with her running shoes, all of which is contrasted with her male partner who is elegantly dressed in bow tie, neat white shirt and pressed black trousers.

Performer / sound experiments proliferate. Breath and footfall may be an aural layer of the work, either live or recorded during rehearsal, with or without musical score. Efforts made not to let the spectator hear the breath and blocked shoe footfall in a classical work is a nexial issue. Removing that noise increases the perceptual distance between dancer and audience, increasing the ethereal and diminishing the corporeal, diminishing the opportunity for performative interaction.

breath and footfall

Pina Bausch, in her choreography for Stravinsky's <u>Sacre de Printemps</u> (1977), gives the audience access to the violence of the theme through the sounds of the movement as the dancers hit themselves, winding themselves, brushing through the peat on the ground, gasping for breath. She provides access to the corporeality of her interpretation through the dancers' sounds as well as their movement. In so doing she draws the spectator into a sensory experience.

Ana Sanchez-Colberg, <u>Futur/Perfekt</u> *Paul Houghton*

In later works her dancers speak to the spectators, as in <u>1980</u>., aand Ana Sanchez-Colberg's in <u>Futur/Perfekt</u> (2001). So too do

speaking dancers

Lloyd Newson's in <u>can we afford this, the cost of living</u> (2000). These dancers are not simply performing for their audience; they are interacting with them in a figure of eight of energy and meaning, in works of a performative art.

sound / space nexus

Where a sound of a dance comes from affects the experience of all concerned. In Bausch's <u>Bluebeard</u> (1977), the sound emerges from the tape recorder which the protagonist operates manually, so bringing the spectator into the event directly. In Bronislava Nijinska's <u>Les Noces</u> (1923), the orchestra and singers are hidden in the pit, underlining the separation of artists from spectators. Ed Wubbe compromises. He chooses to have his piano player on stage in <u>Kathleen</u> (1994) concurrently with a recording of an underlying atmospheric sound score. The performative element of a work is hugely influenced by where its sound comes from. Lea Anderson plans the 'where from' of her sound early on. Replying to Ian Bramley's question as to how she planned to take the performative presence of the musicians on stage in <u>3</u> (2001), she replied

> We have designed Steve and Billy into the new piece. We know already how they will be seen in relation to the movement; they'll have a place on stage that is very much part of the design and won't be just a couple of musicians sitting in a corner. We do think about how live music will be perceived within the performance (Bramley 2001, p.7).

co-existing sound / space

John Cage dragged and scratched a chair slowly around the circumference of the arena stage throughout a work in which Cunningham improvised his movement material on chance-derived cues. Cage's sound started at one side of the stage and gradually travelled around to reach the other, his crouching figure acting as a co-existing foil for Cunningham.[9] The contrast of the two was startling; the ambient scraping noise of Cage with the silently engrossed Cunningham. Their absorbed independence made them seem compatible.

contra-contextual sound / space

Sounds of a radio news bulletin blasting through the open windows intermittently from passing cars was designed to accompany a ballet class as part of a choreological experiment in contra-contextual nexial connections. The outside sound hardly penetrated the liminal space for the dancers. But the viewers were disturbed. The mundane news of atrocities and the aesthetic atmosphere were at odds. The spectators constructed their own interpretation. It appeared that they identified either with the sound or with the dancers while a few just enjoyed the contrast.

integrated sound / space

In Christopher Bruce's <u>Waiting</u> (1993), a dramatic work around the story of apartheid and Nelson Mandela, the performers, both dancers and a percussionist, beat the rhythmical material (composed by Errollyn Wallen) on the rusty corregated iron set (created by Marion Bruce). The combination of the harsh percussive sound emanating through bodily contact with a set that resonated of township poverty created an unmistakable atmosphere of palpable discomfort.

Noguchi describes his working relationship with Graham by commenting:

choreographer and set designer

> Martha was always inventing, using whatever object I gave her. You can call it a prop or a usable thing (Tracy, 2000, p.67).

For his set for <u>Cave of the Heart</u> (1946) Noguchi

> constructed a landscape like the islands of Greece. On the horizon (center rear) lies a volcanic shape like a black aorta of the heart; to this lead stepping stone islands... opposite (stage left) is coiled a green serpent, on whose back rests the transformation dress of gold (metal) (ibid. p.68).

These scuptural objects she used centrally to choreograph the highly charged drama of Medea. The stepping stone 'islands' represented 'the place of passage from life to death'. They provided Graham with an opportunity for all manner of movement in which the emotional danger of not being on terra firma prevailed. Noguchi created a metallic wire object which transformed into a flaming garment which Medea moves into as she is finally overwhelmed. Here the set provides both the ambience for the drama and the source for choreographic invention.

It was designer Arch Lauterer who advised that the dress rehearsal is too late in the creation of a work to contribute the lighting (1959); for him, light was an essential part of the work's generation. For Anthony Bowne, a purpose of his designs is "to reveal meaning in the dance, not merely to give it light" (1989). Ross Cameron's lighting for Dale Thompson's work <u>Intaglio</u> (1999) did just that. His rig is illustrated. He isolated a 'place' by painting the floor with one kind of light, he 'sea' painted the floor around paper boats, he side lit the three figures to underscore their focus on distance.

lighting designer and choreographer

Dale Thompson, <u>Intaglio</u> *Toni Nandi*

9 Performance at Goldsmiths College, London, in 1979 during a residency of Cunningham and Cage at the Laban Centre.

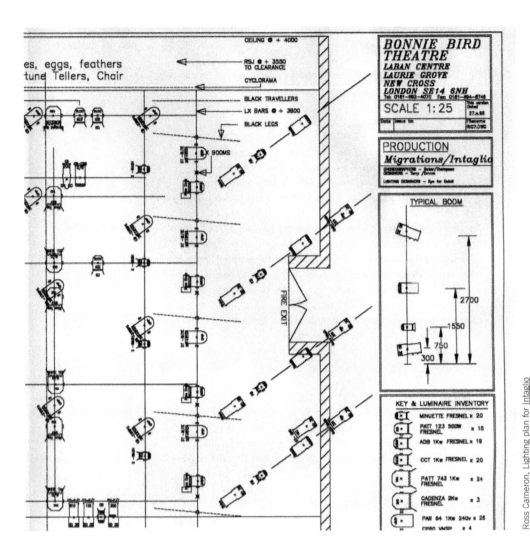

es, eggs, feathers
tune Tellers, Chair

CEILING ⊕ + 4000

RSJ ⊕ + 3550
TO CLEARANCE

CYCLORAMA

BLACK TRAVELLERS

LX BARS ⊕ + 3800

BLACK LEGS

BOOMS

FIRE EXIT

BONNIE BIRD THEATRE
LABAN CENTRE
LAURIE GROVE
NEW CROSS
LONDON SE14 6NH
Tel: 0181-692-4070 Fax: 0181-694-8749

SCALE 1:25

PRODUCTION
Migrations/Intaglio

TYPICAL BOOM

2700
1550
750
300

KEY & LUMINAIRE INVENTORY

MINUETTE FRESNEL x 20

PATT 123 500W x 15
FRESNEL

ADB 1Kw FRESNEL x 19

CCT 1Kw FRESNEL x 20

PATT 743 1Kw x 24
FRESNEL

CADENZA 2Kw x 3
FRESNEL

PAR 64 1Kw 240v x 28

Like Peter Mumford (1985), he aimed for atmosphere and emotional states so that, with the movement material and the title, the required illusion might be put in place. For other artists meaning and illusion are not the issue. Forsythe has ambient lights in place on stage to be spun and shifted around as part of the action. They may refer, or not; they are definitely a norm-flouting actuality.

space / performer

In <u>Smithereens</u> (1999), Lea Anderson's cast dance on platforms that are capable of being pushed and dragged anywhere in the space. She changes the spatial form of the area, sometimes as a long joined-up platform, then as separate Islands, then as walkways, then as obstacles. The dancers shift them with dexterity and speed while their colleagues change costume for the next surprising episode. The physicality of the bodies with the platforms gives the whole event a corporeality in keeping with the topic of the work, Weimar Germany, especially its Berlin cabaret life.

camera / space

Using filmed images in a performance gives an interesting layering of a work's movement content.

Rosemary Butcher, <u>Body as Site</u> *Mark Anderson*

Rosemary Butcher offers both a corporeal dancer and her image, concurrently, in <u>Body as Site</u> (1993). In Ed Wubbe's filmed version of <u>Kathleen</u>, the dancers take turns to film, slipping in and out of being a dancer and a camera operator. The sense of voyeurism pervades the work through the invasive nature of ambient camera people amongst dancers to create an illusion of observed urban promiscuity.

In a workshop, a group of dancers engaged in a tightly structured improvisation while one filmed what was going on from different viewpoints. She was part of the improvisation and her film, projected on the backdrop, created a further layer. From time to time she froze an image and then caught up with the rest of the dance. Phenomenally, the dual happening was full of interesting temporal tensions for the spectator who makes of it what he/she wants - meanings or visual pleasure.

The works cited confront the pigeon-holing and traditional separation of musicians, dancers, composers, set designers. They confront the norm that the choreographer creates the movement work with the dancers which is then 'produced', by adding

choreological perspective

lighting and costumes. The works cited validate the centrality of the concept of the nexus of the medium's strands to choreological theory and practice.

Nexial practice has changed over time. Mary Wigman's space was a physically empty black box. It was her relationship with it which created her magic:

> It is not the tangible, limited, limiting space of concrete reality, but the imaginary irrational space of the danced dimension, that space which can erase the boundaries of all corporeality and can turn the gesture, flowing as it is, into an image of seeming endlessness, losing itself in self-completion like rays, like streams, like breath... Only in its spatial embrace can the dance achieve its final and decisive effect (1966, p.12).

Today, integrated, juxtaposed, co-existing scenography are concepts used as a starting point for understanding how the medium's strands create a variety of images. It is argued here that the nature of the nexus is as significant as the nature of the elements within each strand, both as a signifier between the work and its receivers and in the practical process of creation. The hidden rules and norms that a nexial process might comprise constitute a substantial part of the style and identity of a work of performance. One cannot imagine Cunningham separated from his chosen nexial way of working, co-existing media. One cannot imagine Forsythe without his co-authorship nexus with his dancers, or Balanchine without his music / movement connections.

Contrast Laban's mimetic, musicless <u>Gaukelei</u> (1923) with Amanda Miller's <u>Kunst der Fuge</u> (1999).

The strands of the medium are stated in this text as four. That position serves as a starting point only since today dances are made in films, in videos and in interactive computer happenings, each of which adds its own medium and its own grammar, subverting the corporeal position of a live performance. They have a distinct disruption of normal time and space which allows for fragmentation of the body as well as an ability to transport people from one site to another in the blink of an eye. How the grammars of these more recent media interface and interact with lived dancing, is a topic presented in Rubidge's essay in Part 2.

Amanda Miller, <u>Kunst Der Fuge</u> *Klaus Fröhlich*

Susan and the Saints
and the Neighbours
Barak Marshall
Transitions Dance Company
Toni Nandi

chapter 4
movement mediated by the performer: Laban and beyond

The study of movement remains essential content of any discourse in choreological study, preferably undertaken practically. The perspective that the performer as mediator is ever present in an embodied performative art is the starting point. The nature of this inextricable connection dictates teaching, creating and research methods and the manner in which movement is described on paper. The present discussion is not an attempt to provide a manual of performer/movement practice but to present an introduction to the main issues of a choreological perspective on this aspect of dance.

Mediation by the performer may seem obvious, but scrutiny of manuals on the movement of dance reveal that it is not unusual to write about movement as if it were embodied by an impersonal body rather than by a living personality. Writers may describe movement as if it were a disembodied independent element of dance. Discussing movement in written words is notoriously difficult since the lived experience is never compatible with words. Oral discussion about movement is always accompanied by gestures which embody the very thing that words find beyond their capacity. Writers in the phenomenology of dance, Maxine Sheets-Johnstone and Sondra Fraleigh, have had to provide fresh language to deal with the lived-body, consciousness-body, body-subject and body-object concepts which, to some readers, may sound problematic but which does approach the issue head on. Laban is the writer who most successfully maintains the performer-movement nexus in his language but in so doing his texts are cumbersome to read.

movement in the written word

In an effort to overcome the problem, some practical dance people prefer using the written page as a dancing space, making their marks on paper as spatial compositions (Tufnell and Crickmay, 1988). Choreographers working with improvisation, Miranda Tufnell and Chris Crickmay, make no attempt to accomodate their vision and mode of being to the conventional codes of conduct of book writing in Body Space Image (1988). Preston-Dunlop, in her Looking at Dances: A Choreological

Perspective on Choreography (1998), decided to design her text in the rhythm of verbal language, since her usual way of speaking dance is in a studio, where rhythm and short sentences are more conducive to practical discovery than an argued discussion. In this document the traditional format for discourse is adhered to. However, the reader is asked to read the discussion on movement corporeally with a mover's eye and a dancer's feel for what is beyond the words.

Janet Adshead provides a typical text on movement in dance:

> The moving body has a shape, which may be curved, linear, etc., and it has a size, both in its own right and in relation to other bodies... (1988, p.23).

The text is informative but problematic from a choreological perspective since the performer's mediation is reduced to that of a body, as an 'it' object. Notation manuals by their nature depersonalise the movement, as this example describing the movement in a score shows:

> The timing in steps, gestures, jumps and their combinations are made by the sequential and simultaneous flow of the weight-bearing action and the free leg; fluidity and staccato dynamics are given by the sequential flow from support to gesture and by the sharp juxtaposition of support to gesture (Hackney, Manno and Topaz, in Preston-Dunlop, 1995, p.263).

feeling
To distinguish and create the qualities described above, in performance, the dancer is going to feel one leg supporting her and the other gesturing in space. She has to initiate the flow moving through from her supporting leg to gesturing leg, or in contrast she has to make it happen all at once, on the instant. Notators know that feeling is essential in reading notation scores, through their experience as dancers and of reconstructing works, but the manuals suggest that a reified body is doing something, functioning like an object, not an artist. This not only distorts the reality of the performer / movement nexus but contributes to the alienation felt by many dancers toward notation.

intention
Rosemary Brandt presents the mediating perspective by emphasising the living person's intention and experience of what she is performing: 'Movement doesn't happen to you, you make it happen'.[1]

Laban's writings emphasise the personal attitudes that make the creating of movement possible. Here he is writing on one of the four motions factors:

> The motion factor of Time can be associated with man's faculty of participation with decision. Decisions can be made either unexpectedly and suddenly by letting one thing go and replacing it with another one at a given moment, or they may be developed gradually by sustaining some of the previous conditions over a period of time (1971, p.127).

lived experience
The condition he refers to is the dynamic and spatial content

held in the person's lived experience from whatever movement he or she has just created. Laban goes on to discuss how a person's movement is intimately connected with that person's experience of self and of their interaction with other selves:

> ...mastery of movement is not of value only to the stage artists, but to everyone, since we are all concerned, whether consciously or unconsciously, with perception and expression [of our movement] (ibid. p.89).

The mediating person is present as a perceiving and emitting human being. In choreological writing the problem of how to discuss movement, that is, performer mediated movement, in words, is ever present since in research and academic discourse the word reigns supreme as the accepted means of communication. Most people are unable to read movement notation systems, effort graphs, Motif Writing, ChuMM graphs and so on which are the prioritised choreological marks on paper.[2] But no mark on paper, linguistic or choreological, can capture mediated movement adequately. Performed movement is irreducible.

Transitions Dance Company
Fred Whisker

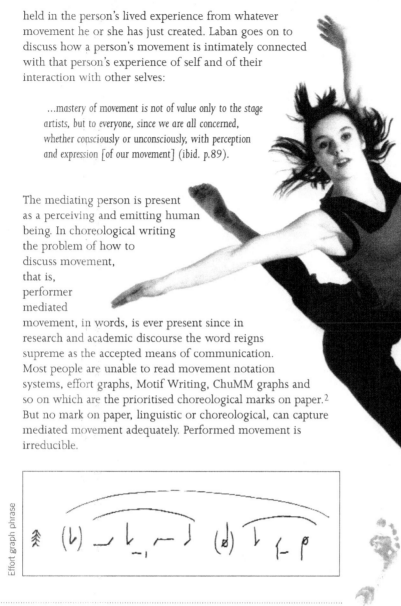

Effort graph phrase

4.1 the ontology of human movement from a choreological perspective

Choreological study, focusing as it does on dance as a performative art, is concerned with those aspects of human movement which contribute to the function and expressivity of movement in the context of dance as theatre, and not in the context of the study of movement per se. While kinesiology and

performative movement

---

[1] Rosemary Brandt, choreological specialist giving a master class in ballet, quoted in Preston-Dunlop (1995, p.222).

[2] See Jeffrey Scott Longstaff's manual (1999) for these and other means of documenting movement on paper.

biomechanics illuminate aspects of skilled bodily movement, and motor control studies illuminate how movement sequences are learned, it is the performative nature of human movement, transactional between art work, performer and spectator, that is the main concern here.

The mix, the nexus, of formal dance vocabularies with the vocabularies of interpersonal behaviour are of particular interest in dance. The manifold ways in which the mundane and the formal merge and juxtapose, in a performative environment, constitute the changing genres and vogues of the dance art. It is this mix that provides layers to the transactional nature of dance performance.

behaviour   It is common knowledge that extensive observation of people socially interacting has shown that tacitly agreed rules exist which govern what is regarded as civilised culture-bound behaviour. Against these rules the machinations of individuality, originality, comedy, tragedy and madness are judged. Psychologists describe these rules through their language and sociologists through theirs since behaviour studies require psycho- and socio-debate. Here we use choreological language.

Behaviour has a kinetic form. This is Laban's way of describing its organicism:

> A movement makes sense only if it progresses organically and this means that phases which follow each other in a natural succession must be chosen. It is therefore essential to find the natural characteristics of the (single) phases which we wish to join together in order to create a sensible sequence (Laban, 1966, p.4).[3]

choreological order   This natural succession he names 'the choreological order'. He is not referring here only to the order in mundane social behaviour but to order in human kinetic behaviour as it appears in the theatre, in dance.

> We must try to find its [movement's] real structure and the choreological order within it through which movement becomes penetrable, meaningful and understandable (ibid. p.viii).

Rosemary Brandt comments that the choreological order is 'that which holds our movement together' through hidden rules. (Preston-Dunlop, 1995, p.222). Just what these laws and 'natural' or 'organic' forms of sequentiality are requires discussion. They are found in the manner in which one movement organically follows another, through the mover preparing her next action, through making organic transitions from one movement to the next. There may be combinations of many of these simultaneously. This kind of compensation of opposites is found in movement that is humane, within the bounds of humanity, not in the movement of objects, marionettes, or computer generated figures.

balance of opposites   The balance of opposites is apparent in the body's muscularity.

The balance of contraction and release in muscle groups enables limbs to flex and stretch, the torso to bend and twist, in an efficient non-stressful manner. With too much relaxation we fail to combat the pull of gravity and so fall to the ground. With too much contraction we sieze up. Laban shows how the balance of movement's dynamic qualities is equally essential. Strong exertion is balanced by light buoyancy. Maintaining a slow pace is relieved by speeding up and vice versa. Holding back the flow of the movement energy is relieved by allowing the energy to flow freely. The maintenance of directly focused movement is relieved by allowing the focus to wander in space. Equally, maintaining continuous three dimensional plasticity is relieved by forming focused, straight movement lines.

The relief in all these counterbalances is experienced by both the moving person and the spectator. Laban's concept of the 'choreological order' holds good for making, performing and receiving dance material. Whether or not organic dance material promotes performative interaction is another matter.

spatial balance

The balance of spatial opposites also contributes to the 'choreological order'. Put simplistically, moving down balances moving up, opening balances closing, moving forward is balanced by moving backwards. In <u>Choreographie</u> (1926) Laban's observations of the spatial balance in classical ballet's vocabulary are detailed. Spatial balance, he found, is complex since we rarely move in the primary directions and more often on oblique and curved pathways. Nor do we return on the same pathway in regular to and fro motion. A dancer may start a curving arm movement that is swinging open to the side but end it by lifting. Her next movement will start by lowering, if the choreological order is followed, but may end by curving backwards. The next will start by moving forwards but may end by inscribing a pathway across her body. These 'natural' compensations constitute a balanced way of moving which Laban called 'harmonic' (as opposed to stilted or grotesque) and 'natural' (as opposed to contrived). The choreological order that he observed and articulated constitutes a base for humane movement.

Norms of order are also described in the canon of non-verbal interaction studies. These inform on the ritualised and socialised manner in which what is regarded as natural within a culture is learned and practised.[4] Included is discussion of proxemic behaviour, also evident in dance, since space between people and their spatial orientation to each other speak loudly of the relatedness or alienation of people to each other (Hall, 1982). Texts on the kinetic form of behaviour in the psycho-socio non-verbal interaction literature focus on eye and body contact, facial movement, head and hand rituals and postures. They barely touch on the dynamic qualities of the movement as

[3] The word 'phase' may be a misspelling of 'phrase', since phrase and phrasing are commonly found in Laban's writings, but not phase.

[4] The seminal work of psychologist Michael Argyle (1967) and sociologist Albert Scheflen (1972) is referred to.

factors of motion as signifiers

He focused on the dynamic content and rhythmical phrasing of the behaviour. That, he observed, is the crux of the semiotic potential of what is non-verbal in social intercourse and presentation of self (1971, pp.114-119). Laban asserted that the factors of motion, its weight / force content, its spatial form, its timing and its flow content are signifiers in all human performance. This is obviously so in behaviour and narrative dance but also, he asserts, in formal, so-called plotless or abstract dance. In such dance material the behaviour patterns described by psychologists and sociologists will not be forefronted - rituals of greeting and grooming, for example, or eyebrow flashes and head nods. But what will be present is the dancer's dynamic and timing. This content, asserts Laban, is not abstract or content-less but the embodiment of inner states of mind. He asserts that dynamic rhythms mediated by the performer are the signs hidden in 'abstract' dance. This is a profound and controversial claim for it is commonly assumed that formal movement material is about itself, not referring to anything else than itself.[5,6]

Iris Fung Chi Sun, Transitions Dance Company *Fred Whisker*

psychic functions / motion factors

Laban articulates and develops the connection between motion factor theory and Jungian psychic function theory. While this is obviously relevant to behaviour studies it is of paramount significance for the performative and transactional nature of formal dance, its making, its performance and its reception, because of what it adds to our understanding of the 'choreological order'. Jung describes the four functions of the psyche as intuitive, emotional, physical and mental. These capacities are functioning as the person engages with the world and with other people (Jung, (trans.) 1971). Laban proposed that these functions are made manifest in people's movement behaviour through their timing, their use of flow, their use of weight or force and their spatial articulation. Laban observed, and deduced a one-to-one correlation of the four psychic functions and the four motion factors. In terms of dance performance, his observations confirm that formal dances, which inevitably are created of content that contains dynamic changes in all four motion factors, embody as content the creators' intuitive, emotional, physical and mental functioning made evident in the movement's dynamics and read subliminally and intersubjectively by an observer / spectator. The proposal explains why formal dance material itself is never meaningless, irrespective of who dances it, but that it inevitably carries semiotic content of human nature in its form.[7]

From a choreological perspective, movement is motion factor clusters and phrases that contain semiotic potential, mediated by the articulation and intention of the mover, and by the engagement of the interactor with it. These clusters and phrases, selected and refined through a choreographer's vision and treatment, are transformed when presented in a theatrical frame to create theatrically coded imagery, while the mover is transformed into a phenomenal presence.

theatrical image and presence

4.2 behavioural and formal dance vocabularies

Behaviour is used as a vocabulary in dance alongside the established formal vocabularies. Ballet, social dance, folk dance, capoiera, and jazz dance are some of the lexicons used today, together with vocabularies established by individual choreographers or schools, including Martha Graham, Merce Cunningham, and the Belgian school. A choreological perspective articulates how choreographers intermix, merge, juxtapose, flout the natural laws of movement in their works in order to create theatre and engage audiences in the performative negotiation. Laban stated:

> Without a natural order within the single sequence, movement becomes unreal and dream-like (1971, p.5).

That 'unreality' is precisely what choreographers want to work with. Artists might not call it dreaming but the aim is to

---

[5] The concept that formal dance can never be content-less because it is danced by a person is well known. It refers to what the performer gives off as a personality either through his personal performative layers added to the choreographed work, or by his physique and charisma, or because the spectator identifies with the performer in some way and sees a personality rather than, or in addition to, the movement material that the person is dancing. Laban goes beyond that. It is the sign content of the movement itself that is his focus here.

[6] Marion North's longitudinal investigation spanning 30 years of the movement prefernces of individuals from birth supports the contention that inner states of mind are evident in movement patterns and are highly influential on personal development. The results of the study will be published in 2003.

[7] To assert that movement material contains meanings is not the same as saying that the spectator will read it as meaningful. It is well known in reception theory that what is in the dance may not be recognised by spectators, and what is not in it may well be imagined to be in it by them.

transcend the mundane or to comment on it. Therefore, using and rupturing the natural order is part of any choreographer's art.

conventions and transcendence

In a choreological perspective, existing conventions of achieving transcendence are taken as a starting point and considered in connection with the triadic perspective on making, performing and appreciating: transcendent making, transcendent performing and transcendent appreciating.

breaking the choreological order

One such convention consists in structuring one vocabulary with several others in the same work, the same scene, the same phrase, even the same movement, so breaking the natural choreological order. In <u>Still Life at the Penguin Café</u> (1981), David Bintley shifts rapidly between ballet, musical comedy, character dance and behaviour, all in one phrase of material, to create a light-hearted idiosyncratic scene of waiters. The sort of movement he puts together is not resonant of widely differing cultures but a gentle shift between material that all belongs within the spectrum of ballet.

conflicting vocabularies

In <u>Duo One</u> (1993) for his company La La La Human Steps, Edouard Locke deliberately juxtaposed ballet steps (danced in running shoes) with athletic 'throw and catch' material between the two dancers, interspersed with aggressive and sexual material. His is deliberate juxtaposing of conflicting vocabularies to create ambiguity. This method is more than a mere formal device. Spectators may identify with one or other of the styles and its culture. Juxtapositioning carries comment on each of its ingredients by inviting the spectator to construct his own interpretation of the mix. The latter may grate on some people's aesthetic taste while amusing others. Some spectators may relish the 'dig' at tradition. Others may view the mix simply for itself as a 'new' phenomenon.

breaking the lexicon rules

Twyla Tharp has used the same method. She choreographed behaviour beside virtuosic and off-balance ballet material for a solo for Mikhail Baryshnikov in <u>Push Comes to Shove</u> (1979) for American Ballet Theater. The audience loved it, as the hilarity on the sound track of the video recording vouchsafes. These kinds of structuring break the rules with which each lexicon is held together so inevitably giving rise to a jolt in spectators' perceptions. Running shoes with ballet steps? BARYSHNIKOV grooming his hair after a triple tour?[8]

treating behavioural material

A second convention of combining mundane and formal elements to transcend comprises selecting behavioural material, retaining it unaltered and subjecting it to formal choreographic devices such as repetition, retrograding or speeding up. Pina Bausch in one episode of her tanztheater work <u>1980</u> took the ritual of 'goodbye' - people's habituated statements as they take leave of each other. One after the other, each company member speaks his or her own version of goodbye - 'Adieu', 'I'm sorry to see you go', 'Give my love to your mother', facing the departing person, seriously and deliberately. Other compatriots cluster around awaiting their turn to participate in the ritual.

This exaggerated repeated treatment is recognisably a familiar dance device but combined with speaking it begs the question: is this dancing or is it not, as well as offering a message on the superficiality of human rituals.[9]

In her work <u>Les Six Belles</u> (1997), Lea Anderson collects the minutae of behaviour, tiny shifts of eyebrow, mouth, neck taken from an interpersonal context. She fragments them, re-organises them so that the natural order is flouted. The natural phrasing of the original material has disappeared. She replaces it by unnatural just-off-beat metric phrasing, so transcending the mundane. Is this dancing? The spectator new to Anderson may wonder, her deliberate awkwardness unfamiliar.

**rhythmicising
behaviour**

Lea Anderson, <u>Les Six Belles</u> Fred Whisker

Using a third convention choreographers enlarge and exaggerate behaviour so that a generous smile, for example, is danced as a sweeping upwardly curving gesture of arms supported by a deep plié and rise, the performer giving the soft dynamic of the original smile and its outward focus. Doris Humphrey, in her classic work <u>Day on Earth</u> (1947), transformed in this way the actions of a farming family into what would be described as an abstract expressionist work. Her farmer ploughed his ground. Humphrey used spatial form particularly to carve out the line of the furrow disappearing into the distance through a deep curving progression of the man's arm ending extended forward and downwards, the dancer's intention and focus going on in the line of movement, way beyond his hand, confirming his arm movement by lungeing deeply into the 'earth'. His wife's femininity and firm motherly nature was choreographed not mimetically but through deeply etched curving-surrounding torso-arm gestures, the dancer's focus remaining within her own kinesphere in architectural, grounded, rounded forms.

**exaggerating
behaviour**

---

[8] The same work was mounted almost 20 years later on the Royal Ballet and danced, expertly, by a less well known dancer. There was not a chuckle to be heard. The original joke, dependent on time, place and person, was no longer there.

[9] The same device is used throughout <u>1980</u>, each scene transcending a mundane situation.

behaviour with 'steps' A fourth method, and possibly the most used in traditional ballets, is the overlaying of behaviour on to choreographed formal dance material through the dancers' dramatic interpretation of their roles. Sylvie Guillem and Jonathan Cope have that challenge in the Royal Ballet's remounting, for the 2000 season, of Ashton's tragic ballet <u>Marguerite and Armand</u> (1963). Ashton uses more than one mix of behaviour and formal material. He creates original material on love and dying for both dancers in which the material is an enlargement of behaviour. Added dramatic interpretation is given by the performers. Additionally, the behaviour is up to the artists' feeling for the 'steps' and what they offer as evidence of the tragedy. Lastly, Ashton gives traditional mime to Armand's admonishing father. Because of these mix of methods in one work, is it difficult to believe in or identify with the protagonists' distress?[10]

4.3 the components of movement material

The structural components of movement are stated variously by choreographers and teachers, structural being interpreted as the kinetic elements present in the form of performed movement material:

spatial factors, temporal factors, force aspects...

weight, space, time and flow...

a cluster of spatial and dynamic elements combined with a particular use of the body in action... (Lockhart and Pease, Laban, Adshead, in Preston-Dunlop, 1995, pp.222-3)

five components of movement Together, these strands of the movement seem to be the dancer's body and his coordination, actions of his body, the spatial forms of his movement, the dynamics, rhythm and timing of it and the relationships between the various parts of his person and between one performer and another (Preston-Dunlop, 1986).[11] This five part view is derived from working with what must be clarified, structurally, in order to create and perform the bare bones of movement material, and, what can be appreciated / coached / rehearsed in someone else's movement to achieve the basic form. Always, additionally, and indivisibly, the dancer's mediation makes it happen. In formal dance material the intention and lived experience of the dancer may be of a structural nature also, since in that kind of material there is no referential field or narrative to inform intention. In material that is referential, the structure is there to support the embodiment of an intended image while in formal material the performed structure is the dance.[12]

Choreographers also provide dancers with all manner of imaginative realms and ideas in order to rehearse the quality of performance that they envisage, that is, to help the dancer to find the bodily, actional, spatial, dynamic and relational subtlety required. These may not have any connection with the choreographer's vision of the work's content, a vision that many artists keep to themselves. Teresa Barker, long standing collaborator with Lea Anderson, was observed in a workshop on excerpts from Anderson's early repertoire. Having almost achieved what she wanted from the dancers, namely, 'a head movement in the table plane', she added:

See a mouse on the floor beside you, it is running round your feet to the other side; watch it all the way. [13]

She was after a clear formal horizontal semicircle with the head, to be danced in unison. The mouse may have had nothing to do with the theme of the dance - only the dancers need know it. Such transient images are not expected to penetrate to the spectator; they facilitate the creation of a phenomenon but do not symbolise.

Choreographers' attitudes to the bodies of their dancers fall somewhere along a continuum from reified objects to gendered, individual and fully human people. The extreme reified body is the one in the computer manipulations of Merce Cunningham's BIPED (1999). Less extreme but still reified are the men and women in the minimalist unison intricacies of Krisztina de Châtel's Paletta (1992) and the figures in Oskar Schlemmer's Triadic Ballet (1922). In these works the dancer's person is manipulated as an object. The head is almost faceless, the chest is breastless, the legs are hairless, the pelvis genderless. In Cunningham's case, the unitard unisex costumes almost confirm the computer generated reification. But he has always said that he enjoys seeing the same movement on different bodies. Unison for Cunningham never obliterates individuality.

In de Châtel's case, her reified male figures, dancing absolutely in unison, gradually appear as men trapped in their own routine:

What would appear to fascinate de Châtel is the feeling of enslavement inflicted by self imposed constraint (Utrecht, 1992).

The uniformly trained male bodies, with minimally individual

private images

the body / action nexus: reification versus individuality

---

[10] Was it easier to look at the event as a brave attempt to make a new interpretation of what was one of Margot Fonteyn and Rudolf Nureyev's most celebrated performances, and thereby to focus on Guillem and Cope rather than on Ashton?

[11] The study of spatial form in movement is known as choreutics, and the study of dynamics timing and rhythm is known as eukinetics.

[12] It oversimplifies to say that the danced structure is the work. The artists dancing it, especially soloists, will add something more, something indefinable to do with personal charisma. That something may be intended or entirely spontaneous.

[13] Workshop held at Laban Centre London, 1990.

Kristina de Châtel, *Paletta* *Ben Van Duin*

physiques, moving in tight formation, are given material which moves through the stage space while the reified, almost identical female bodies are encased in huge perspex tubes. Their material is the physical and tactile exploration of their tube. The women's last action of the work is their first look outwards. The tension between potential opportunity of an individual for freedom and imposed constraint of that freedom creates a powerful image. De Châtel's reification of her dancers underlies her narrative sign, as well as giving her the opportunity to make a visually powerful work to be engaged with for its own sake. Cunningham's reification of his figures is there for itself, without narrative; that is, unless we, the spectators, choose to give it one.[14]

Schlemmer wrote in his Diaries:

> *One might ask if the dancers should not be real puppets, moved by strings, or better still, propelled by means of a precision mechanism... (ed. trans. 1972).*

His three heavily costumed and disguised dancers did not, apparently, sufficiently fulfill his wish to present extreme reification.

Lloyd Newson, *can we afford this, the cost of living*
Michael Rayner

Other choreographers look on the body as humanly physical, where hair, sweat, nails, buttocks and private parts are presented for public view. Male nudity is now no longer uncommon. De Frutos' nude self is on the cover of Dance Theatre Journal, Autumn 2000 issue. Lloyd Newson's male nude performed in can we afford this, the cost of living (2000). In Newson's case, human bodily difference in age, sexuality, physique, rotundity and impairment, in fully human thinking, feeling, speaking individuals, are what is forefronted and celebrated.[15]

A choreographer's attitude to the human person's body spills over into the actional material he/she creates for that body. In BIPED, the dancers are dancing computer generated, and manipulated, actions which provide them with almost none of the preparation, action and recovery phrasing of humane motion. Their movement is constructed of fragmented body parts co-ordinated in a manner where 'the natural order' is deliberately and rigorously eschewed. In particular, the dancers' head movements are isolated from the movement of their torso, and on several occasions are tilted backwards, so that the dancers face the ceiling while dancing other fragmented motions with their limbs. The technical demands on balance and coordination are immense. In line with Cunningham's treatment method that every strand co-exists with every other strand, this concept is pushed to its limits in terms of any bit of the dancer's body co-existing with any other bit.

fragmentation

The movement given by de Châtel for her men is primarily step / gesture patterns for their legs in the primary directions of forwards, backwards and in place, repeated with minimal changes. Not a glimmer of behavioural content is present. By contrast, her female figures, sometimes inverted, sometimes upright, use their encasing tubes in rounded, sliding leans and supports, never giving off an image that they enjoy the encasement or dislike it. They continue the same embodiment to the last expressionless 'look' out at the world beyond their tube. The women's movement is grossly limited by their environment but humane in nature, while the men's movement is grossly regimented but not confined to the spot. These juxtapositionings of stricture and freedom in body use and action create de Châtel's emergent statement. The statement may only be recognised on a second viewing because the dance may also be seen as an almost abstract minimalist play of the space/ movement/ dancer/ sound nexus that de Châtel has put in place.

Ways that performers co-ordinate their limbs, torso and focus are used by choreographers to embody points of view. The European expressionist ausdruckstänzerin of the 1920s and 1930s used co-ordination congruency of her whole person. Simple deeply felt movements coming from the centre of the body were prioritised. There was no reification here,

co-ordination as signifier

---

[14] See Preston-Dunlop's essay 'Looking at Dances' in Part 2 for further discussion of BIPED.

[15] See Preston-Dunlop's essay 'Looking at Dances' in Part 2 for further discussion of Newson's work

no fragmentation, no hiding of the person behind her body. The erlebnis of the action, (the lived experience of it) was crucial. The dancer did not extend, she reached; she did not step, she strode; she was not gesturing, she was striving. The actions of the ausdruckstänzerin contrasted in her time with those of Schlemmer. His was a deliberate counter move to 'those body people'- the German expressionist dancers and body culture groups that dominated the period's dance (Schlemmer, ibid.). Counter tension was an ausdruckstänzer favourite as one half of the dancer pulled against another, creating and expressing feelings of angst and spannung, anxiety and tension. Listen to Mary Wigman's empassioned description of her <u>Whirl Dance</u> (1928):

> ...now the body is stretched high, lifted on tiptoe, with the arms thrown up, grasping a non-existent support. A breathless pause, an eternity/long, lasting, however, only a few seconds. And then the sudden letting go, the fall of the relaxed body into the depth... (1966, p.39).

Choreographers ask for specific co-ordination, possibly by demonstrating it rather than talking about it. Some require centering of weight around which limbs function. Another uses fragmentation so that the dancer's limbs and joints work independently of each other. Where the movement is initiated in the dancer's body is an issue for many. In a Graham class or Graham-derived choreography, the contraction deep in the pelvis has to be found as the source of all movement while in a ballet class the dancer may learn that her port de bras does not start in her shoulder joint but in her sternum. The flexible and articulate use of the spine in Alvin Ailey's dancers, the sophisticated isolations of Bob Fosse's jazz sequences contrast with the mundane co-ordination of the torso and limbs in the opening of Wim Vandekeybus' <u>Roseland</u>, as his dancers run and pass their bricks to each other.

issues of posture
and gesture

Body use is selected for a purpose, for it is clear that one kind of co-ordination follows 'the natural laws of movement' while another creates 'movement that becomes unreal'. One natural law is discussed by Warren Lamb (1965) who observed the significant co-ordination of 'gesture' with 'posture' in human interaction.[16] His research suggests that a person's dynamic gesture supported by a posture with a similar dynamic reads as an authentic presentation of the person's intention. In contrast, gesturing independently of postural support is seen as contrived or 'untrue'. Through the merging of posture with gesture the person is seen as giving off personal conviction while unsupported gestures are read as learnt or superficial. This is evident in the dance studio where posture is understood as the core of the person through the spine and weight, gestures being any movements of single limbs, joints, the head, even eyes and brows. Supporting the gestures, however small, with the core of the person, however subtly done, makes a considerable difference not only to the performance but to its reception.

Contrasting dynamic within the body is also a signifier. Laban's

research, as reported by Marion North, uses the term 'body attitude' where Lamb introduces 'posture'. Laban suggests that a person's expressivity in the core in their body always signifies self, and so too do their gestures, in variety - although the latter may be acquired and in conflict with the body attitude. The mix gives off authenticity, or conflict, or disinterest and so on (North, 1972)[17]. The range of possibilities can be explored in dance workshops.

Motif writing action phrase

What artists and schools regard as their basic action material is peculiar to them. There are no such things as agreed basic actions beyond the anatomical bend, stretch and twist of limbs. Ballet is clear that it regards its steps as basic actions which, in Cecchetti style, are categorised as one of seven:

action

> plier, entendre, relever, glisser, sauter, élancer, tourner.

For Geoffrey Hearn, renowned coach of social dances, basic actions include:

> spot turn, step, kick, brush, swing, change hands...

In Roseland, Wim Vandekeybus' basics for his dancers as they handled bricks were

> throw, catch, pass, carry, drop, over-balance, pick up, release... (Preston-Dunlop, 1995, p.239 et seq.)

An action base for a dance work, or a dance style, is not the same thing as a basis for action in dance, per se. The former is idiosyncratic and fluctuates with the work in progress while the latter aims at some sort of overall starting

action base of a work

---

16 The theory is known as 'posture gesture merging', or 'pgm'.

17 North's research into the dynamic behaviour of babies shows that innate patterns of body attitude / gesture are present at a very early stage in a person's life, and are signifiers of personality.

point. Notation systems, through their analysis of motion, take a position on what is the essential data in terms of action that can be said to satisfactorily document a piece of movement material. Labanotation is the method referred to here since it is grounded in an analysis of the structural components of movement, including action. One of the problematic areas of any notation system is that it records the dance in the notation's action grammar which (may or) may not equate at all with the action grammar of the choreography being recorded. The finite number and formal nature of the action categories that are contained in Labanotation are identified as basic in Motif Writing, the simplified symbol system derived from Labanotation. Here action categories, not embodied actions themselves, are discerned and these can be regarded as a 'starter pack' for action exploration.

action categories

Action categories taken from Motif Writing include locomoting, turning, jumping, transferring the weight, gesturing without weight change, over-balancing and rebalancing, extending and contracting, twisting, axial movement around a joint, inward and outward curving gestures and pausing.[18] Embodying these actions, combining them, timing them, phrasing them, retrograding them, intending them, spacing them, giving them a sound, constitute possible topics for practical compositional and editing research in the studio.

These action ideas are useful when a choreographer wishes to alter received formal material. The CDRom of Forsythe's improvisation method shows him holding a classical port de bras pose and twisting it to find new movement. Balanchine is known to take a leg extension in second, and contract the ankle. In Push Comes to Shove (1979), Twyla Tharp takes a pirouette and off-balances it. Contemporary dance techniques take classical feet positions and rotate the legs to parallel. Action alteration is one way of breaking norms and rules and so finding new movement.

kinetic possibilities

Straightforward and deep exploration is another way in which a choreographer will push to the limit the kinetic possibilities that the body offers him. This 'lived experience' way of working requires some kind of control or schematic motivation to avoid a tendency for the person to find himself trapped in his own habitual patterns. Ideas taken from the structural components are used in this capacity. For example, from body / action ideas, concentrating on the surfaces of the limbs produces quite different movement material from concentration on the joints. Focusing on off- and on-balance produces different movement from transferring the weight with play on the size of the space covered.

kinetic motivation

Since all dance movement is mediated and intended, dancers who train with a particular school learn not only the required bodily co-ordination and actional choice but the school's manner of thinking about movement generally. Adina Armelagos and Mary Sirridge (1978) wrote on 'the motivation of a vocabulary' as being inseparable from its surface style. For a dancer, part of learning repertory successfully is letting go of habitual ways of motivating movement and taking on not only the visible movement style but its kinetic motivational core. The inscription in a dancer's body of a style is made by both her kinetic motivation and her kinetic action.

4.4 relatedness between people and within the body

Categories of bodily and spatial relationship articulated in the non-verbal interaction literature prioritise their sign-carrying nature. Argyle (1967) focuses on 'bodily contact' as a prime interpersonal signal but is vague on the form that the contact needs in order to read. Touching is the category of bodily contact prioritised in his writing where it is presumed that the touch will be made by the person's hand or arm (apart from sexual touch). Where the touch is received on the body of the touched person is of significance to Argyle because of the taboo areas associated with male / female touches, parent / child touches, single gender touches, as well as the taboos of whole cultures.

touching, norms and taboos

In the performing arts these rules and norms are the subject of rupture. For making and performing in dance, Argyle's points are inadequate in their exploration of the possibilities of touch but significant for appreciation. Spectators will bring with them their norms for touching that enable them to interpret the semiotic content of the touch material in dance works. Because of the cultural norms and rules of touching, creative rule-breaking and norm questioning take place in performative dance works, copiously. The opening scene of Bausch's <u>Bluebeard</u> (1977) does just that, with the man shifting between obsessive listening to his recording of Bartok's opera[19] and obsessive lying, curled up, on the stomach of a woman as she pushes herself along the leaf-strewn floor. What kind of tactile interaction is that?

Proxemic behaviour, articulated in the psychology and sociology of interpersonal signs, shows how the spatial orientation of people to each other carries meaning within a culture. Hence vis-a-vis, side by side, diagonal spacing, higher and lower than each other, the distance between, all carry culturally-bound meaning. In dance, these categories are available to a choreographer to use if she wishes to refer to human intimacy or alienation. They are also explored as formal material with no references in mind.

proxemic behaviour

---

[18] See Hutchinson-Guest's developments of Motif Writing, (1983).

[19] Bela Bartok's opera <u>Duke Bluebeard's Castle</u>.

Spectators, however, may bring cultural norms of proxemic behaviour to their appreciation of a work. A formal work such as Cunningham's Points in Space (1986) may be interpreted as containing all manner of human care, friendship, tenderness and so on, because of the proxemic forms that appear in it by chance through Cunningham's choreographic processes.

Hélène Blackburn, Black Embrace *Chris Nash*

timing

Timing of an interpersonal gesture carries meaning. Who offers a handshake first, synchronising one's walking rhythm with another person, using a similar or dissimilar pace of gesturing, may be a way of establishing a power position, of diffusing aggravation or of establishing togetherness. In verbal conversation, interrupting someone, using the alternating timing of conversation, speaking at the same time as another person, carry signs beyond what is being said. Behavioural timing is observed and explored (and ruptured) in narrative episodes in dance works. In the section of Vandekeybus' Roseland in which men dominate women in duo material, the intimidation through touching is heightened by timing. The man moves first, the woman countering the male move through immediate timing, and vice versa. Timing between dancers in formal works may also read. The synchrony, syncopation, arbitrariness of the performers timing in relation to each other is (maybe) interpreted as having interpersonal resonances.

interpersonal flow

The flow of energy passing from one person to another, or its denial in rigidity, stopping, holding back, signifies, both in behaviour and in dance. In the Roseland duos, the women are rigid; they do not respond one centimetre to the invasive energy of the men. Denial of interaction is the message. Similar rigidity is used by Lester Horton in his powerful duo The Beloved (1948), again as embodiment of a woman's defence against male intimidation. Not only does she sit on the edge of her chair, hands clasped on her knee, head bowed, but she moves only her eyes to watch her husband - seated at the table, his hands on the Holy Bible. An excerpt from the score of The Beloved is on page 287.

Ulysses Dove both confronts and uses these devices in **duet**
Dancing on the Front Porch of Heaven (1992). His episode on
'friendship so deep that nothing can come between it', is a duet
for two men. He aims to create a male duet articulating
friendship, not erotic love. In order to do so he needs to
observe the cultural norms of friendly single-sex touch.
Spectators may well presume that he will explore 'love', since
his dancers are the Royal Ballet of Sweden where, as in most
ballet companies the romantic duet is common, albeit usually
between a man and a woman. In any case, when two people are
alone on stage a personal intimacy of some sort is anticipated
by the spectator, whether realised or not.

Ulysses Dove, Dancing on the Front Porch of Heaven *Mats Bäcker*

A close engagement with Dove's material and his dancers' performance of it illuminates how he managed to compress in a duet of brief duration a relationship of complexity, intimacy, trust and depth. He had to do it by creating movement material that contained human feeling for, as he said in his documentary introduction to the work's performance for video, the training and expertise of his Swedish dancers did not include an appreciation of the traumatic feeling of love and loss through death that inspired Dove's work (Macrory, Lockyer and Venza, 1995). He was accustomed to getting intensely felt performances from his New York performers, a response not available from these classical dancers. Dove used touch and weight sharing, lifts and leans as a basis - material that demanded dextrous and virtuosic performances, which he shaped through the sculptural form, the proxemic spacing, the precise timing, and very occasionally through the fluidity, with minimal use of transitional material. It is a duet that presents space, time, weight and flow-relatedness to create an image of deep engagement of two people with each other.

relationship categories

It is the research of movement notators that has given rise to identification of the categories of relatedness necessary to record a work in dance notation. That resource provides categories useful in workshops on making, performing and appreciating. They are: focusing on (by any body surface), approaching, going away from, near to, surrounding without touch, physical touching, surrounding with touch, supporting/carrying, supporting by surrounding. The articulation identifies whether each of these is mutual or created by one party, is instantaneous or gradual, retained or given up, sliding contact that brushes off or slides that stay in contact. Possibilities are impossible to describe verbally but Labanotation and Motif Writing can prescribe, suggest or document contact ideas through a set of relationship symbols and scores.

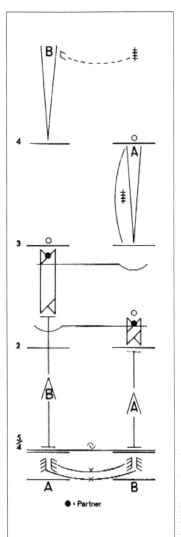

Motif Writing partner phrase

These formal relationship categories are a necessary supporting part of choreological study, used in the service of dance as a mediated and performative art. Studied in themselves they offer limited material. Used with the triadic perspective of making, performing and appreciating, they begin to function performatively. One way is through the theory of natural affinities, based on Laban's articulation of the 'natural' affinity in movement between certain dynamic qualities and certain spatial forms (Laban, 1971). This concept is used in workshops to alert dancers to habitual and clichéd choices of relationship material.

Breaking the 'natural' way of embracing one another can be seen in Robert Cohan's Cell (1969) and in Lloyd Newson's Strange Fish (1992), both works exploring alienation. When we embrace we tend to do so with the arms and upper torso, while Cohan's performers do so with one person's torso surrounding another's feet, with one person grasping another's ankles, with one person supporting another only to let her drop. The expected response to the embrace is not given so we read the alienation. We embrace and touch with palms inward to feel the other person's body. Twisting the arms breaks the 'natural' way, altering the gesture radically in form, in feeling and in sign content. Touch a beloved's face slowly with soft fingertips or, in contrast, with the back of the hand, the fingers taut and stretched, vibrating. Newson directs this alienating contact for his socially inept character Nigel, who attempts to make physical contact with a woman. A natural gesture is turned into an unnatural one by changing his hand surface, the route he took to achieve the touch, the dynamic he gave to it, how long he kept it there, how he supported it posturally or did not, and by his focus.

ignoring the norms

Contact Improvisation explores all manner of weight sharing and touch in a mutual relationship of bodies but is confusing in theatre. While it is a means of experiencing and sometimes of embodying the relationship between people, by its nature it ignores the norms of touch. Since the physical contact is agreed to by the participants, is mutual but is not intended to contain

Robert Cohan, Cell Anthony Crickmay

signs of intimacy while actually containing them, the spectator is left to make of it what he can. Such spatial and touch intimacy would 'normally' result in a response, negative or positive. In Contact Improvisation it does not. The response is a technical one, not one of timing, or flow, or sculptural form or proximity change, or drama or power play. What remains for the spectator is to engage phenomenally with the material, to enjoy it for its own sake. However the enjoyment of such material is primarily in the participants' experience which excludes a spectator. The negotiating aspect of dance as a performative art has little to negotiate about.

Relatedness between dancers and relatedness within the dancer's own body are both potentially choreographic. Material using relatedness within the body explores, articulates and presents all manner of ways in which the body's limbs, joints and surfaces make contact with each other, deliberately in both formal and referential material. The categories described above - touch, surround, focus on, carry - are useful across the triadic of dance. They provide themes for improvisation leading to making, and for articulation and intention leading to performing, and for observation leading to appreciation, editing and coaching. For example, moving to stand in second position can be intended as a parting of the feet. If relatedness is not a theme then the same movement may be simply a shift of weight or as establishing a horizontal inscription in space between two feet. The intention for each alters the embodiment and the sign. If a dancer is asked to focus on her own hand she can intend it narratively, or, the purpose may be to

Ed Wubbe, Kathleen Hans Gerritsen

establish a virtual spatial inscription to be used in counterpoint, or, to prepare for her head to move towards her hand as a formal manipulation.

Body relatedness is a frequent theme in making. It is used by Ed Wubbe as a metaphor. In <u>Kathleen</u> (1994), he has a male dancer grasp and hold his own leg as he moves unevenly across the space, his leg being dragged along by his arms, as he advances towards and retreats from the women, uncertainly. Later in the same work, Wubbe gives a dancer material based on counter-tension, the top half of his body against his lower half, as a metaphor for not wanting to involve himself in something (in this case, in drug taking).

body relatedness as metaphor

4.5 choreutics with proxemics and the phenomenology of space

Choreutics is the study of the spatial form embodied in movement, in particular of the harmonic content of spatial form and its performativity. The term, coined by Laban in the early part of the 1920s, was a contributory part of his effort to establish choreology as the practical theory for and of dance. He saw choreutics at that time as comparable to the study of harmonic principles and practice in musical composition and to the study of form in the visual arts.[21] Choreutic study includes micro-choreutics which articulates and researches the spatial content of movement within the kinesphere and macro-choreutics which studies, practically and theoretically, the spatial forms of a work as a whole including the use of the whole performance space by locomotion and group forms, lighting and any content that is spatial.

choreutics

Micro-choreutics is studied through the inscriptions that the dancer and her movement create in her kinesphere and how that spills over into the surrounding space, and also through understanding the three-dimensional geometry on which much performed formal dance material is based. By inscription, the forms created in space and in the dancer's person offers abstract material of unlimited design and complexity, and a means to embody narrative images, abstracted or corporeal according to their treatment (Humphrey, 1959). The geometric principles of counterpoint through clustering of embodied lines and planes are a starting point in choreutic practice.

inscription and geometry

The manner in which Laban organised choreutics is seen as both problematic and fundamental for several reasons. He described certain prototype spatial forms, rings and scales,

Laban's choreutics

---

[21] Both Laban and Arnold Schönberg published under the term Harmonielehre (harmony studies). See Preston-Dunlop in Louppe (1990).

known as 'Space Harmony', while giving minimal advice as to how they might be useful to making and performing; that is, as anything other than forms to be experienced by the mover for their harmonic content. The practice of the scales constituted his labile dance technique in the 1920s and 30s. As such, it started an expansion of movement possibilities from the constrained harmonic forms of danse d'école.[22] It has taken Forsythe to show both the potential for theatre art of Laban's original ideas and their limitations.

The scales and rings are all forms traced in and around the perfect solids: the tetrahedron, the cube, the octahedron, the icosahedron and the dodecahedron. For Laban, these were much more than exercises or bases for bodily technique. He saw the scales as perfect or harmonised prototypes of the fragmented movement patterns of human behaviour. His observations showed him that human beings do not naturally move in the cardinal directions although the cardinal directions are what are used commonly in dance parlance to conceptualise and idealise movement. Such directions are incompatible with the way the skeleton controls human movement. Instead we move primarily in three-dimensional labile curves (Longstaff, 1996). The scales constituted a kind of lexicon of formal prototypes of these curves drawn in space (Laban, 1966, p.88 & Part Two).

Additionally, because of the harmonised nature of the scales and their basis in perfect geometric 'scaffoldings' their practice was, for Laban, a participatory experience as well as a tool for negotiation in the theatrical sense; a communal spiritual ritual and/or an element for theatrical invention. However, Laban's choreutic material, and the concepts on which it is based, are a potent resource for choreographers, as Forsythe has demonstrated. The first step is to recognise that the geometricised forms in the choreutic canon are spatial ideas, not spatial movements. The embodiment of the forms in danced material is a separate process open to individual imagination. For the embodiment to have an integrity, the embodying artist has to set up ludic rules with which to improvise and to find possibiliities, and also to set up criteria of excellence for the selection or rejection of the resulting materials. In Laban's case, in the role of embodying artist, his criteria were (for his community dance works) an enhanced experience of harmonic relations in space and between people, and for his theatre works, material that satisfied his 'delight in line' as a viewer. For someone else, the criteria might be fragmentation of form requiring virtuosic technical performance. To make use of the choreutic resource it is neccessary to separate it from Laban's own artistic preferences for its performance which were inevitably coloured by the expressionistic time and place in which he worked. Choreographic embodiment of any resource is individual.

harmonic counterpoint principles

Hidden in the welter of geometry in Laban's writings on choreutics are several choreological concepts that have general application in dance. They contain movement counterpoint principles. The vector[23] content of lines embodied by performers in their motion and in their design cut across and reverse each other, parallel and right angle each other, axis and equator each other, creating spatial clusters, spatial intervals and spatial tension (Laban, 1926)[24]. These constitute the elementary principles of harmonic counterpoint, which are used and expanded in composition. Choreutic counterpoint are by no means confined to practice in the 1920s and 30s. It appears in contemporary choreographed works; in Trisha Brown's MO (1995), in Ulysses Dove's Dancing on the Front Porch of Heaven (1992) and, copiously and fragmented, in William Forsythe's repertoire for the Frankfurt Ballett (Figgis, 1996). It appears in classical dance since ballet is a geometrically founded lexicon. Where two people dance classically, counterpoint of a choreutic sort will be present as it is in the duos in Forsythe's Steptext.

Choreutic counterpoint is the concurrent or immediately successive presence of at least two choreutic units, placed beside each other in such a way that a further resonance is given off. Counterpoint can be embodied in a work by the deliberate act of a choreographer but that is not the only way that it appears. In the documentary on the creation of Brown's MO she discusses how she devises a phrase - a 'gem' - from a random selection of directions and then devises a second phrase counterpointing the gem - a 'satellite'. Each of her dancers has a gem and a satellite and these are constructed together according to her aesthetic decisions to form an ensemble counterpoint and a counterpoint with Bach's Musical Offering she is working with. In Anastasia Lyra's improvised work for some forty dancers in alfresco city sites, Sxedia Polis (1996), the dancers move in incredibly slow motion so that the spectators have time to make connections between dancers that have arisen by chance. Some connections are pure counterpoint, others are narrative, both of which are constructed by the spectators. Lyra did not put them there. They arose by chance through the sensitivity and discipline of the dancers.

counterpoint embodied

Counterpoint can be created by the relationship between dancer and spatial content of the stage / performance space. It is present in Sxedia Polis as a dancer's choreutic content is seen in the context of city architecture. It is present in de Châtel's Paletta as the dancers move in and through the cylindrical tubes encasing the women, seen against a vivid blue backdrop. Neither of these choreographers may have had counterpoint in mind. Nevertheless, their treatment and editing gave rise to an inevitability that counterpoint would be construed by a spectator with an eye for spatial forms.

counterpoint and scenography

---

[22] For the geometric basis of ballet see Space module of the arms and legs 1 & 2, pp. 2 & 20, Kirstein, L. & Stuart, M. (1977).

[23] Vector is used to describe the directional content of motion rather than the direction of the destination of a movement. The need for both terms is not evident in movements that pass through the body's centre, but it is in movement that is peripheral or transversal. For example, the vector of an arm movement starting from backwards at low level and ending sideways at middle level is diagonal.

[24] Trans. Longstaff, J.S. in press for 2003.

Anastasia Lyra, Sxedia Polis *Takis Anagnostopoulos*

choreutic units and manner of materialisation

What Laban literature contains is a complex and competent analysis of the 'trace forms' notionally inscribed in the kinesphere but almost nothing on their performance. In Preston-Dunlop's manual of scales and rings an introductory section outlines 'the manner of materialisation' of these forms in performed movement (1984). While the study of space harmony forms themselves has to be regarded as a specialist activity for the few, the principles contained and their embodiment have wide application in articulating the complexity of choreutic practice in all dance forms. Preston-Dunlop goes beyond the normal description of spatial form; that is, a description of the actual performed movement (Dell, 1972). She discerns the virtual choreutic forms that the dancer and the spectator create between them. Virtual spatial forms are lines/forms in space that are perceived to be there but are actually not there. They occur as spatial projections when energy is thrown into the space through the dynamic of the dancers' performance. Their focus - in face or chest, or energy projected out beyond their fingertips, out beyond the thrust of a knee, for example - creates virtual lines through the space. These virtual projecting spatial forms are one element of the manner of materialisation analysis (MM)[25].

MM articulation of spatial form in performative dance includes virtual spatial tensions seen as existing across the space between people or objects or limbs, and spatial body design in which the human being's physicality 'disappears' and his spatial geometric form 'emerges' through the dancer's way of performing. The line is literally embodied in the dancer's flesh. The spectator 'loses' the person dancing and 'sees' the form being created. The fourth manner of materialisation and the most common, spatial progression, is seen when the dancer's motion seems to leave behind a trace of lines and curving shapes in the space.

These virtual choreutic lines are as potent in some choreographers' counterpoint as actual motion. Their absence or presence in spatially choreographed material is highly significant to style. As already described, Humphrey's style of using virtual space for <u>The Man in Day on Earth</u> illustrates how virtual and actual lines were clustered by her to create a narrative character. Virtual projection in space is evident in Jane Dudley's classic solo <u>Harmonica Breakdown</u> (1940), as her defiant woman pushes her way across stage. Dudley was embodying what it is like to be on a treadmill, pushing forward but getting nowhere, endlessly. She did it by what Lois Balcom described as

> a queer stiff-legged flat-footed progression like nothing on earth (Sears, 1984).

The projecting spatial force seems to jab into the void in front of the performer, a metaphor for endeavour against all odds.

In the geometric choreography of Brown's <u>MO</u> the choreutic embodiment remains within the actual body, not projected. <u>MO</u> is not a metaphor; it is itself, a dance about spatial counterpoint and the interdependence of Bach and Brown. Cunningham, as one would expect, is interested in actual forms in his dancers' bodies. The absence of virtual projections is part of his style.[26]

Manner of materialisation theory and practice articulates the manner in which spatial forms are created, performed and appreciated, in clusters. It also articulates for dancers choices of how formal material might be danced. A ballet combination contains choreutic clusters in its movement form and offers the dancer of it performance choices through manner of materialisation possibilities.[27] Is this arabesque to be seen as a contained body design or is the curved progression into the arabesque what is wanted? Is it projected into the space through fingers, through chest, or not? Or are we to see a man moving rather than an embodied spatial form?

[25] ChUMM analysis (Choreutic Unit and Manner of Materialisation) is discussed in Preston-Dunlop (1983).

[26] Discussion between Cunningham and Preston-Dunlop in 1981 during his residency at the Laban Centre.

[27] See Paula Salosaari's essay 'Multiple Embodiment in Ballet' in Part 2 of this text.

Forsythe and choreutics

Forsythe's improvisational method is choreutically based. He discusses how he and his dancers inscribe space with lines and curves developing on from Laban's 'manifold options' (Baudoin and Gilpin, 1989). Forsythe ruptures Laban's concept of centre being in the dancer's body centre:

> Laban's model suits the movement vocabulary of classical ballet particularly well, since both employ one central point in the body as their structuring element. But what if a movement does not emanate from the body's centre? What if there were more than one centre? What if the source of movement were an entire line or plane, and not simply a point? (ibid.)

Forsythe's structuring comprises a whole gamut of spatial actions arising from and returning to centres, lines and planes, created and decided upon in and around the dancer's body. Extrude the line, replace it, collapse it back to centre, bridge, replace, invert, curve to floor, are examples of his language for embodied spatial actions.[28] This sequence might constitute a cluster of choreutic inscriptions in space, achieved in any size, by any body part, into any of 26 directions that radiate from any centre, in normal, minimal or 'superzone' extension.[29] His concept of choreutics in performative art goes beyond the aim of showing what actually happens by forefronting what he wants to be shown and allowing the rest to 'disappear'. With deconstructionist architect Daniel Libeskind, the concept of disappearance and disequilibrium is seen to work for both men, in solid architecture for the one and in 'the living architecture' of dance for the other. While Laban restrained his exploration of space to retain or return to a state of equilibrium, Forsythe

> searches precisely for those superkinespheric moments when the limits are transgressed, falling is imminent (ibid. p.75).

William Forsythe, *Quintett Dominik Mentzos*

The cross of axes theory which came about through an analysis problem of notators, looks at the way in which human beings orientate themselves in space, variously, while moving.[30] One might expect there to be one view of orientation, one direction forwards, one direction upwards. Dance uses (at least) four and they manifest themselves in dance techniques and forms of choreography.

Human orientation comes about by people engaging with space. It is a power game between the body and space. If the body dominates a mover's consciousness then upwards is conceived to be above the mover's head and forwards to be in front of the mover's chest.[31] When lying on your back on the floor where is upwards? To the ceiling or 'above' your head? Where is backwards? Down through the floor or 'behind' your head? Above and behind may appear to be in the same place..? It is a matter of choice of orientation. If 'up' is regarded as towards the ceiling then the vertical line of gravity in space dominates and 'down' is directed to the floor; forwards and backwards are conceived as at right angles to that dominating line. If the body's perception of itself dominates then 'up' is seen as 'above' the top of the head and 'down' as towards the feet, forwards and backwards being judged in relation to the front and back of the body's surface.

In daily life, human beings normally compromise between the dominance of the body and the space. We tend to think of upwards as to the ceiling or sky and forwards as wherever our chest is facing. On stage, dancers think of space differently because there the fourth wall and the presence of the auditorium gives a second front to be concerned with - each person's front and the common stage front. If a director says 'please step forwards' does he mean 'step downstage to the front of the performance area' or 'step into your own forwards, whatever front you personally are facing'? The same request made by a director from the auditorium or said while on stage with the dancers might mean something different because the director's orientation may change from being dominated by the spectator's view or the individual performer's view.

Merce Cunningham works with the cross of the body's axes as part of his selection of movement material. He does not prioritise stage front but rather each individual's front. A Cunningham-based technique class orientates the standing exercises primarily according to the body's cross. As a result, the dancer focuses on her own body in preference to considering herself as viewed from stage front. In contrast, the ballet dancer orientates according to the cross of the stage space and simultaneously

---

[28] Forsythe, W. CDRom, (1999).

[29] Superzone is a Laban concept introduced in Choreutics, p.23.

[30] Knust, A. 'Crosses of Axes Theory' in papers of the International Council of Kinetography Laban (1972).

[31] The only way to understand the experience of cross of axes choices is by moving; hence, a workshop example is suggested.

according to the compromise standard cross. In ballet, en haut is conceived of as vertical, in the line of gravity. Ballet's verbal language expresses this dual orientation since there are words that express the stage space dominance: croisé, effacé, en face, and others that orientate the dancer's own space: fourth position, en avant, derrière, à coté. The term 'alignment' means aligned in stage space and in the body in ballet, while in Cunningham work it usually means aligned in the body.

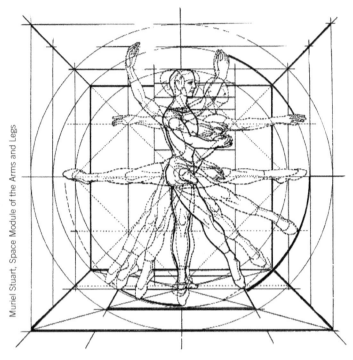

Muriel Stuart, Space Module of the Arms and Legs

The kind of choreographic group work that emerges from these contrasting spatial orientations is recognisable in that Cunningham's works are to be viewed from anywhere, with every bit of space of equal value. Traditional ballets are still choreographed to be seen from the front with a hierarchy of centre for the ballerina and her danseur noble. Darcey Bussell is accustomed to dancing centre stage in front of the corps de ballet, as she did with Jonathan Cope in Michael Corder's <u>Dance Variations</u> (2000). Forsythe set out to rupture that hierarchy. <u>In In the Middle Somewhat Elevated</u> (1988), the ballerina is choreographed to work from time to time in the dimly lit corner of upstage left. In a choreological perspective such spatial use is, as always, the embodiment of ideas. In this work, ideas are both formal and about social structure and social priviledge. Forsythe puts his point of view through his use of the performer - space nexus.

proxemics   Proxemics has already been touched upon in the discussion of relatedness. It is further articulated here. Proxemics is a term used by sociologist Edward Hall in his discussion of how space and proximity to another person is used in social interaction in different cultures. As he writes: 'space speaks' (1966).

Hall has identified distances as providing thresholds indicative of one kind of social relationship or another, from intimacy to public speaking. Dancers' habitual distance from one another in class, necessitated through the avoidance of one another's arms and legs, is the least theatrically potent of distances, one that signifies social order of a functional rather than an interpersonal sort. Invasion of someone else's personal space, or dancing together across a wide distance, provokes interest. Proxemics includes the study of the sign content of spatial orientation to one another: face to face, vis-a-vis, diagonal, back to back, on the same level as, higher than / lower than, the other person. These orientations and distances are manipulated by choreographers in every ensemble work through their performer - space nexus, providing potential for meaning.

Stuart Hopps, Dr Dolly's Follies *Chris Nash*

Because Forsythe slips between behaviour, virtuosic partner work and occasional quasi sign language in Steptext, the proxemic content slips too. It is functional when Deborah Bull and Peter Abegglen, Michael Nunn and William Trevitt lift and support each other. Enough space is used for efficiency and safety. When a pair stand close to each other, waiting in behaviour mode, the space between them becomes pregnant with expectation giving a complex polysemantic mix of theatrical image with mundane interaction. They all slip in and out of being themselves and being superlative performers. Their proxemic behaviour is one way of achieving the slip.

Choreutics and proxemics have been treated in the past as separate subjects, one in dance and the other in sociology. Choreological research practices them as essentially intermingled. The phenomenology of space, or as Gaston Bachelard and Peter Brook name it, the 'poetics of space' is also included (Bachelard, 1994; Brook, 1968). Bachelard describes

phenomenology of space

the experience contained in a corner, an attic or a corridor, a shelf or a drawer, a doorway or a box. Such spaces contain all manner of phenomenon: secrecy, transition, opportunity, memory, privacy, public display and so on. Brook takes this into the phenomenal content of performance spaces and its effect on the performativity of a theatre work.

Phenomenal space was a starting point, for Rosemary Butcher in her works for the Jerwood Space (1999) and the Whitechapel Gallery (1987). For Butcher, a gallery space has its identity in which its own modes of making, performing, and appreciating have their existence. Gallery visitors can look at a painting for as long or as short a time as they wish. They can ignore, ponder, pass by at will. Butcher respected and worked with that mode in her Whitechapel performances. When her dancers exited, the space resumed its unbroken identity. For the Jerwood Space she created her own dancers' square through lighting and surrounded it with benches for the spectators. She restricted herself to working within that 'canvas'.

Kirsi Heimonen (1989) researched the phenomenon of dancing in alfresco spaces in her native Finland inspired by writings on the phenomenology of architecture. A bridge was simultaneously a bridge for pedestrians and a performance space for Heimonen. It took on two kinds of phenomenal content - the dynamic link of bridge and the static spot of stage. Pedestrians became interactors in a performative event. Following a similar research pattern, April Nunes choreographed and directed <u>Newness at Lessness</u> (1998) in the ruins of an abbey in South London. She paid attention to the purpose and feel of the space, now a recreational space, leading her spectators in procession from the mundanity of a busy road to the sacred auditoria where her multi-stranded 'dance' emerged from and merged with the surrounding history-laden environment and local population.

4.6 eukinetics: rhythm, timing and dynamics

eukinetics and choreology

Eukinetics is the term coined by Laban, as the partner discipline to choreutics, in his preparatory studies for establishing choreology. At that time, he saw eukinetics as comparable to the study of rhythm and dynamics in musicological theory and practice, a study particularly relevant in the light of the innovations in rhythm being introduced by such iconoclastic artists as Igor Stravinsky and Arnold Schönberg. What Laban undertook was practical research into the rhythms of the moving human being and thence of the principles of rhythm, timing and dynamics of an autonomous dance art for the twentieth century, freed from music's metre. Eukinetics was the term he proposed for this study (Maletic, 1987).

Today, the central eukinetic issue to be addressed in this text is how rhythm, timing and dynamics function in the performing, making and spectating processes of any performative dance situation. To do that, choreographers' attitudes to and use of rhythm, timing and dynamics is discussed. Eukinetics functions as micro-eukinetics, which is the study of the individual dancer's generation of dynamic and rhythmic dancing and as macro-eukinetics, which is the study of the overall dynamics and timing of a work, or programme, or season of works. Debate and discussion, both written and in the studio, lead to a historiography of the rhythm, timing and dynamics of dance embodiment.

In choreological study, eukinetic terms are articulated, eukinetic differences in the dancer's experience are discerned, use of eukinetic preferences by artists is discussed (in relation to the interdependence of making, performing and appreciating) and eukinetic experimentation takes place in the studio. This text is not a manual of eukinetics but some basic principles are presented relevant to the performative.

eukinetic terminology

Rhythm is regarded as beginning whenever two or more 'things' occur beside each other in time and in space. The elements that create rhythm in movement are regarded as its timing, its various embodiments of stress through manipulation of weight and force, and the fluidity or abruptness of the change from one thing to another. Accenting is regarded as a rhythmic happening in which something is made to become more significant than something else; that is, significant to the onlooker and / or to the mover. It is achieved in movement by the dancer emphasising one movement (part of a movement) by giving it more (or less) energy, more (or less) weightiness, increasing (or decreasing) its speed, making it bigger (or smaller), pausing it, giving it a clear preparatory move, sounding it, looking at it, and more.

Timing is a broad term covering several concepts. In the phenomenology of time, primordial temporality and objective timing are distinguished as, on the one hand, a fundamental lived experience of the flux of past, present and future, and on the other, as the manner in which we organise time in metred units, seconds, hours, counts, etc. Long and short durations, quick and slow pace, accelerating and decelerating speed are primarily experiential, while a long duration over fourteen counts, or a slow pace at metronome 32, have to have objective organisers brought to bear. Psychological timing is variously defined but apparent in the timing of hesitation or repetition, or whatever is needed, to achieve a performative relation with the audience.

Dynamics in dance is also variously defined. The narrow definition equates dynamic with the element of force, as it is in musical ff and pp. The dynamics of movement is distinct from the dynamics of a dance work. The opposite of dynamic is stated as static, in equilibrium, equally balanced, still. But one can have dynamic stillness, stillness that is pregnant with motion. A strict definition of static or of dynamic can be reductive rather than productive. All manner of dance strands can be dynamic: a dynamic relationship between two dancers, a dynamic episode in a work, a dynamic off-balance movement, a dynamic pause. What links these events together as all having dynamic quality is their energy content, either perceived or actual, energy being vibrant and in flux.

The manner in which these elements are considered by artists is idiosyncratic as is the verbal and non-verbal language used to express them. Technical terms and metaphors abound in the studio in the attempt by artists and rehearsal directors to help dancers embody what is wanted, for micro-eukinetic qualities have fundamentally to be felt and performers have to commit themselves to produce extreme qualities as well as nuances.

rhythm embodied

Following Laban's initial researches, his outstanding student Mary Wigman had, by 1919, built up a picture of what embodied rhythm in dance was for her:

> The same way as music, dance too is called an 'art of time'... It would be little else than stale theory were we to determine the rhythm of dance solely from the element of time... the element of strength plays its part in the dance - the dynamic force, moving and being moved, which is the pulsebeat of the life of dance... dynamic breath is the mysterious great master who reigns unknown and unnamed behind all and everything (1966, pp.12-13).

Rhythm became the felt rhythm of action - not metric, not counted. The inner resolve of the dancer dictated the rhythm through her attitude to timing, to strength and energy, to breathing and continuity.

effort rhythm

The rhythm of bodily action that Laban, with Wigman, researched developed into what is known today as 'effort rhythm'. Wigman's feeling for breath in her movement Laban saw as the motion factor of flow in his effort theory. The changes in timing, in strength, in flow and in spatial plasticity constituted the elements of effort rhythm. The dynamic flux of a person's movement comes about by their lived experience of change. The development of a dancer's corporeal awareness of the nuances of effort flux and of the range from delicate to crude of effort experience is the crux of eukinetic practical studies. Ability to produce a middle range of effort qualities is not enough for a dancer. One of Laban's observations was of the individual effort habits and preferences that constitute a person's effort profile.[32] Helping dancers to recognise their own profile and go beyond the barriers that their preferences set up is part of choreological workshop practice.

The term 'effort' is an unhelpful one since the common understanding of 'effort' is a reduction of what the term means in eukinetics. It is as effortful for a dancer to generate lightness as strength, and to use restraint and fluidity, but the common usage of the term 'effort' suggests strength and stress. The term is not widely used in general studio work butit is in choreological workshops. To date there is no better term to replace it.

Bodily rhythm is by its nature both metric and non-metric since those two kinds of rhythm are present in the human body. Stepping and jumping lead to metricity, or as Humphrey called it, the motor rhythm of a movement material. The feeling of heartbeat and pulse give one a sense of regularity and of pace. Breath is regular when a person is calm and still, but in activity and under emotional excitement it is not.

metric and non-metric rhythm

All the regular rhythms of the body speed up and slow down.

Pace and tempo are changeable. Bodily rhythms are many layered and complex.

Some technique classes pay little heed to rhythm, timing and dynamics beyond counting, usually in groups of eight counts and always in a metre. Since technique is the strongest influence on a dance student - usually the aspect of dance that they first encounter - it is counting that a workshop in eukinetics has to abandon. Counting inhibits experiencing dynamic change and it is the ability to experience that has to come first in effort mastery.

The theory of natural affinities shows that certain dynamic qualities cluster together naturally (Maletic, 1987). Strength, speediness, directness and controlled flow tend to cluster. Ask a dancer to speed up a movement and he will most likely increase its strength as well. It is much less likely that he will speed up with lightness. Ask for a strong movement and he will probably generate one that is controlled in flow and stops rather than one that flows on strongly. Qualities of lightness, free flow, indirection in space and slowing down in time tend to cluster. Crossing over from one natural cluster to the other requires more skill. Speedy lightness is much more difficult than speedy

natural affinities

Iris Fung Chi Sun, Transitions Dance Company *Fred Whisker*

---

[32] Developed in Lamb (1965) and North (1972).

strength; speedy plasticity in space is more difficult that speedy directness. All dynamic colours are needed in dance and Laban's effort theory and practice offers an invaluable basis for dancers. From the eight beginning effort qualities, all manner of combinations of quality can be generated in motion and stillness, in phrases, in strings, in sequences, in metres, ranging from pale quality to extremes of force, extremes of slowness to almost still, extremes of plasticity to knotting, extreme heaviness to collapse, and so on.

choreographer specific eukinetics: Taylor's organic rhythm

Effort content was evident in variety in Paul Taylor's season at Sadler's Wells Theatre in the 2000 season. The fluidity and fleetness of the organically composed opening work, Cascade (1999), contrasted with contrived and percussive material in The Rite of Spring (rehearsal) (1981). Here the rhythms of Stravinsky's music organised satirical material, highly metric, danced with energy, mimetic articulation and effortful fun. The dynamic of the third work, Piazzolla Caldero (1992) was emotionally charged, the eukinetic content arising partly through the ethnicity of the music and inspiration - a poem of Neruda - and manifest by the dancers' wholehearted entering into their roles. Although the works were surprising in their difference, Paul Taylor used organic rhythms, thoroughly humane in their preparation / action / recovery phrasing, coloured and interrupted by the dynamics of dramatic intent.

Humphrey's suspension fall and recovery

Returning to the historiography of eukinetics, Humphrey's Water Study (1928) was her experiment with musicless dance. She was not however looking for a completely autonomous movement art as Laban was, free of music and free from narrative image. In Water Study it was the ebb and flow of water's rhythm that Humphrey sought to embody. In general she researched a basis for the eukinetic content of her own theatre work. Suspending against the pull of gravity, falling with it and recovering from the fall was her phrasing of the movement of dance, coloured dynamically by all manner of variants on 'sharp and smooth' and controlled by the observance of metre. The rhythmical counterpoint of one set of timing and dynamics for the movement and another in the music is one of her innovations (Humphrey, ibid.). Like Wigman, Humphrey used the breath; Wigman inspired by the passion and feelings of breath, Humphrey by the phrasing possibilities it gave to movement material.

breath rhythm and phrasing

Breath rhythm use today includes feeling breath to organise the phrasing of material, using the ebb and flow of breath as a means of generating material, and using irregular breath to embody emotional states. By feeling the breath in her movement the dancer imbues a humane quality to the material. Breath rhythm carries semiotic content, for humans breathe and objects do not. Reification of the dancer and breath do not go together. Although Ashton uses the dramatic interpretation of the roles in his works to enhance the dynamic content, in her performance in Marguerite and Armand, Sylvie Guillem uses her breath to aid her interpretation of the highly charged tragedy that she is dancing. Three layers of dynamic content - musical, dramatic and breath - are there to help the spectator to engage with her as a woman, not as a dancing technician.

Martha Graham, searching concurrently with Humphrey in New York, found her own dynamic and rhythmic base for her work. The contraction and release from the dancer's pelvis, the origin of all movement, she overlaid with rhythmic patterns inspired by the emotional states of her characters and archetypes. Susan Sentler recalled how sometimes the movement's timing and dynamic were dependent on the intense collaborative feeling of the company, not metrical, but the embodiment of the passions of the idea.[33] Graham's contraction and release motivation dictated the use of taut energy in her works. She used eukinetic leitmotifs to express characterisation. In Diversion of Angels (1947), the White Girl's calm sustainment with the suspicion of soft impulse contrasted with the Red Girl's fiery attack, percussive contractions and vibrant stillnesses, contrasted with the Yellow Girl's fleetness, flexibility and fluidity.

Graham's contraction and release

As has been articulated in this text elsewhere, Merce Cunningham and the Judson Church pioneers discontinued the mainstream Modern Dance way of making work. Their attitude to rhythm, timing and dynamics was one way of achieving a new direction. Yvonne Rainer's strategy of denial contains the phrases:

functional rhythm

> no to transformations and magic and make-believe... no to involvement of performer (Banes, ibid. p.43).

In eukinetic terms she is not going to use dramatic, emotional, dynamic timing, nor is she going to use effort with its dependence on the attitude of the dancer to the material she is dancing. No connection with humane movement, or material that would offer a behavioural life line to the spectator was to be included. She specifically wrote in her Analysis of Trio A in 1963 that she would:

> eliminate or minimise... phrasing... development and climax... variation; rhythm, shape, dynamics... (ibid. p.55).

Sally Banes wrote:

> In sum, the movement style is factual (matter-of-fact, non-illusionistic), unexaggerated, unemphatic. Neither weight, nor time, nor space factors are noticeably stylised or emphasised. The one factor that is obviously altered and manipulated is the flow of movement (ibid. p.47).

She continued:

> Treating dance as an object to be examined, dance material as a series of tasks to be presented, Rainer becomes a workman (ibid.).

With the change in choreographic method and dancers' performance, the way spectators looked at the works altered,

---

[33] Susan Sentler, Graham dancer and teacher in conversation with the authors, 2000.

inevitably. Searching for meaning, hoping for illusion, was clearly pointless, made explicit by the change of venue from theatre to loft. It was at this time that the Snoopy cartoon voiced the current opinion on art: 'Mean, mean, does it have to mean something?'

No it doesn't, was the answer. Phenomenal engagement with what was happening took over from a search for semiotic content. The performative was reduced to a minimum.

Later, experimenter Lucinda Childs, who embraced the minimalist repetitious aesthetic being presented in music by Steve Reich et al, required her audience to look for minutiae. The score of Melody Excerpt (1977) gives the geometric floor patterns of the work. Rhythmically it holds to a continuous unchanging pulse, dynamically it is 'virtuosic in terms of endurance, precision, clarity, composure and memory' (ibid. pp.142-3). No drama, no narrative, no hidden evidence of complex psychic function, no added effort colouring, just functionally metred motion, repeated again and again with spatial variations.

action rhythm

In these experiments, interest shifted from creating dreams to presenting everyday happenings as happenings. Everyday spaces became dance spaces, everyday sounds became dance sounds and everyday clothing took over from costuming. Sneakers and jeans, piazzas and buildings, barking dogs and police car sirens became familiar material. Using rhythm functionally became a norm, taking everyday actions and their everyday rhythm as dance material. With similar values, Cunningham focused on the functional rhythm of dance movement. In order to distance his movement from behaviour and the illusion of human feeling, he used chance methods to determine actions of bodies in space and in time. Each movement was of equal value, to be danced by individuals each of equal value, in any part of the equally valued space. The term 'action rhythm' was coined for his eukinetic choice, the rhythm required by the action, no more and no less. Choreographing ensemble works with this aesthetic requires that the duration of each dancer's material becomes an organising time principle. Dancers need to be as sensitive and accurate in their pace as they are in their space (Denby, 1968).

mundane and idiosyncratic rhythm

In Pina Bausch and the tanztheater movement in Germany, effort returns but with her treatment. She presents the mundane in movement, in speech, in costume and in space and in the here and now performance of her company. The eukinetic elements are mundane too in the matter-of-fact manner of performance, albeit exaggerated to carry through the proscenium arch. Dancers speak as they speak, walk as they walk, sit down, lie down as they would in a mundane environment, but precisely, articulate with Bausch's aesthetic. But since Bausch is commenting on that behaviour, she structures it, repetition of the same material several times being a favoured method. Because material is repeated by several performers, their individuality being the interest, idiosyncratic timing and dynamics becomes a feature of her work. In <u>1980</u> each performer repeats the same verbal phrase, differently, each person settles himself to sunbathe, differently, each person reacts to a mouse in the house, differently. She includes its opposite for she shifts between presenting each person's way of doing things to showing, in unison, highly stylised walks and gestures. This idiosyncratic material is the focus in <u>Café Müller</u> (1978) where four characters have eukinetically distinct leitmotifs as they interact with discomfort and dislocation amongst the table and chairs of an eating house.

Pina Bausch, <u>Café Müller</u> *Gert Weigelt*

macro-dynamics

The macro-dynamic profile of an full evening's work, or of a triple bill, is not by any means achieved through the dynamics of the movement only. Dynamics of the movement and dynamics of a work are not synonymous. Neither are the two concepts - macro-eukinetics and macro-dynamics - but they overlap. Eukinetics refers to the qualities in performed movement, whether at a macro- or a micro- level. Dynamics must be a broader concepts for performative dance since dynamic change is embodied in all strands of the dance medium and since dynamic change is experienced by makers, performers and spectators.

The tripartite perspective suggests that dynamic content is put in place through a making process by the whole creative team.

Lighting designer, costume designer, set designer, composer, choreographer, video controller, et al, have means at their disposal to create dynamic change. Because colours contain dynamic energy, lighting and gels, pin-pointed white focused light followed by dim overall steel blue flooding, create a lighting rhythm. The speed at which slide images are changed on a screen is dynamic. Scattered ensemble dancing followed by a solo, provides macro-dynamic change.

In the pioneering work of the American Modern Dance people, the criteria for the dynamic of a work was proposed by Louis Horst in what was the first ever course in composition in America (1928). Using the visual arts and music as models, Horst urged dancers to structure their works as well as spontaneously allowing them to arise from feeling, that being the expressionist mode of the time.

His concepts on structure derived from the interplay between existing dance forms and new dynamic introductions, mirroring the diversity of the modernity of artists in other fields:

> Distorted like Picasso; impressionistic like Debussy; linear like Klee; dissonant like Webern; linear like Gregorian chant and medieval drawings; jazzy and wide open spaces like America: cerebral (dehumanized) (Madden, 1996, p.68).

Through and with Louis Horst, musician and mentor, Graham developed her ability to use micro- and macro-eukinetic content as a means of theatre. The performative in her works was palpable.

Fernando Crespo undertook an analysis of Bausch's 1980 to discover how she achieved the macro-dynamics in her episodic works (1986). Most of her episode changes are seamless, one gradually grows out of the other. He found that she introduced a new episode in one strand while all the rest remained in the previous activity. Each strand gradually changed over until, almost without the audience realising it, a new episode was in full flood. Sometimes it was a solo figure that was introduced. Sometimes speech began. Sometimes the lighting changed, or an object was brought on stage. As each of these events occurred, the dynamic tension on stage started to shift as, inevitably did the performative engagement of the spectators. In that piece, Bausch contrasts ensemble parts where the company are shouting and careering haphazardly around the stage space, with stately walking in unison. Later in the work, a solo man sits eating his porridge slowly and repetitively; in another section the company enter one by one and settle down, each with their own blanket, to end in attitudes of sleep. In another scene the company are huddled together, giving a density to the dynamic.

Ed Wubbe's Kathleen has a high level of dynamic throughout, but Wubbe gives it rise and fall through his structuring as well as his company's performance. The work opens with a women's

Ed Wubbe, <u>Kathleen</u> *Hans Gerritsen*

counterpoint ensemble, rich in its micro-dynamics, watched by
still men, and accompanied by a strident theme on the piano
with a second layer of discordant sound. This is followed by a
man's brief solo and an intense and vigorous duet. None of
these fragments are long; they merge into each other changing
the pace and energy level enough to give an overall sense of
shifting uncertainty. The structure continually moves on to a
trio, to a male quartet, to an ensemble, to a second duet, and so
on. The hard rectangular set adds an abrasive feeling which the
graffitti scrawled on the backcloth exaggerate. Wubbe has given
the work a macro-dynamic rhythm which never drags.

In 2001, any and all of the rhythm, timing and dynamic modes
discussed, macro- and micro-, are to be found in dance
practice. Many more exist in Britain alone, where the multi-
ethnicity presents multi-eukinetic performances. Dancers
entering the professional field are required to prepare
themselves for almost anything. It is not possible to say that the
turn of the century has prioritised one kind of eukinetic over
another. Anything may be present. It is not, however, the
dynamic that will make a work performative, for dynamic
performance can be admired but not engaged with - it is how
the dynamic is directed toward the spectator to require and
elicit a response that makes the difference.

Crabs
Hervé Jourdet
Transitions Dance
Company
Chris Nash

chapter 5
a'binocular vision': semiology and phenomenology of dance

In the previous chapters of this enquiry it has been proposed that the focus of a choreological perspective lies in the nature of the dance medium - its structures, methods and processes. By doing so, choreological study is shown to share comparable aims to those of recent developments in semiotics and phenomenology of theatrical performance. In particular, the enquiry into the relationship between the phenomenon and signs in theatre and performance praxis shares similar aims to those of this enquiry. When performative dance artists are border crossing between dance and other forms of performance, this connection is particularly relevant.

Phenomenology aims to describe happenings, events, subjective experiences focusing on an understanding of the nature of an initial encounter with the phenomenon, before cognition and a search for causes takes place. In dance this includes focus on the intuitive subjective experiences of the maker, the performer and the spectator. Semiotics, the study of the signs embodied in performance praxis, looks at how artists create visual, aural and kinetic images of a kind that can be recognised, within a culture, as meaning something. While words are a useful medium for the discussion of signification and meaning, they are not at all good at getting at subjective experience. It will be argued here that for an adequate account of the making, performing, spectating complexities in dance both a semiotic and a phenomenal perspective need to be approached, in tandem. While the duality is not difficult to work with in the studio, the following discussion is an attempt to verbalise a connection that is non-verbal in reality.

Since a choreological perspective locates dance within the field of theatrical performance, writings on semiotics and phenomenology of theatrical performance are seen as relevant to this enquiry.[1] The focus does not imply that choreological study is only concerned with activity that happens in a theatre

dance performance and theatrical performance

---

[1] For a detailed discussion of the concept of 'performance' see Carlson (1996), Kaye (1994) and Schechner (1988).

building, but rather one which takes place within a theatrical framework organised by theatrical codes. By locating the study of dance within the field of performance, choreological study adopts and supports the position that the analysis of performance (and dance specifically) constitutes a discourse on its own terms requiring its own specific methods and systems of analysis.

phenomenon and sign

Current thinking on the nature of 'performance' suggests that theatre and performance provide a framework for communication and for the participation in behaviour of a certain kind. On the one hand, as the Prague Linguistic Circle proposes, 'all that is on the stage is a sign'. On the other hand, as States proposes, objects and persons in theatre are not only signs standing in for something else, but are also the thing itself (1985, pp. 28-29). Dances as performative events also contain signs as well as the fabric of the dance itself which is there to be engaged with for itself. Choreological study is, therefore, located at the plane of intersection of these two perspectives which is referred to here as the interpraxia, that is, the analysis and practical exploration of the connections between the two positions. On the one hand, a choreological perspective tries to explain dance as a communicative art form, whilst on the other proposes that it is an art form of a particular singularity because of its embodied nature; that is, dance is both semiotic and phenomenal.

'binocular vision'

This interpraxia requires two distinct but interdependent ways of knowing dance; the experiencing of the phenomenon and the creating/interpreting of the signs within the phenomenon. This duality has been aptly named by States as a 'binocular vision' (ibid. p.8) which sets out to understand the objects / subjects within a theatrical event as they oscillate between their 'experiential and referential' dimension. All three of the processes of dance - namely creating, performing and interpreting - are experienced and understood through both phenomenal encounter and through sign interpretation, by engaging with the work and its processes simply for themselves and by engaging with them in a search for meanings. Intuition, perception and cognition are all active in this dual process.

theatre signs

In studying the relevance of semiotics to the analysis of performance, consideration needs to be given to the fact that theatre semiotics has developed away from orthodox semiotics, linked as it is to verbal language, in recognising the way in which theatrical discourse is different from other linguistic-based models of signification. Whereas in conventional linguistic semiotics the interpretation of the sign is based on notions of consensus and conventionalisation (ie: the sign refers to something else outside of itself which can be recognised), in theatre the sign is open to a process of 'desemiotisation' (ibid. p.23) based on ambiguity, excess and negation of meanings. The consensus would apply if a person nods after the question "May I ?", in that it has become a norm that a nod signifies agreement and permission. The conventionalisation is the process by which the nod, in those circumstances, becomes a recognised sign. In dance, in a theatrical frame, a nod as part of a movement sequence can be nothing more than a head movement offering nothing more than itself, a down and up gesture, while simultaneously suggesting agreement but possibly without clarification of what the agreement is for, and hence both a phenomenon and ambiguous.

The negation of meanings in the process of desemiotisation, may occur through excess and redundancy, such as that seen in Forsythe's Loss of Small Detail. It is a work in which umpteen individual signs are presented concurrently by an ensemble moving independently of each other in chaotic counterpoint, kinetic, visual and aural, so that the spectator's eye can well become satiated and overwhelmed with 'information' deliberately placed there. Semiotic transaction becomes drowned out and phenomenal appreciation becomes the alternative option.

As States points out, 'the referential urgency of the sign' in linguistic-based discourse is transformed in theatre into emphatic response, an expressive density through exaggeration (ibid pp.24-25). In dance the exaggeration of performance is even greater in an effort to create a sign. Ed Wubbe, in Kathleen, exaggerates the initial contact between a man and a woman by repetition of the act of touching, by enlarging the normal size of the gesture and slowing down its timing.

Moreover, it is now generally agreed that the theatrical sign is polysemantic, not only because it is open to multiple interpretations but also because a theatrical sign (contrary to conventional signs) can be formed from a conglomerate of features belonging to a diversity of sign systems. In Kathleen, Wubbe creates a series of concurrent and sequential signs for the tensions and promiscuity of urban youth, through graffitti on the backdrop, through his choice of layered electronic music, through the physicality of his costuming, and the sexual nature of some of the movement material. There is no one primary system, but a diversity of systems in a complex network - each with its own subcodes - of lighting, movement, text, decor and sound, for example.

This polysemanticism ruptures the process of conventionalisation of the sign. Departing from Derridean description of the sign (for a sign to be a sign it must be repeatable), States argues that in performance we witness imagery, made of materials of the medium, which

> does far more that is necessary in order to mean whatever it may mean
> (ibid. p.25).

He proposes that a study of theatre must then consider the way in which theatrical imagery becomes conventionalised into theatre-based signs and from signs into systems of theatre-based codes and how simultaneously, it destroys and ruptures this process through the multiplicity of its layers. The tension between polysemanticism and desemiotisation exists for directors and choreographers to play with in theatre works and works of theatre dance. Multiple meanings or chaotic excess result.

observing and rupturing codes

The presence of codes in a performance sets up an expectation in the spectator that some things will be included and some things will not. A classical ballet work is coded through the artists obeying the rules of the genre. Certain theatrical norms will be observed: the curtain will open; the lights will go down; the spectators will sit on their seats and watch; certain movements will be included and others excluded. A range of musical styles will be expected and others not and so on across the whole spectrum of features of that genre. Tradition is maintained by work that observes the codes.

But an innovative choreographer will play with the rules, from adopting slight personal touches to downright subversion. The subversive codes eventually become accepted as a norm. They become conventionalised and subsumed into the existing codes of dance performance. As has already been articulated in this text, Martha Graham subverted the codes of her forebears in dance and continued to state those subversions until they became a code in their own right, the Graham code. Cunningham subverted the expressionist rules set up by Graham and her co-pioneers. Again, his coherence and stability led to his ruptures becoming a norm, the Cunningham / Cage code of co-existing strands. The contemporary postmoderns addressed the formalist codes of Cunningham et al and disrupted the methods that reduced movement to codified vocabularies. In so doing, they question the relationship between dance and 'reality' and explore the inherent tension between theatrical codes and the cultural codes of everyday mundanity. The relationship between these two sets of codes is present in the multitude of experiments and events in postmodern dance today. The practice of such complexity constitutes an area of interest in choreological study and one that links it to larger socio-cultural/historical discourse.

theatrical semiotics

Starting from a recognition of the way in which polysemanticism operates in theatre and the specificity of theatrical codes, discussion of theatrical semiotics is triadic, as it is in choreological discourse. It considers the relationship between:

> **1.** directorial intention,
> **2.** the way the intention is materialised and interpreted in the work and its performance and
> **3.** the manner in which that will be interpreted by an audience.

Pavis suggests that the key to understanding the particularity of theatrical communication lies in the notion of the mise-en-scène, seen as a 'synchronic confrontation of signifying systems' whose interaction produces meaning (1982, p.19).

Pavis' concept of the mise-en-scène is compatible with that proposed by the nexus of the strands concept but the latter goes much further and is broader in its praxis for dance.

In discussion, it has been suggested that mise en scène is an established and sufficent term for what is proposed by the concepts of the strands of the dance medium. That is disputed here. Mise en scène arose with a presumption that there is a text to be 'put on stage' (Aston & Savona, 1991, p.121). Although that position has now expanded to include non-text based perfomance the term is associated with text and with directorial decision making. That concept is too narrow for the range of dance theatre practice, a range that the nexus of the strands of the dance medium encompasses. The strands concept applies to making, performing and appreciating processes and is by now sophisticated in its use of nexial clusters.

mise en scène

As previously discussed, the concept of the strands attempts to articulate the specificity of the dance medium through an understanding of the complexities of dance theatre practice. It includes Pavis' view that the theatrical event (the dance) cannot be reduced to a description of 'isolated units described in their minutest detail' (ibid. p.15). The notion of the strands as a nexus supports the notion that the reduction of the theatrical sign to its elemental constituents is perverse. Theatre engages through clusters not through single items; that is, in conventional functions of meanings, in combination, and in their polysemantic ambiguity.

Matthew Bourne's <u>Swan Lake</u> with Adventures in Motion Pictures can serve as an example, focusing on the male swans. Taken singly, the swans are bare-chested men in feathered trousers in place of the traditional women in white tutus. Theatrically, they suggest layers of ambiguous reference and confound audience's expectations. Bourne's meanings are deliberately polysemantic. His feathered men dance with familar music associated with other images, which confuse, amuse, excite or enrage according to personally held views. To open out the phrase 'functions of meaning', Jacobson's communication functions (in Guiraud, 1975) may act as a starting point. These are discussed further in Werner's and in Preston-Dunlop's essays in Part 2, in which Jacobson's functions are individually discussed. Here, Bourne's swans are ambiguous and polysemantic. In Jacobson's communicative categories:

functions of meaning

1. they arouse all manner of responses and questions in the spectator
2. they confront the conventions of ballet, of gender, of tradition
3. they dance superbly and musically thereby representing extremes of human capacity, skill and virtuosity
4. they are part of a coherent and worthful event thereby eliciting an aesthetic response
5. they suggest all sorts of references, to flight, swanness, idealism, masculinity......

6. they contribute to a continuously maintained interaction between stage and auditorium giving rise to spectatorial engagement and intention to watch, and interpret.

These images cluster with others in the work to function polysemantically.

transaction

The notion of the mise en scène carries with it a concern not only with what happens on stage through directorial intention and performative concretisation, that is, embodiment in all strands of the medium, but also the manner in which the world on stage discloses itself to the audience and is disclosed by the audience. The activeness of the audience's response is essential for the disclosure to 'work'. The notion of the mise en scène as proposed by Pavis (and further developed by States and Garner) carries with it a tripartite perspective which suggests that the identity of the performance (and for our inquiry, the identity of the dance) is transactional and, therefore, gives emphasis to the cooperative/complementary role of maker/performer/audience in the creation of the identity of the work (Garner, 1989, pp.10-11; Bennett, 1997). The meanings in the work are not only created by the artistic team but also by the recipients of the work, who do much more than passively receive what is given. They (can) interact with the work's images and allow their own knowledge of the world and imagination to stimulate their own sense of the significance of what is going on.

However, it is the discussion of the particularity of this collaborative process which prompts States to suggest that semiotic analysis, although useful, is incomplete. He suggests that to consider theatre only from the perspective of signification is to negate one of its key aspects, namely, the way in which theatrical devices liberate the theatrical experience from the purely referential and restore its corporeality, that is, its intersubjective bodiedness. The notion of intersubjectivity focuses on the subjective, personal experience of one person in contact with another person who is seen as an equally subjective and personally experiencing 'other', not as another 'thing' to be looked at as an object. The restoration of corporeality prevents theatre from being seen as yet another type of 'passage of information' (States, 1985, p.12), such as that achievable by the written word or morse code messages. Theatre is much more than a cognitive exchange.

What theatre as performance constantly reiterates is the inability of ascribing to the theatrical event a 'pure sign' function without eliminating its own inescapable physical presence - its 'thereness' as actual bodies, persons, sounds. This is acutely so when dealing with the performer's physical presence on stage, as States argues, which will inevitably have direct relevance to dance since dance performance is a theatrical event based on physical presence through performer-mediated movement. The 'twinness' of dance is in itself double. It is of the dancer who is both himself as a particular individual and not himself as a dancer playing a role, and of the movement which can be just itself and/or may refer to something else.[2] Therefore, the theatrical paradox acquires maximum complexity in the dancer's body in space.

Twyla Tharp's <u>Push Comes to Shove</u> can illustrate the point. Baryshnikov is both himself, famous, with a reputation, and the phenomenally talented dancer dancing Tharp's material. Her material is simultaneously itself and a rupture of classical ballet, referring to both that sub-culture and to the modernity Tharp espouses. This reflects back on Baryshnikov who becomes caught up in the politics of art making. His costume and bowler hat, the well known music, all refer while being themselves. The audience engage with whatever of this complexity they reach for (plus their own extras). States' view suggests that if they only try to comprehend Tharp and Baryshnikov they will miss half the dance. It is there not only to carry meaning but to BE, to be seen for its being. It is a phenomenon, a happening, an event, an occurrence alongside being a complexity of signs.

First attempts at a phenomenological perspective specifically on dance include the writings of Sheets-Johnstone (1966) and Fraleigh (1987). The authors draw upon Merleau-Ponty's and Ricoeur's theories of phenomenology to elaborate their position. Their writings illuminate those instances in dance

---

2 Twinness is present in the strands of the sound and space of dance performance since the sound is both itself and referential, as is the space.

when "thinking about what I am doing" and the actual doing come together as a present moment of lived experience. The thinking about it disappears and the living it happens. The contrast to this lived moment is the feeling of the dancer who treats her body as an object which she causes to move, so separating herself from what she is doing. While this unified way of working is pursued and practised in daily class, it is another matter when the dancer functions in a theatrical framework in which the theatrical paradox exists. She is her lived experience of role, personally subsumed into her material, but also seen as both individual artist and role, both Martha Graham and Medea, both Dominique Mercy and his Bausch role. Fraleigh invokes Susanne Langer's theory that what is evoked in any art medium is virtual, not actual. In Langer's terms, and the works that she writes about, the dance and the dancer are subsumed into a virtual world of illusion. By phenomenally living the part the dancer 'disappears' as herself, so denying the corporeality of her presence. The essential duality accounted for by States is not allowed for by Langer and hence not dealt with by Fraleigh and Sheets Johnstone. Performative work, tanztheater, physical theatre, operate on direct intersubjective relationships between performer and spectator, both of them corporeal people not illusory but very real. Disappearance of the dancer is not only demonstrably impossible but also fails to take into consideration ways in which the body in performance serves to rupture the idea of illusion, not create it. This is particularly true of contemporary postmodern works from Yvonne Rainer to Bausch, to Forsythe to Mats Ek and most certainly of Alain Platel. Illusion and disappearance are not on their agendae; physical personhood is. Hence, Fraleigh and Sheets-Johnstone's position is not a tripartite, contractual perspective on performance. Rather it sustains a teleological perspective on the event, one coloured by 'expressive' notions of dance; that is, dance as 'expression' being something sent from the dance to the receiving dance audience.

choreological perspective

What a choreological perspective proposes is a more detailed examination of how the experience and expression of dance is a result of an 'intersubjectivity' whereby knowledge of ourselves and the world is not self-contained but contingent upon interaction with the other (Jones, 1998). This is proposed as an alternative to the semiotic notion of 'intertextuality' in which the 'text' of the art work and the 'texts' in the memory of the spectator interact, ignoring intersubjective experience.

The information and experience of dance, gained through studying its processes and products through phenomenology and semiotics, is maximised when the issues debated above are taken into account. In this way, we can establish the phenomenology and semiotics of performative transactional dance. When these two perspectives are assembled, inform and complement each other, we come to the choreological position that the plane of intersection of these two perspectives provides the way for attending to the complexity of embodied theatre works of dance.

The discussion of the interpraxia in this text is regarded as an introduction, a statement of a position that requires an expanded discourse on both phenomenology of performative dance and semiotics of performative dance, as well as of their complex connection. None of the extant writings within these two areas have subsumed into their arguments the issues raised by transaction, embodiment, corporeality, the nexus of the stands of the dance medium, the tripartite perspective on making, performing and appreciation, the connection between process and product, or the mediation of movement by the dancer. This text is a beginning.

Futur / Perfekt
Ana Sanchez-Colberg
Theater enCorps
Max Thielmann

chapter 6
what next ?

In this text an attempt has been made to focus on the performative in dance practice and to present for debate parameters for a choreological, dance-specific perspective. The authors have drawn from current published documents and the European tradition of dance theory and have introduced new concepts and associated terms where necessary. The aim has been to consolidate a range of thought and practice and to suggest directions for practice-based research and practice-interrogated theory and so further the debates in current dance discourse.

A choreological perspective, like the art form from which it is derived, is necessarily in flux since performative dance practice continually nudges the borders that surround it and attempt to stabilise it. Embodiment and corporeality have been argued as central to dance while at the same time including an essay on current performative interactive digital installation work that, at least partially, eschews the live human body. Since a choreological perspective arises from dance practice it has to articulate a position and concurrently allow for expansion and contradictions of this sort.

The medium of dance, as multi-stranded and nexial in nature, has been presented as the manner in which the mise en scène of theatre appears, variously, in dance theatre. Since the timing and manner in which the various bits of 'scène' are put in visual and aural place in dance, it has been argued that the strands of the medium terminology and concepts allow for the multiplicity and layering of practice and its verbal articulation. With the advent of technology-based works traditional concepts of mise-en-scène will have to be re-thought, a situation for which the 'strands' theory is in place and ready to accomodate.

The manner in which the processes and skills of making, performing and appreciating overlap and co-exist in performative events has been presented. Current practice suggests that ways of preparing young people for careers in the performative dance theatre of the future require debate, for practitioners need to be dextrous in all three processes as well as able to collaborate with other contributing artists. Training dancers to dance only is unhelpful as the shortage of choreographers coming from the classical companies and schools demonstrates.

The increasing use of technology in the dance domain has been touched upon only. Forsythe uses it with a CDrom to communicate his improvisation method, something that words could never achieve. Cunningham and others use technology to find new movement for their works and integrate it scenographically into their productions. Rubidge shows its use in digital installation work. The extract of Hutchinson Guest's notated score was computer generated. Lighting and stage transformations are computer controlled. Many more imaginative ways are currently in use. Certainly choreological method and publishing, and probably much of performative dance will before long be technology compatible.

A choreological perspective, rooted as it is in practice, has been presented to function as a complement to existing perspectives emanating from cultural studies. Links between practice and theory are common in research and writing in the arts. What a choreological perspective argues is that the assumed dichotomy between theory and practice is unhelpful since practice embodies its own theoretical base. It has been argued that it is unhelpful to use dance practice to illustrate theoretical positions 'borrowed' from other disciplines when dance practice is perfectly capable of 1. interrogating theory and 2. of generating theory.

The fluidity of process and product in dance theatre has been shown to be in sharp contrast to the traditional division of the two, where processess are completed in the rehearsal period and a dance artefact is put in place to be marketed on a par with other manufactured products. The living nature of corporeally-based dance is arguably incompatible with the concept of completed product. It is ironic that Laban developed a dance notation system designed to 'fix' a dance's form when his own choreographic output was essentially in works that were rarely, if ever, complete or repeatable since they were purposely co-authored and collaborator-dependent, as well as responsive to audiences. 20th - 21st century choreographic practice has developed through a period of stabilisation and notation compatibility to one where the idiosyncratic nature of movement vocabularies and the 'becoming' nature of events challenges methods of documentation.

While Part 1 of this book has concentrated on putting in place an introduction to choreological concepts and discourse, in Part 2 some of these "what next?" issues are presented through discussion of the research undertaken by a group of practical scholars. The two Parts together should show the continuities and contradictions of both dance practice itself and of a choreological perspective.

Adshead, J. (1988). *Dance analysis: Theory and practice*. London: Dance Books.

Armelagos, A. & Sirridge, M. (1978). The identity crisis in dance. *Journal of Aesthetics and Art Criticism*, Vol. 37, No. 2.

Anderson, J.(1983). Idealists, materialists and the 32 fouettés. In Copeland and Cohen (Eds), *What is dance?: Readings in theory and criticism*. New York: Oxford University Press.

Argyle, M. (1967). *The psychology of interpersonal behaviour*. London: Penguin.

Aston, E. & Savona, G. (1995). *Theatre as a sign system*. London: Routledge.

Bachelard, G. (Ed.) (1994). *The poetics of space*. New York: Orion Press.

Banes, S. (1980). *Terpsichore in sneakers: Postmodern dance*. Boston: Houghton Mifflin.

Baudoin, P. & Gilpin, H. (1989). Proliferation and perfect disorder. *Programme for William Forsythe/Reggio Emilia Festival Danza, Bk. 2.*

Baumann, R. (1989). Performance. *In Encyclopaedia of Communication,* Vol. 3. Oxford: Oxford University Press.

Benesh, R. & J. (1969). *An Introduction to Benesh Movement Notation - Dance*. New York: Dance Horizons.

Bennett, S. (1997). *Theatre audiences: A theory of production and reception*. London: Routledge.

Bowne, A. (1989). Lighting Design and Contemporary Dance. *Sprung Floor*. June.

Bramley, I. (2001). 3-way conversation. *Dance Theatre Journal*, Vol 17, No. 3.

Brook, P. (1990 - original 1968). *The empty space*. Harmondsworth: Penguin.

Burian, J. M. ed. trans. (1993). *The Secret of Theatrical Space: memoirs of Josef Svoboda*. New York: Applause Theatre Book Publishers.

Caplan, E. & Cunningham, M. (directors) (1986). *Points in Space*. (BBC TV programme made with Cunningham Dance Foundationd Inc.). London: British Broadcasting Corporation.

Carlson, M. (1996). *Performance: A critical introduction*. London: Routledge.

Carter, A. (1998). *The Routledge dance studies reader*. London: Routledge.

Clarke, M. & Vaughan, D (1977). *The encyclopedia of dance and ballet*. London: Peerage Books.

Cooper-Albright, A. (1997). *Choreographing difference: The body and identity in contemporary dance*. Hanover/London: University Press of New England.

Crespo, F. (1986). *A justification for the inclusion of the strands of the dance medium in dance analysis*. Unpublished MA dissertation, Laban Centre London.

Croce, A. (1982). *Going to the Dance*. New York: Alfred A Knopf.

Cunningham, M. (1952). Space, time and dance. In R. Kostelanetz (Ed.)(1992). *Merce Cunningham / Dancing in space and time*. Chicago: a capella books.

Dell, C. (1972). *Space harmony*. New York: Dance Notation Bureau

Denby, E. (1968). Essays, stories and remarks about Merce Cunningham. *Dance Perspectives*, No. 34.

Desmond, J. C. (1997). Embodying difference: Issues in dance and cultural studies. *In Meaning in Motion: New cultural studies of dance*. Durham/London: Duke University Press.

Deutsche Rundfunk (1985). *Mary Wigman Ausdrucktänzerin*

Donaldson, A. (1993). *The choreutic parameter: A key determinant in choreographic structural style*. Unpublished PhD Thesis, Laban Centre London.

Eco, U. (1980). *The semiotics of theatre and drama*. London: Methuen.

Figgis, M. (director) (1996). *William Forsythe* (in Channel 4 series Dancing Around) (TV programme made by Euphoria) London: Channel 4.

Forsythe, W. (1999). *William Forsythe improvisation technologies: a tool for the analytical dance eye*. (digital arts ed., special issue) [CD-ROM] Karlsruhe, Germany: Zentrum fur Kunst und Medienttechnologie.

Foster, S.L. (1995). *Corporealities: Dancing Knowledge, Culture and Power*. London, New York: Routledge.

Fraleigh, S. (1987). *Dance and the lived body: A descriptive aesthetics*. Pittsburg: University of Pittsburg Press.

Garner, S.B.Jnr. (1989). *The absent voice: Narrative comprehension in the theatre*. Urbana: University of Illinois Press.

Garner, S.B.Jnr. (1994). *Bodied spaces: Phenomenology and performance in contemporary drama*. Ithaca: Cornell University Press.

Goodman, N. (1976). *Languages of art*. (2nd.ed.). Indianapolis: Hackett Publishing Co. Inc.

Grimm, T. (producer). (1984). *An Evening with Martha Graham.* (TV progamme by Martha Graham Center of Contemporary Dance Inc. & Danmarks Radio). Copenhagen: Danmarks Radio.

Gruen, J. (1976). (Host) 1976 March 8. *The sound of dance: Interview of Kurt Joos by Patricia Birch.* WNCN, New York.

1 sound cassette in the New York Public Library Dance Division.

Gubernatis, R. & Bentivolio, L. (1986). *Pina Bausch.* Paris: Théatre de Ville et Centre Internationale des Lettres.

Guiraud, P. (trans. G. Gross) (1975). *Semiology.* London: RKP.

Hackney, P., Manno, S. & Topaz, M. (1977). *Study Guide for Elementary Labanotation,* (2nd. ed.). New York: Dance Notation Bureau.

Hall, E. (1966). *The hidden dimension.* New York: Anchor Books.

Hall, E. (1982). *The silent language.* New York: Doubleday.

Heimonen, K. (1989). *Places.* MA unpublished dissertation, Laban Centre London.

Hodson, M. (1996). *Nijinski's Crime against Grace: Reconstruction Score of the Original Choreography for Le Sacre de Printemps.* Styvesant: Pendragon Press.

Hodson, M. & Archer, K. (1999/2000). To catch a nightingale: reconstructing the Chant du Rossingol. *Dance Now,* Vol. 8, Winter.

Hoghe, R. (1980). The theatre of Pina Bausch. *Theatre Review,* Vol 24, No. 1.

Humphrey, D. (1959). *The art of making dances.* New York: Rinehart & Co.

Hutchinson Guest, A. (1970). *Labanotation.* New York: Theatre Arts Books.

Hutchinson Guest, A. (1991). *Nijinski's Faune restored.* London: Gordon and Breach.

Hutchinson Guest, A. (1983). *Your move: A new approach to the study of movement and dance.* London: Gordon and Breach.

Hutera, D. (2001). Re-imagining Romeo and Juliet. *Dance Theatre Journal,* Vol 17, No. 3.

James, M. (director) (1998). *Trisha Brown.* (in the Channel 4 Series Dancing Around) (TV programme made by Eupohoria) Channel 4.

Jones, A. (1998). *Body art: performing the subject.* Minneapolis: University of Minnesota Press.

Jordan, S. (1996). Musical/choreographic discourse: method, music theory and meaning. In G. Morris (Ed.). *Moving words: re-writing dance.* London: Routledge.

Jung, C.G. (1921 - trans 1971). *Psychological types,* Vol 6. Princeton: Princeton University Press.

Kaye, N. (1994). *Postmodernism and performance.* New York: St Martins Press.

Knust, A. (1979). *Dictionary of Kinetography Laban (Labanotation).* Plymouth: Macdonald & Evans.

Kirstein, L. & Stuart, M. (1977). *The classic ballet: Basic technique and terminology.* London: A&C Black.

Laban, R. (1926). *Choreographie.* Jena: Diederics.

Laban, R. (1950). *Mastery of movement on the stage.* London: Macdonald and Evans.

Laban, R. rev. Ullmann L. (1971). *Mastery of movement.* (3rd ed.). Plymouth: Macdonald and Evans.

Laban, R. ed. Ullmann. L. (1966). *Choreutics.* London: Macdonald and Evans

Lamb, W. (1965). *Posture and gesture: An introduction to the study of physical behaviour.* London: Duckworth.

Lange, R. (1988). Dance notation and the development of choreology. *Musica Antiqua VIII: Bydgoszcz.*

Lange, R. (1985). Laban's system of movement notation. *Dance Studies.* Vol. 9.

Lange, R. (1980). The development of anthropological dance research. *Dance Studies.* Vol. 4.

Lange, R. (1984). Guidelines for field work on traditional dance, methods and checklist. *Dance Studies.* Vol. 8.

Langer, S. (1957). *Problems in art.* New York: Charles Scribner's Sons

Liu, F - S. (1986). *Chinese ritual dance* 1766 BC - 1279 AD. PhD thesis, Laban Centre London.

Loader, K. (executive director) (1986). *Face to Face with Jeremy Isaacs: Merce Cunningham.* (TV programme). London: British Broadcasting Corporation.

Loney, G. (1984). Creating an environment: Pina Bausch redefines dance with peat moss, autumn leaves, sod, tables and chairs. *Theatre Crafts,* Vol. 18, No. 8.

Longstaff, J.S. (1996). *Cognitive structures of kinesthetic space: Re-evaluating Rudolf Laban's choreutics in the context of spatial cognition and motor control.* Unpublished PhD thesis, Laban Centre London.

Longstaff, J.S. (1999). *Selected methods of documentation and analysis in choreological research: A diversified Laban analysis approach.* London: Neue Aura.

Louppe, L. ed. (1990). *La Danse Tracée.* Exhibition catalogue, Paris: Centre Pompidou.

Lyra, A. (1999). *A European urban dance event.* Athens, Sxedia Dance Company.

MacGibbon,R. (director/editor) (1997). *The Royal Ballet in William Forsythe's Steptext.* (TV programme in the series Summer Dance) London: British Broadcasting Corporation.

Macrory, A., Lockyer, B & Venza, J. (producers) (1995). *Two by Dove*. (collaborative TV programme by BBC and Thirteen / WNET), London: British Broadcasting Corporation.

Madden, D. (1996). *You call me Louis, not Mr. Horst*. London: Harwood Academic.

Maletic, V. (1987). *Body - Space - Expression / The development of Rudolf Laban's Movement and Dance Concepts*. Berlin; de gruyter

Margolis, J. (1984). The autographic nature of the dance. In M. Sheets Johnstone. *Illuminating Dance*. Associated University Press

Marion, S. (1990). Authorship and intention in re-created or notated dances. *Notation Papers of the Hong Kong International Dance Conference*.

Marti, S. & Kurath, G. (1964). *Dances of Anahuac*. Chicago: Aldine.

Martin, J. (1965). *Introduction to the dance*. New York: Dance Horizons.

Melrose, S. (1994). *A semiotics of the dramatic text*. Basingstoke: Macmillan.

Merleau-Ponty, M. trans. C. Smith. (1962). *Phenomenology of perception*. London: Routledge.

Merriam-Webster. (1993). *Collegiate Dictionar, 10th edition*. Springfield: Merriam-Webster Inc.

Miller, J. (1986). *Subsequent Performances*. London: Faber & Faber

Morris, G. (ed) (1996). *Moving Words: Re-Writing Dance*. London: Routledge.

Moustakas, C. (1994). *Phenomenal Research Methods*. London: Sage Publications.

Mumford, P. (1985). Lighting Design. *Dance Research*, Vol III, No2, Autumn.

Nattiez J.J. (trans. C. Abbate). (1990). *Music and discourse*. Princeton: Princeton University Press

North, M. (1972). *Personality assessment through movement*. London: MacDonald and Evans.

Ots, T. (1994). The silenced body - the expressive Leib: On the dialectic of mind and life in Chinese cathartic healing. In Thomas J. Czordas (Ed.). *Embodiment and experience: The existential ground of culture and self*. Cambridge: Cambridge University Press.

Pavis P. (1993). *Languages of the stage*. New York: Performing Arts Journal Books.

Preston-Dunlop, V. (1964). Martha Graham. *The Laban Art of Movement Guild Magazine*, No. 32.

Preston-Dunlop, V. (1983). Choreutics: Concepts and practice. *Dance Research, Vol I No 1*.

Preston-Dunlop, V. (1984). *Point of departure: The dancers's space*. London: Verve Publishing.

Preston-Dunlop, V. (1986). *Choreological studies: A discussion document*. Unpub. Laban Centre London.

Preston-Dunlop, V. (director) (1986). *In The Laban Tradition: Sylvia Bodmer*. (Video). Laban Centre London.

Preston-Dunlop, V. (director) (1986). *Recreation of Laban Dances 1923-28*. (Video). London: Verve Publishing.

Preston-Dunlop, V. (1990). Laban, Schönberg et Kandinsky, 1899 -1938 In L. Louppe (Ed.). *La Danse Tracée*. Exhibition catalogue, Paris: Centre Pompidou.

Preston-Dunlop, V. (1995). *Dance Words*. London & New York: Harwood Academic.

Preston-Dunlop, V. (1998). *Looking at Dances*. London: Verve Publishing.

Preston-Dunlop, V. (1998a). *Rudolf Laban: An Extraordinary Life*. London: Dance Books.

Redfern, B. (1983). *Dance, art and aesthetics*. London: Dance Books.

Ricoeur, Paul (1966). *Freedom and Nature: The Voluntary and the Involuntary*. Chicago: North Western University Press.

Richter, H. (1965). *Dada art and anti-art*. New York and Toronto: Oxford University Press

Rubidge, S. (2000). *Identity in flux: A theoretical and choreographic enquiry into the identity of the open work*. Unpublished PhD thesis, Laban Centre London.

Rubidge, S. (1995). Reconstruction and its problems. *Dance Theatre Journal, Vol 12, No. 1*.

Sanchez-Colberg. A. (1988). Style and the dance: A clarification of the concept of style as applied to dance and a methodology for its research. *CORD Conference Proceedings, Dance and Culture Conference*. Toronto.

Sanchez-Colberg. A. (1996). Altered states and subliminal spaces: Charting the road towards a physical theatre. *Performance Review, Vol.1, No.2*

Schechner, R. (1988). *Performance theory*. (Revised and expanded ed.). New York and London: Routledge.

Scheflen, A. (1972). *Body language and social order*. Englewood Cliffs: Prentice-Hall.

Schlemmer, T. (Ed.) (1972).*Oskar Schlemmer: Letters and diaries*. Evanston: Northwestern University Press.

Sears, D. (1984). Breaking down Harmonica Breakdown. *Ballet Review, Vol. XI, No. 4. pp. 58-69*.

Shahn, B. (1975). *The shape of content*. Cambridge: Harvard University Press.

Sheets Johnstone, M. (1979). *The phenomenology of dance*. (2nd ed.). London: Dance Books.

Siegel, M. (1971). Nik. *Dance Perspectives, No. 48*.

Soares, J. (1992). *Louis Horst: Musician in a dancer's world*. Durham NC: Duke University Press.

Sorrell, W. (1986). *Looking back in wonder: Diary of a dance critic*. New York: Columbia University Press.

States, B. (1985). *Great reckonings in little rooms: On the phenomenology of the theatre.*Berkeley: University of California Press.

Sutton-Smith, B. (2001). *The ambiguity of play.* Cambridge Mass: Harvard University Press.

Sutton-Smith, B (1997). *Performance: A critical introduction.* London: Routledge

Szeemann, H. (1980).*Monte Verità.* Milan: Electa Editrice.

Taper, B. (1974). *Balanchine: A Biography.* New York: Collier Macmillan Publishers.

Terry, W. (1956). *The Dance in America* New York: Harper and Brothers

Tracy, R. (2000). *Spaces of the mind: Isamu Noguchi's dance designs.* New York: Procenium Publishers

Tufnell, M. & Crickmay, C. (1990). *Body space image: Notes towards improvisation and performance.* London: Virago

Turner, V. (1982). *From ritual to theatre: The seriousness of human play.* New York: P A J Press.

Utrecht, L. (1992, October 26). *Review.* Der Volkrant.

Valesquez, J. (1986). *Lenguaje, verdad y mundo: Modelo fenomenologico para el analisis semantico.* Barcelona: Antropos.

Van Zile, J. (2001). *Perspectives on Korean Dance.* Hanover, NH: Wesleyan University Press.

Veltrusky, J. (1964). Man and object in the theatre. In Paul L. Garvin. *A Prague school reader on aesthetics, literary structure and style.* Washington: Georgetown University Press.

White, E.W. (1966). *Stravinsky: The composer and his works.* London: Faber & Faber

Wigman, M. (trans. W. Sorrell). (1966). *The language of dance.* London: Macdonald and Evan.

Amagatsu, Ushio	Butoh	Sankai Juku	1990
Anderson, Lea	Smithereens	Cholmondeleys & Featherstonehaughs & Victims of Death	1999
	3	Cholmondeleys & Featherstonehaughs & Victims of Death	2001
	Les Six Belles	Transitions Dance Company	1997
Ashton, Frederick	Marguerite and Armand	Royal Ballet	1963
	Symphonic Variations	Sadlers Wells Ballet	1946
Balanchine, George	Agon	New York City Ballet	1957
	Apollo	Ballets Russes	1929
	Ballade	New York City Ballet	1980
	Le Chant du Rossignol	Ballets Russes	1924
	Symphony in C	New York City Ballet	1948
Bausch, Pina	1980	Wuppertal Tanztheater	1980
	Bluebeard	Wuppertal Tanztheater	1977
	Café Müller	Wuppertal Tanztheater	1978
	Iphigenia in Taurus	Wuppertal Tanztheater	1991
	Sacre du Printemps	Wuppertal Tanztheater	1977
Bintley, David	Still Life at the Penguin Café	The Royal Ballet	1981
Bourne, Matthew	Swan Lake	Adventures in Motion Pictures	1995
Brown, Trisha	MO	Trisha Brown Company	1995
Bruce, Christopher	Swan Song	London Contemp. Dance Theatre	1987
	Waiting	London Contemp. Dance Theatre	1993
Butcher, Rosemary	Body as Site	Rosemary Butcher Dancers	1993
	Scan	Rosemary Butcher Dancers	2000
	The Site	Rosemary Butcher Dancers	1983
Childs, Lucinda	Melody Excerpt	Lucinda Childs Company	1977
Cohan, Robert	Cell	London Contemp. Dance Theatre	1969
Corder, Michael	Dance Variations	Royal Ballet	2000
Cunningham, Merce	Biped	Cunningham Dance Co	2000
	Beach Birds	Cunningham Dance Co	1992
	Points in Space	Cunningham Dance Co	1986
	Rainforest	Cunningham Dance Co	1968
de Châtel, Krisztina	Paletta	de Châtel Dansgroep	1992
Decoufflé, Philippe	Codex	Companie DCA	1993
Dove, Ulysses	Dancing on the Front Porch of Heaven	Royal Swedish Ballet	1992
Dudley, Jane	Harmonica Breakdown	Dudley	1940
Ek, Mats	Smoke	Guillem, Niklas Ek	1995
	Swan Lake	Cullberg Ballet	1987

dance and the performative

Forsythe, William	Artifact	Frankfurt Ballett	1985
	In the Middle Somewhat Elevated	Paris Opera Ballet	1988
	Loss of Fine Detail	Frankfurt Ballett	1992
	Steptext	Royal Ballet	1997
Graham, Martha	Appalachian Spring	Martha Graham Company	1944
	Cave of the Heart	Martha Graham Company	1947
	Clytemnestra	Martha Graham Company	1958
	Diversion of Angels	Martha Graham Company	1947
	Errand into the Maze	Martha Graham Company	1947
	Night Journey	Martha Graham Company	1947
	Primitive Mysteries	Martha Graham Company	1935
Harris, Rennie	Rome and Jewels	Puremovement	2001
Horton, Lester	The Beloved	Lewitsky, Boden	1948
Humphrey, Doris	Day on Earth	Humphrey Company	1947
	Water Study		1928
Hopps, Stuart	Dances for Turnage's The Silver Tassie	English National Opera	2000
Jooss, Kurt	Gaukelei	Folkwangbühne Essen	1930
	Die Grüne Tische (The Green Table)	Folkwangbühne Essen	1932
Laban, Rudolf	Gaukelei	Tanzbühne Laban	1923
	Prometheus	Hamburger Bewegungschöre Laban	1923
	Sang an die Sonne	Wigman, Bereska, Perrottet et al	1917
Locke, Edouard	Duo One	La La La Human Steps	1993
Lyra, Anastasia	Sxedia Polis	(City Specific Auditions)	1996
Macmillan, Kenneth	Romeo and Juliet	Royal Ballet	1965
Madden Dorothy	Zero Six	Maryland Dance Theatre	1971
Marin, Maguy	Grossland	Maguy Marin Company	1988
Morris, Mark	Hardnut	Mark Morris Company	1991
	Liebeslieder Waltzes	Mark Morris Company	1989
Newson, Lloyd	Can we afford this : the cost of living	DV8 Physical Theatre	2000
	Strange Fish	DV8 Physical Theatre	1992
Nijinska, Bronislava	Les Noces	Ballets Russes	1923
Nijinsky, Vaslav	L' Aprésmidi d'un Faune	Ballets Russes	1912
	Le Sacre du Printemps	Ballets Russes	1912
Nikolais, Alwin	Kaleidoscope	Nikolais Dance Theatre	1956
Nunes, April	Newness at Lessness	Laban Centre London	1999
Platel, Alain	Lets op Bach	Le BalletsContemporain de la Belgique	1998
Rainer, Yvonne	Terrain	Rainer dancers	1963
	Trio A	Rainer dancers	1963
Robbins, Jerome	West Side Story	Bernstein musical	1957

Schlemmer, Oskar	Triadic Ballet	Schlemmer and dancers	1922
Taylor, Paul	Cascade	Paul Taylor Company	1999
	Piazzola Caldero	Paul Taylor Company	1992
	The Rite of Spring (Rehearsal)	Paul Taylor Company	1981
Tharp, Twyla	Push Comes to Shove	American Ballet Theater	1979
	The Fugue	Tharp and dancers	1970
Thompson, Dale	Intaglio	Thompson dancers	1999
Vandekeybus, Wim	La Mentira	Vandekeybus Company	1995
	Roseland	Vandekeybus Company	1990
	What the Body Does not Remember	Vandekeybus Company	1990
Wigman, Mary	Hexentanz	Mary Wigman	1914
	Whirl Dance (in Celebration)	Mary Wigman	1928
Wubbe, Ed	Kathleen	Scapino Ballet Rotterdam	1994

MACHINE RHYTHMS

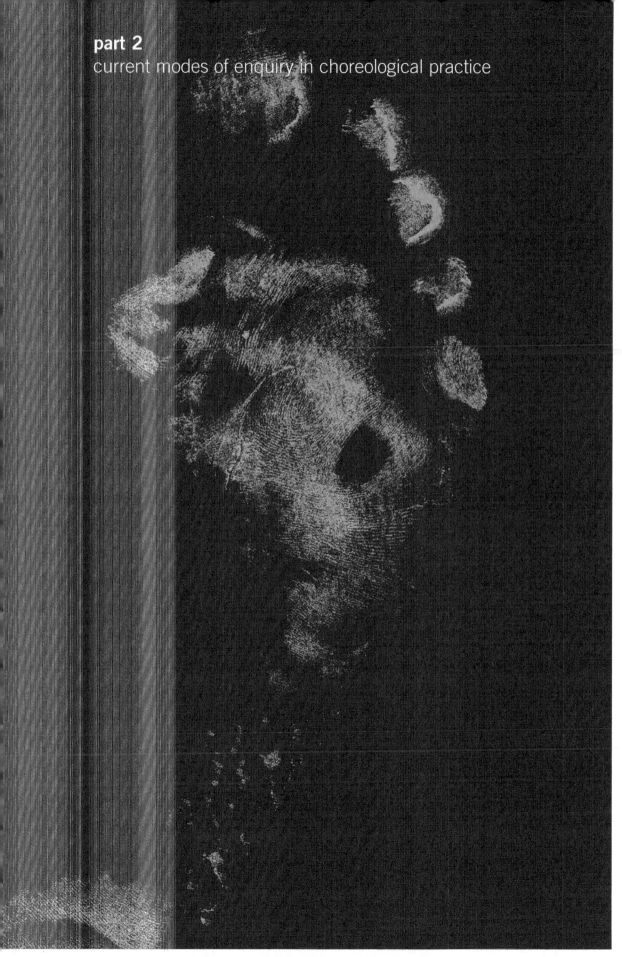

part 2
current modes of enquiry in choreological practice

Oben und Unten
Laban 1923
(re-created Valerie
Preston-Dunlop 1990)
Toni Nandi

chapter 7
current modes of enquiry in choreological practice
Valerie Preston-Dunlop and
Ana Sanchez-Colberg

The diversity of dance knowledge and ways of coming to know dance and to experience it in Merleau-Ponty's terms (1962) dictate the complexity of modes of enquiry currently practised in choreological study and research: practical knowing in the viscera; engagement with works and with one's own performing; propositional knowledge and debate about theoretical positions on dance practice; aural, visual and kinaesthetic perception of the nexus of sight, sounds and physicality of dance; understanding the complex networks of the contractual nature of the event. These are some ways in which a choreological perspective and the performative in dance are explored.

Because the dance studied is so diverse the methodologies available have to take account of the continuities, discontinuities and severe ruptures that have occurred over time of the traditions in the dance profession. The study modes used need to enable fruitful research, articulation and debate, in practice and in verbal discourse, on the diversity of process, product and transaction. It is not uncommon to find that a proven method or theoretical position is insufficient or misleading for adequate articulation of current performative dance practice since many theoretical positions have come about through considering a dance as a cultural object, a completed artefact to be appreciated from the spectators' perspective. The complex multiplicity and flux of performative dance practice requires a wider mode of enquiry than that.

Because choreological study operates both practically and theoretically, concurrently, the methods used centre on practical scholarship. Currently four perspectives are prioritised. Broadly these come under the headings of: experiencing, experimenting, documenting, and analysing, distinct in nature and purpose but interdependent. The knowledge from one mode interacts with the knowledge from another through confirmation, questioning and debate.

The purpose of prioritising experience is to encourage a

corporeal attitude which leads to an ability to discriminate differences in the experiencing person's own acts of making, performing and spectating. Engaging with whatever is the subject of the experience is the essential feature of workshops that concentrate on experience: of the dancer's self; of other participants in an artistic event; of a performative event by other people; of the sources for choreographic making.

Experiencing bodily facilitates a corporeal attitude toward whatever is beyond the boundaries of the body. Shifting inter-subjectively from proprioception to exteroception is dependent on the perceiver having developed a facility to attend, to engage. Rather than 'seeing' everything 'out there' as objects to be scrutinised and dealt with, people 'out there' are experienced as subjects to be engaged with as co-subjects. The facility of dance people attuned to experiencing enables empathetical connection with what other dancers feel kinetically. This is far removed from casting a critical eye as a detached observer on another body-object 'doing' movements. In this respect Laban principles and understanding of movement as mediated are a starting point in that they act as a bridging facility between the experience and intent of one's own movement and the appreciation of another's. His work provides a language of kinaesthetic feeling that combines with his observation method.

Experiencing moving subjectively is starkly different from 'doing' movements. The question of ownership of the material is raised and thence the capacity to take on its innate flux and changeability. Movements are not fixed objects but subjectively created entities, primarily in a permanent state of becoming, with occasional moments of arrest, created anew each time. The mix of proprioceptive and exteroceptive attending, kinaesthetic searching for feeling with openness to phenomenal experiencing brings about a profound change in dancers' sense of ownership of their own material and their own person.

Paula Salosaari's studio-based research has taken an experiential perspective into the dilemmas of teaching ballet in a period when the ballet profession is struggling with how to move forward into the twenty first century. Her essay discusses the traditional way of teaching ballet and proposes a broader method. She articlulates the transition that her dancers made from striving to master a received vocabulary to experiencing it, multiply, and thereby taking possession of it. A further strand of her research was the effect that possession had on her dancers' relationship with their tradition.

Professor Stephanie Jordan, her examining "opponent" in the public defense of her doctoral thesis in Helsinki's Theatre Academy, quoted Susan Crow and Jennifer Jackson's remark

> Ballet as we know it to-day will, overburdened by nostalgia, limp into the 21st century

as indicative of the relevance of Salosaari's research into a radical re-think of how to approach the demise facing ballet's artistic future.

For Sanchez-Colberg, the idea of 'experiencing' is a key focus of her performance project <u>Futur/Perfekt</u>. Central to the practice-based research is a concern with the role of 'physicality' and 'corporeality' in performance. The starting point is the experience of the dancer, in the form of a memory, which becomes a source for the work and has an effect on the fluid thematic of the various events that have constituted the project. The work explores the implication of the various dimensions of experience: experiencing at the moment of performance; the dancer's physicality as a tool; the formal structuring of the work around corporeality; the actual material of the work in that the dancer's physicality is the main production strand of the event from which movement develops. With experience as a main feature, the work is not regarded as a completed object but encourages a consideration of performers as agents of an event-in-the-making initiating a network of impact on the audience's own memories and physicality.

The purpose of experimenting is to alert dance people to new possibilities within their medium and art form. Putting together things that have not been together before is part of any creative endeavour. In workshops, classes, rehearsals and research, explorations take place in order to develop a climate of experimentation, in an atmosphere where anything is possible. This kind of exploration inevitably takes place in choreographing a work but there the outcome sets out to be a performative art work. Choreological experimentation is not necessarily so structured: it may result in a series of studies; be a process of learning to be used in whatever way the learner requires; facilitate the flux of experimental risk-taking during a performance.

experimenting

Sarah Rubidge's discussion of her research delineates the symbiotic relationship between her philosophic and choreographic modes of enquiry, leading her into choreographic experimentation. Her use of the term 'interrogation' for choreographic activity underlines the position that practice can and does offer a great deal more than an illustration of theory. It 'interrogates' theory in a way that verbal research cannot. As she says, the choreographic interrogation led to a theoretical shift, since the traditional stance on identity in dance did not hold for open works of dance, at any rate for the open work that she authored and directed. The shift in theory to one on flux led her into a further choreographic enquiry in another dance medium - performative interactive digital installations - itself a form of experimental open work.

Rubidge's mode of investigation is one that is championed within choreological study. The performative nature of the works she discusses enlarges the genre of works beyond those discussed in the text of Part 1 where, apart from Merce

Cunningham, choreographers have had the feet of all their dancers on terra firma. In Passing Phases and Halo this is not so or not so entirely. Rubidge homes in on the 'interactor' as a participant in the performative activity. The traditional notion that receivers of a work are spectators not makers, questioned in the discussion of the triadic perspective in Part 1, is soundly ruptured, for Rubidge's spectators become interactors who 'initiate' the flux in the installation.

Rubidge's work also addresses the traditional stance on process and product. Her works never become products or artefacts but are permanently 'becoming'. The reader may wish to compare her interactive event with the 'becoming' nature of Laban's Kammertanz works discussed by Preston-Dunlop and the 'becoming' of Sanchez-Colberg's project Futur/Perfekt.

documenting
Documenting through whatever means is a way of capturing dance, overcoming its ephemeral nature. Documenting begins in the body through making the transition from improvising to recalling and stablising the material so that it is saved, corporeally. The main 'library' of dance material resides in dancers' bodies.

It is not until performers have to put data on paper, or have to dance material themselves, that they realise that they do not know, have not seen, have not heard, have not felt. Much documenting is intended as a learning process and not productive of a manuscript. Simply the process of experiencing that, for example, movement dynamics can be written underlines for a novice that dynamics is not just an intuitive personal interpretation but the serious stuff of dancing. Writing a lighting plot or a story board, or drawing a costume design, or notating a string of jumps may all occur in learning processes in workshops.

In analysis, documenting consists in collecting data in a form that can be shared with someone else, sometimes stored in the body, sometimes written on paper, sometimes recorded by film and technology. Data about the processes, participants, the choreographic treatment, the ideas treated, surface form, sound, et al., is collected, collated, discussed, transformed according to the problem that initiated the documentation.

Writing a score to safeguard a work, to copyright it and to enable the work to be kept in the repertoire, is one of the responsibilities of a company choreologist. There is much debate on the advisable content of a dance score. Some company notators expect to remount the work themselves, at least to undertake the first rehearsals. With that in mind decisions can be made on the kind of movement detail and ancillary information to be included, the legibility of the score, the use of personal shorthands, for example. With a time lapse between the notating and the remounting of a work a debate surfaces on the nature of the identity of the work. Rubidge discusses the ontology of identity while Preston-Dunlop questions whether an understanding of a dance work lies in the score or in a recognition of the much more complex performative elements of it, its embodiment and nexial form.

Choreographers' notebooks are forms of documentation that give a glimpse into the poietics of a work rather into the work's trace, which a score gives. Martha Graham's Notebooks, Mary Wigman's annotated drawings in her Language of Dance show the reader something of a choreographer's way of working. Lea Anderson's private notebook for Smithereens is filled with her response to the politics and performances in Germany during the Weimar Republic. Ana Sanchez-Colberg's discussion of her work Futur/Perfekt is a form of its documentation. Preston-Dunlop's essay "Beyond Communication to Transaction" shows how the article written by Lloyd Newson on his physical theatre piece can we afford this: the cost of living affected her appreciation of the work's poietics. Critical reviews of performances give insight into layers of a work, as Peter Williams' critique of Schéhérazade in Preston-Dunlop's essay on revivals and re-creations shows.

If the structure of the work is of interest then a score is extremely helpful. If the performance of the work were of interest then a video recording might constitute a more usable form of documentation, as would access to a dancer who had performed the work. Combining the three media, score, video and dancer, may prove enough but video recordings have their own syntax and cameramen do not have an impartial eye. The particular performance filmed cannot / may not constitute an adequate record of the work; the video is a record of one version of the work, danced by one cast, in one interpretation, on one occasion, filmed by one cameraman. If the work contains improvisation, is an open work (see Rubidge's essay) or an event (see Sanchez-Colberg's essay) or a process work (see Preston-Dunlop's essay) then one video recording can only misrepresent the work.

When documenting methods are used in research formal criteria of legitimacy and legibility apply. They must be in shared symbol systems, that is, systems that can be read by someone else since the verification of data validates the findings of a researcher, or questions them. Published notation methods are regarded as shared systems on a par with verbal language. Any published system is legitimate which in dance may include effort graphs, linear effort graphs, ChUMm graphs, floor plans, morphological graphs, lighting plans, musical scores, costume designs, stage management diaries, historiographical data.

In her essay Preston-Dunlop concentrates on the process-product issue essential to archeochoreological work. What she undertook in the research project over several years to refind Rudolf Laban's performative works involved experiential engagement with the dance culture of the period and experimental workshops on his methods. The project included documentation of the research in three formats, 'documentation' in the bodies of the participants of re-created dances and their processes of making, video recordings of all the rehearsals, discussions and performances, and discursive articles and a film on the process. In this respect the project included all four of the current choreological workshop methods : experiencing, experimenting, documenting and analysing.

In looking at other archeochoreological projects the whole notion of what a performative work of dance is comes under the writer's scrutiny. Dance history is 'normally' taught theoretically but what the perspective on history in this essay proposes, and practices, is the role of experiential workshops in coming to know dance cultures other than one's own. Thereby, historiography expands from having primarily a verbal and film method to one that is also workshop based. It is well known that baroque dance is taught practically, with an aim to get at the corporeality of authentic steps and carriage of the body. What Preston-Dunlop's workshop-based historiography shows is that, even when the surface form of the works is lost, experience of the processes gives insight to participants. It shows that even when an 'analysis of immanent structures of the work', as Nattiez puts it, is required, experience of the poietic processes offers a deeper engagement with the work and with the artists involved.

It may be of interest to the reader to compare the issues raised from this project by its thoroughly corporeal method with those raised by Rubidge on the identity of open works that conclude with the creation of a non-corporeal digital installation.

Both of these projects look at works in flux rather than stable works as artefacts. Rubidge discusses theories of flux, especially of Deleuze and Guttari, to help her articulate the problems of identity when a work has no stable surface form. Both essays rupture the concept that a stable surface form is the norm for dance works, a belief strengthened wherever a notated score is made and used. Sanchez-Colberg's project demonstrates the opportunities such a fluctual event offers for an expansion of the debate on dance documentation.

analysis and engagement

Analysing usually has a product in the form of discussion, backed up by data, leading to findings around a particular enquiry. While that kind of articulation and debate is a valid goal, a preliminary goal to develop an attitude of engagement with a work, has to be set. The wealth of content that is there to be discovered in the making and performing of a dance can only be revealed gradually through layers of cool analysis accompanied by personal transaction. Knowledge and experience of a work's wealth leads directly back into studio-based experiential work, for the more that is understood about layers, the more there is to engage with in corporeal practice. Skill and sensitivity in the process of analysis should develop a conceptual discipline which in turn helps a dance person to organise exploratory work.

Analytic methodologies are established procedures in which an object or event or person is addressed in order to discover what overt and hidden processes might be in action. Choreological methods do this with reference to the notions of embodiment and of the triadic perspective of dance, together with the concept of the nexus of the four strands of the dance medium. Methods of analysis, including corporeal analysis during practice, are selected appropriate to the problem being addressed, together with suitable documentation. Frank Werner's essay is one example.

Because knowledge of a dance cannot be confined to knowing it as an object, strict objectivity used to validate a hypothesis, associated with scientific method, is rarely a useful criterion when coming to know dance. Appreciating a dance includes a subjective process partly through the embodiment issue. Because movement is made anew every time that the dancer dances it, the material cannot exist outside the dancer, it is essentially coloured / created by each embodiment of it. Hence it is unsatisfactory to treat dance only as a disembodied object (although this might be one perspective of a dance score reading). A subjective element to appreciation is inevitable partly by the manner in which the perceiver decides to attend to the dance.

Werner, rather than participating in the work that he discusses, was a spectator and ultimately an analyst. Analyses of dances can and do take various perspectives: a Labananalysis of the dynamic form of a work; or the interpretation by more than one performer of a work; the manner in which musician and dancer interact in a work. Adshead (1988) gives several examples. Many topics concentrate on the evident form of the work, its immanent structure. Werner uses his own corporeal knowledge as a dance practitioner to look at 'how' Trisha Brown created meaning in the structure and performance of her dance, not at 'what' she meant by it. Practical experience informed his method, rather than constituting a studio-based part of his method.

He refers to the communication theory of Jacobson as explicated by Guiraud, a theory also referred to by Preston-Dunlop in her engagement with the performative works of Bailey, Newson and Cunningham. Here Werner pursues the manner in which Brown has communicated since she makes clear that she wishes so to do, to give an homage to Petronio, while Preston-Dunlop shows how the concept of communication is neither sufficient for, nor true to the experience of, spectating performative work especially when the layers of the work generate the other half of the 'binocular vision' - phenomenal engagement.

Preston-Dunlop is not undertaking a formal analysis of works but engages with them as a whole. To do so she turns to Nattiez's suggestions for analytic methods (Nattiez, 1990, p.140) that attempt to connect the spectator with the maker and performer. Nattiez applies semiotic theory to musical analysis which Preston-Dunlop makes clear cannot be used directly for dance performance without considerable reconsideration. Adaptation is possible through identifying what aspects of Nattiez's proposals are problematic for dance, revisiting the original semiotic writings and using choreological concepts to replace, shift, develop, wherever a problem in relevance presents itself. Nattiez lists:

1. Immanent analysis, that is, analysis of the surface form of the work and its structures, irrespective of any interpretation or reference to creative processes.
2. Inductive poietics, by which data from the surface form is discussed in order to come to propositions about aspects in the creative process that might have occurred to produce form.
3. External poietics reverses the inductive method. Evidence of process (an article, a letter, a workshop) is taken and the work looked at with that inside information to gain a deeper understanding of the work's content.
4. Inductive esthesics grounds itself in defending a personal perception or interpretation of the work, citing data to prove that a particular interpretation is a valid one.
5. External esthesics begins by collecting perceptions and interpretations of the work from various spectators and comparing those with the evidence in the work itself. This is where reception theories and intertextuality analyses focus
6. Communication between all levels is the final method listed by Nattiez in which the poietic content (making processes and referents), the neutral trace or data from the actual performance, and esthesis responses (spectators' interpretations) act upon each other symbiotically.

In her engagement with three performative works Preston-Dunlop starts from these methods to develop a personal **6.** She precedes her use of Nattiez by referring to Jacobson's communication theory which she acknowledges is a perverse reference when looking at a Cunningham work that purports to eschew communication. She continues by discussing how 'living' the performance as it unfolds is a vivid alternative and complement to searching for understanding and meanings.

Each of these essays is, or is about, an amalgam of the four basic choreological modes of enquiry and illustrates how one mode informs another and the symbiotic nature of corporeal and verbal modes of engagement.

<u>Dithyrambus</u>, Laban 1923 (re-created Valerie Preston-Dunlop 1990) *Toni Nandi*

Halo
Sarah Rubidge
and Simon Biggs
still image

chapter 8
identity in flux: a practice-based interrogation of the ontology of the open dance work
Sarah Rubidge

In this article I will be describing a practice-based research project, begun in 1994, which constituted a choreographic interrogation into the nature of the open work, and an examination of the implications of questions raised by this choreographic investigation into the theories of identity which had traditionally been invoked in discussions of identity in dance. During the research process, the choreographic interrogation gave rise to developments in theoretical debates on identity in dance, inasmuch as it demanded a re-examination of theories grounded in an ontology of substance which had previously dominated the debate on identity in dance. This led to a theoretical shift which embraced an ontology of flux. This in turn served to propel the choreographic interrogation into a new artistic dimension, namely that of performative interactive digital installations. Such installations embody the theoretical framework concerning the ontological status of the open work which emerged during the research, and consequently provided a particularly appropriate context for further choreographic interrogations into the open work.

practice-based research

The paradigm of the open work used in this research project was quite specific, that of a work which is designed in such a way as to exhibit radical differences in surface features and/or form from presentation to presentation.[1] The open dance work, as a work, is designed as an open-ended system and thus has, in the long term, no point of closure, although it might exhibit temporary moments of closure in the form of performances, presentations or productions. Thus, open dance works not only privilege, but embody in their intentional logic the inherent disjunctiveness of the relationship between the strands of the dance medium noted by Sanchez-Colberg and Preston-Dunlop in Part 1.

an open work

---

[1] The claim could be made that any dance work is an open work, inasmuch as every performance of any dance work differs from all other performances to a greater or lesser extent. Classical ballets, because their material features are subject to change in different productions are, for example, 'open' dance works, as are works by contemporary choreographers who modify details of their works when they are revived. However, these are not paradigms of the genre of artistic practice which produces what have become known as 'open works'. This genre of compositional practice saw its genesis in the 1950s and 60s in music and dance with the compositional experiments of composers such as Pierre Boulez and Stockhausen, and in the work of 'post-modern' dance artists.

Open dance works present intriguing questions to the dance theorist when issues concerning their identity as works, particularly those concerning their ontological status, come up for discussion.[2] Since the 1970s it has been recognised that paintings and sculptures might have a different ontological status to performance works (Wollheim,1980; Wolterstorff, 1980; Margolis,1981 and Goodman, 1966). In my research I explored the notion that open works might have a different ontological status to closed works. One of the distinctive features of the radically open work is that it cannot by any stretch of the imagination be identified as an artefact. Rather, it is a dynamic, open-ended 'work-system' constituted from variable movement materials which are subject to modulation according to a series of authored intersecting systems of rules for behaviour. The openness of dance works are articulated variously through manipulations of kinaesthetic impulse and eukinetic profile of the movement material, through differences in the movement material performed, or through manipulations of the temporal progressions of the compositional units from which the work is constructed. Different rule systems may be developed for different strands of the work. Any artefacts (productions, performances) which might emanate from the work are momentary stabilisations of the work-system, one of many possibilities it presents, not the work itself.[3] Productions of an open dance work necessarily exhibit significantly different profiles of the work, some of which may be so different that it would not be possible to recognise two performances as being of the same work from their concretised features alone.[4] This in itself differentiates open works from closed works, which are identified through the similarities between performances.

choreographic interrogation

The first of my choreographic interrogations into the open work, Intimate Memories (1994), was a performance work for three dancers composed only of duets. Its surface theme concerned the shifting nature of relationships between the three protagonists. It was not a narrative piece, however; rather, it provided the framework for an exploration of the variability of human relationships, and the variability of meaning embodied in movement and gesture. As such it had an expressive choreographic intent. The intentional logic of this work lay in its openness, not in its surface themes, inasmuch as it consciously thematised the openness of the Barthian 'texte'. Intimate Memories took a particular approach to openness. It was not an improvised work, which is, perhaps the paradigm of the open work in contemporary dance practice. Rather, each production was composed, rehearsed and presented by a director as a 'closed' production of the work.

Thus, in contrast to the tendency in modern dance to reconstruct the original production as closely as possible, the dance-text Intimate Memories was designed to be open to a multiplicity of alternative scenarios and ambiences which would not be available if the 'original' production-text was taken as a paradigm of the 'work'.[5] When I devised the performance directives[6] for this work I designated five duets as

the compositional 'units' from which the work was constructed.
The performance directives stated that the movement materials
from which the compositional 'unit' were composed were open
to radical alteration with respect to their eukinetic features, that
the units were open to juxtaposition in different temporal
progressions, and that the mise en scène (sound
accompaniment, setting and costume) were not determined in
any way by the originating author. As choreographer, I
generated two productions of this work, in 1994 and 1996.[7]
Each differed radically in its eukinetic features and mise en
scène. (The first production favoured continuity of flow in the
movement, and partnering, saw the performers in costumes in
sepia tones, and used a medley of Bessie Smith songs as the
sound accompaniment. The second production favoured
staccato, impactive movement, saw the performers costumed in
black and used a Xenakis piece as sound accompaniment.)

---

[2] Although they are linked (the former being dependent upon the latter), issues of identity and issues concerning the ontological status of the dance work are concerned with different philosophical issues. The former is concerned with the means through which we individuate individual works of art, the latter is concerned with the mode of being of works of art. The individuation of the work of art is predicated on an ontological position concerning the mode of being of works of art.

[3] The same claim might be made with respect to the relationship between performances of a closed dance work and its 'score'. Indeed the history of discussions concerning the identity of the performance work have continually had to address the fact that the performances are not the work, as such, although they are the actualisations of the work. No agreement has been reached as to where the work is sited with respect to concrete art object, ideal art object or score, however.

[4] Thus challenging common-sense perceptions of what counts as the 'same' work, and with it Julie van Camp's "lay observer test of recognition" as a means of identifying a work (van Camp, 1980).

[5] This is standard practice in classial ballets, but much more rarely used in the world of modern dance.

[6] A term used by Wolterstorff (1980) in place of 'score'.

[7] At the Barber Festival, Birmingham in 1994 and at the Place Theatre in 1996.

In 1998, two productions were generated by two different independent directors, one of which used video projections as a further strand of the work. Whereas, as director, I focused on exploiting the openness of the eukinetic features and mise en scène, generating two productions which exhibited a shared temporal progression of the compositional units and within the compositional units, each of the independent directors deconstructed the assemblages of movement material (the duets) that I had designated 'compositional units' into smaller units. These they reconfigured into 'new' duets.

Thus it was the modulation of the expressive elements of the dance-text, in particular the eukinetic features, setting, costume, and sound environments, that served as the focus of the first two productions. The second production of Intimate Memories differed significantly from the first in terms of its surface movement style, and its setting, and clearly 'represented', or 'denoted', a different 'world'. As such these productions constituted an interrogation of certain positions concerning the identity of the dance work, in particular those proposed by Armelagos and Sirridge in their seminal essays of 1977 and 1978.[8] Under the conditions of identity proposed by Armelagos and Sirridge, who argue that: a) movement style is a condition of the identity of a work and b) deviations from the mood and tempo of the 'original' movement text disqualify a performance, or production, from being a performance of the work (Armelagos and Sirridge, 1978), these productions would be considered to be different works. Although these essays have been interrogated theoretically (e.g. Margolis, 1981), they have not been overtly interrogated choreographically.

openness of form

The independent directors embarked on a different line of investigation. Another aspect of openness invoked in open dance works, and incorporated into Intimate Memories, is openness of form.[9] Open works which emphasise open form draw on strategies closely aligned with the practices of mid-twentieth century composers Karlheinz Stockhausen, Earle Brown and Christian Wolff, and the Judson Church, a generation of dance artists who were working in the 1960s and 70s. Their works tended towards the formalist, and included both improvisations in which the movement materials were subject to improvised modulation during performance and works in which the compositional 'units' were not subject to such treatment during performance prior to the performance event. Their works were generally articulated in a 'score' of some kind,[10] as an unorganised collection of elements, which needed to be organised into unified totalities from presentation to presentation, rather than as pre-unified totalities in and of themselves.[11] In many open works of the time not all of the compositional units presented in the performance directives were required to be used in individual presentations of the work. Although this compositional device was not explicitly introduced into the performance directives, the two independent directors of Intimate Memories incorporated this approach into their reading of this work.

It became clear during the choreographic interrogation embodied in <u>Intimate Memories</u> that radically open works (particularly those which are couched in such a way as to be open to directorial interpretation not only with respect to material features but also to the originating choreographer's performance directives) raise new questions with regard both to the 'nature' of such works as works, and to the means through which they are individuated.[12] In particular, the question was raised as to the effect on the identity of the work if material properties (e.g. small-scale choreutic parameters of given larger-scale compositional units) which had been originally designated as individuating features of the work were modified by directors in subsequent productions. The very 'nature' of the work would, surely, be put into question. Under the auspices of an ontology of substance, such action would necessarily lead to that production being transformed into a different work. (It was this very concern which led Nelson Goodman to impose such strict conditions of identity on performance works.[13] Within this philosophical framework at a particular point in its transformation, the work must become a different work.

However, any claim made with respect to the boundaries of a work's identity is necessarily seen through the prism of a particular ontological position. The accepted framework for the discussion of the ontological status of the art work has been, until recently, an ontology of substance.[14] It became clear during my choreographic interrogation of openness in the dance work, that this philosophical framework not only problematises notions of 'identity' with respect to the 'work', but also obscures the particularity of the open work, and thus crucial features concerning the nature of this type of work as work. It became equally apparent that framing questions concerning the ontology of the open work through the prism of an ontology of flux was a more appropriate approach to take with regard to the subject under investigation.

That said, theories of identity developed under an ontology of substance cannot be summarily dismissed. During the heyday of discussions of the identity of the dance work, indeed - any performance - a work was necessarily identified through certain

identity as substance

---

8 Armelagos, A. & Sirridge, M. "The Identity Crisis in Dance" (1978) and "The Ins and Outs of Dance: Expression as an Aspect of Style" (1977). Their claims are frequently implicitly invoked by dance critics when ascertaining the 'authenticity' of a production of modern dance works.

9 Indeed Earle Brown (1966) suggests that open works are more correctly called 'open form' works.

10 These were often articulated in verbal form as a set of instructions for performers.

11 Rainer's <u>Terrain</u> (1963) is a particularly good example of an open work of this kind (see Banes, 1983) for a detailed description of this work.

12 The individuation of a work allows the viewer to ascertain whether two productions of a work are productions of the same work. This differs from establishing the 'nature', or mode of being of a work, which entails determining its ontological status.

13 Goodman argues that any performance of a work which does not follow the performance of its notated score to the note (or letter, or step) is not strictly a performance of the work because the score "...has as a primary function, the authoritative identification of the work from performance to performance." (Goodman, 1966, p.128)

14 An ontology of substance has dominated western philosophy since Plato and Aristotle, suppressing the move towards an ontology of flux made by pre-Socratic philosophers such as Heraclitus.

essential features, generally embodied in some form of performance directives.[15] (Goodman (1966), the early Margolis (1980, 1981), van Camp (1980) and later Thom (1993) and McFee (1994), proposed that performance directives were a condition of identity of performance works.) Thus, if a production complies with the material and formal features of the work laid down by the originating artist, it is a production of the work, however different its surface features might appear. This is inarguable. However, the claim was also made that any major modification or omission of the 'essential' features preserved in the performance directives would render a production of the work a production of a different work. The search for what constituted 'essential' features dominated discussions in dance. Armelagos and Sirridge argued that movement style was the essential condition of the identity of a dance work.[16] Margolis (1977), Wolterstorff (1980), van Camp (1981), amongst others, countered this view, arguing that a modification in style would not necessarily lead to the presentation of a different work, but merely an interpretation of the work.

However, it became increasingly clear that, although they could individuate individual open works, neither of these approaches to conditions of identity for the dance work accommodated the particularity of the open work, which is predicated on change, not similarity. Both conditions of identity which underpin these theories focus on the ontic features of the work; that is, its features as a 'thing', an artefact, rather than on its mode of being, or of becoming, and it is this which is of central importance in the ontology of the open work

type - token theory of identity

Other theories of identity which attempted to address the ontological status of the art work also appear to accommodate the nature of the open dance work with greater ease. The type/token theory of identity (which relies implicitly on the thesis of notationality for the individuation of the work) is one such theory. The type-token theory (championed by philosophers such as Wollheim and Margolis) posits that the artwork is an abstract particular (the type), which is instantiated in material 'tokens', but is distinct from that token. The token is a material object. The artwork, the type, is not. It is an intentional object, and thus exceeds any physical features its tokens might exhibit. It cannot be denied that, like any work, the open work (the type) is manifest through tokens which emanate from an authored performance-directive.[17] As such the open work can be subsumed under the umbrella of the type-token theory of identity. The argument for the applicability of this theory to the open work is strengthened further by the fact that it specifically allows for differences in the instantiations of any work which has multiple instantiations. Under this theory any performance work can support multiple tokens which differ one from the other to a significant degree.[18] Further, tokens need not contain every property exhibited by the type, nor need the type exhibit all of the properties exhibited by its tokens. If the latter obtains, the token can be said to 'exceed its type' (Margolis,1981), to go beyond the properties of the work-type specified in the performance directives, yet still remain a token of the work-type. The open performance work frequently, and deliberately, 'exceeds its type'.

Now it could be argued, justifiably, that if the variations in its productions which identify an open work as an open work are accommodated into the type-token theory there is no need to invoke new, or alternative, theories of identity with respect to such works. I would suggest, however, that this is not the case. The very generality of the type-token theory, along with its reductionist tendency to subsume the complexity of the composition of process works under a general framework which favours the ontic, leads to the elision of significant differences between open and closed works. Closed works are clearly articulated, highly specific expressive forms, with a more or less stable macro-structure and clearly identifiable extensional properties. Open works, conversely, are open-ended *systems*, constituted by active processes, which come to rest from time to time as forms of expression. They are *designed* to be continually open to deconstruction and subsequently to reconfiguration and renewal. These processes of deconstruction and reconfiguration are a central part of what the open work is, and are not addressed explicitly by the type-token theory of identity. For that reason, its adequacy for articulating the particular ontological status of the open work is open to question.

identity, process and procedure

To a very great extent, the identity of open works lies in the processes and procedures through which they are brought to being as work-events. Indeed, the intentional logic of the open work lies in its focus on the articulation and rearticulation of a process of thought in action, not in the products of that process. Thus, whilst there is no doubt that recourse to the type-token theory and the related thesis of notationality can be made to numerically identify open works,[19] this approach does not reveal its intentional logic. What matters in the open work are not merely the differences, but the varying differential relations that exist between the elements from which it is constituted. Simply noting substantive differences in instantiations does not suffice as a means of understanding such works. For this reason the type-token theory, like other theories of identity developed under the aegis of an ontology of substance, does not account adequately for the underlying nature of open works as works.

---

[15] Wolterstorff and Thom use the term 'performance directives' to accommodate all forms of instruction for performance, whether these be a score, a recording of some kind, or even the memories of performers.

[16] However, despite noting a multitude of exceptions to the rule in works which did not fit into their paradigm of the dance work (which was modelled on mainstream modern dance works of the 1950s, 1960s and 1970s), they still came firmly down on the side of movement style as a general condition of identity in dance.

[17] This performance directive might be in the form of a pre-existent score, or in the case of ongoing 'instructions' the performer gives him or her self during an improvisation.

[18] What counts as significant with respect to works of art is work-specific, and may change during the course of the work's 'career'.

[19] To numerically identify a work is to individuate instances of a work.

Intimate Memories highlighted this inadequacy. Because the conventionally conceived 'conditions of identity' of Intimate Memories (i.e. the original compositional units) were substantially modified during its 'career', genuine problems are encountered in individuating the work. Intimate Memories directly problematises the 'conditions of identity' proposed in previous paragraphs at two levels. Not only was it in flux with respect to the observable features of its instantiations, as are all open works, and of its movement style; it was also in flux through different interpretations of performance directives.

If Intimate Memories, as a work, is conceived as some kind of artefact - an 'object' - it could prove difficult to pin down what constitutes the identity of this work. Although the work can be individuated through recourse to the performance directives, the 'work' Intimate Memories - that is the 'work of the work'-[20] is not embodied in either the performance directives themselves or in any material features which might be derived from its performance directives. Rather, the 'work' is embodied in the very fluidity of form and structure that is implicated in those performance directives. It is there that the intentional logic, and thus identity, of the work lies. If Intimate Memories is characterised as a 'work-system'- that is, as an authored set of procedures which generates a multitude of related, but in no way similar actualisations - [21] it becomes easier to see the work as the kind of work it is.

As a system, the work Intimate Memories is dissimilar in kind to the forms of expression it will cause to come to being. It is, rather, a fluid, unformed 'state'. It is defined, as a work, not merely by its elements, but also by the fluctuating network of fluid, but undefined, connections through which those elements can be formed into temporary unified aggregates. The framework within which Intimate Memories operates only minimally constrains the form that the work's instantiations take, and, as has been seen, even those constraints are themselves subject to change as the boundaries of the work's 'identity' are stretched and redefined with successive encounters with directors and/or performers. The very openness of this framework allows for the work to reveal a multiplicity of perspectives through its engagement with different ways of 'thinking the work'. As such, the work could be said to be in a continual state of becoming.

This mode of understanding the nature of the open work is clearly derived from the analyses of the work undertaken by post-structuralist thinkers such as Barthes (1977) and Foucault (1969). The directorial strategies of fragmenting the compositional units from which Intimate Memories was constructed adopted by the independent directors brought to the fore the inherently 'post-structuralist' conceptual framework which characterises open works. In doing so they demanded that I shift the philosophical focus of my theoretical enquiry. Both independent directors demonstrated clearly that an open work such as Intimate Memories is constituted as a mobile

network of changing movement images, which can generate a
multiplicity of structural and expressive forms, not all of which
might have lain within the author's original imaginative
framework.[22] Through their interpretations of the performance
directives, which went beyond that originally envisaged by the
originating author, the original compositional framework of
<u>Intimate Memories</u> was destabilised and the work transformed
into a far more fluid and complex network of elements than
had been conceived by its creator. The interpretations, however,
did not counter the intentional logic of the work, inasmuch as
the independent directors complied with the performance
directives as written, but at the same time actualised, and
advanced, the notion of trans-formation which was a central
focus of this work. The directorial interventions of the directors
of the third and fourth productions of <u>Intimate Memories</u> thus
served to extend not only the authorial conception of the
boundaries which I had tacitly limited <u>Intimate Memories</u> in
my own productions of the work, but also the nature of the
work itself.[23] <u>Intimate Memories</u> was clearly revealed as a
variable 'text', not only in terms of the organisation of the
compositional units which had originally been designated as
the building blocks of the work, but also in terms of the
boundaries suggested by those compositional units.

Under an ontology of substance, this would be the point at
which any claims that the productions created by the

a work as texte

[20] Andrew Benjamin (1994) argues that the modern art work is defined by the work it undertakes as a work, by, for
example, the questions it asks.

[21] Different philosophers use different terms to describe materialisations of performance works. In this chapter the term
'actualisation' is favoured when discussing open works, in accord with the terminology employed by Deleuze and Guattari
(1987) with respect to open-ended entities. The term 'instantiation' is used, however, when discussing the work of
philosophers whose writings employ this term.

[22] It has long been accepted that this is a feature of any art work with respect to the way viewers construct their
interpretation of the work. It is less common to apply this notion to the concretisations of the works themselves.

[23] In spite of the difficulties of using the term 'nature' with its implications of essentialism, I will continue to use the term in
this essay, invoking the later Margolis as the framework for my usage.

independent directors were productions of the same work, rather than new works, would become shaky. Indeed, it was found that continuing to argue from this perspective did nothing to illuminate the particularity of <u>Intimate Memories</u> as a work. At this point in the research, it became clear that a reconceptualisation of the ontological status of such works was needed; one which acknowledged that, rather than constituting a traditional 'work', <u>Intimate Memories</u> constituted Barthean texte through which directors can

> fabricate text and meaning from another's text in the same way that each speaker constructs individual sentences and entire discourses from another's grammar and vocabulary and syntax (Landow 1994, p.117).[24]

The dance-text <u>Intimate Memories</u> thus must be conceived of as a work-system which, whilst it might guide its productions, does so only to the extent that a language system guides discourse.

influence of practice on theory

As can be seen, the relationship between practice and theory continually influenced my own understandings of the 'work' in both a theoretical and a choreographic context. As <u>Intimate Memories</u> became increasingly open and undifferentiated, and

Sarah Rubidge/Will Thorburn, <u>Intimate Memories</u> *video still*

increasingly open to modulation and transposition, I was led inexorably towards an investigation of a different conception of the ontology of the open work grounded in an ontology of flux. It was apparent that few theoretical positions concerning the identity of the dance work invoked in dance theory had been able to explain the ontology of the open work satisfactorily, even though it was clear that theories of identity developed by dance theorists have a value with respect to understanding of particular open works at certain levels of description. It was equally clear, however, that open works are accounted for by such theories at only one level of description, that which applies to actualisations of the work, for the theories

dance and the performative

do not address the particularity of the mode of being of open dance works, and it is this which is important with open works. The emphasis in open works is on variation as a *mode* of being. As a result, the identification of samenesses across productions, though still necessary for numerical individuation, assume less importance than understanding these works in terms which acknowledge that it is a more or less undifferentiated plane which is subject to a multiplicity of types of interaction and interconnection between its elements, its behaviours, its intensities.

It was becoming increasingly clear, as a result of my choreographic practices, that, if the 'identity' of open works is to be accounted for adequately, a theory which did not merely accommodate the issues of continuity and difference with which we have to deal in open works, as does the type-token theory, but which specifically addressed the issue of the nature of change, could prove to be a more productive framework in which to achieve this than those grounded in an ontology of substance.

the open work and ontologies of flux

Inasmuch as dance is ineliminably a processual art, it is, perhaps surprising that, with few exceptions (e.g. Sanchez-Colberg, 1992 and Kemp, 1996) dance theorists have been so slow in adopting theoretical frameworks which acknowledge, indeed embrace, an ontology of flux in their discussions of the identity of the dance work. It is even more surprising that, in spite of the insights provided by the writings of Barthes, Foucault and Derrida in the 1960s and 70s, that discussions of the ontology of the open performance work continued to try to force it into the framework of an ontology of substance.[25] An open work, as noted, is more of a work-system than a work. It constitutes a set of (protean) elements, which can be organised in a multitude of different configurations through a set of (protean) structuring strategies. Any production is but one of this potentially infinite set of possibilities inherent in the work-system. As such it is, as a work, a semi-formed field of possibilities, rather than a more or less closed form of expression articulated through a relatively limited range of performance possibilities.

These works retain their integrity, even though in some of the extant productions of the work the original intentions of the performance directives, as initially conceived by the originating

---

[24] As such it was also a form of 'hypertext'.

[25] See Armelagos and Sirridge (1968), Thom (1993) and Sparshott (1995) on 'free' improvisation, and Saltz (1997) on performative interactive art.

artist, might have been extended. Transformations of the authorial intentions of the performance directives resulting from directorial interpretations of those directives, such as those evidenced in <u>Intimate Memories</u>, is entirely in keeping with what Benjamin (1994)[26] calls the 'work of the work', its intentional logic, which I would venture to suggest is intimately linked to the identity of the work. Indeed, it is part of the nature of open works that they constitute

> *a dynamic network of discursive relations of which any material record can represent only a subset* (Moulthrop, 1994, p.103).

Although any performance work can be said to be in accord with Moulthrop's statement, the dynamic network which constitutes the open work is radically more flexible and open-ended than that of the 'closed' performance work. Further, the performance directives from which actualisations of the work are generated may themselves constitute another such dynamic network. Rather, the network of connections and differential relations between elements and facets of the work are constantly dissolved and reformed as each new mind acts upon it. Whilst, as has been seen, it is not impossible to accommodate such a model of the work into the philosophical positions discussed earlier in this paper, these positions do not account as adequately for the work as a dynamic network as do those developed by thinkers such as Roland Barthes, Michel Foucault, and Gilles Deleuze.

The open work, I would suggest, constitutes an artistic interrogation of the traditional concept of the 'work' which runs parallel with the theoretical challenges to the work concept forwarded by philosophers such as Foucault, Jacques Derrida and Barthes, and later Deleuze. It actualises many of the conceptions of the work proposed by Barthes in <u>The Death of the Author </u>(1977) and <u>From Work to Text</u>, (1977) and by Foucault in <u>What is an Author?</u> (1969). Open works are characterised by their 'textuality' (using the term in a Barthean sense); that is, by their openness, their malleability, and the multiplicity of forms of expression and meanings they can generate. Any discussion of open works must be conducted in recognition that their character as a mobile network, within which images and ideas are configured and reconfigured, is central to their nature as works.[27] That is, it must accommodate an understanding of the 'work' which emerges in the writings of Foucault, Barthes and Deleuze and Guattari, which allows that its identity, such as it is, is constituted by a fluid, underdetermined network of interlocking, overlapping, modulating strands and elements (not all of which are work specific, for example, conceptual frameworks), the structure of which is constantly dissolving and reforming from presentation to presentation. From this perspective the significant individuating features of an open work are located as much in the features of its structure, which facilitate but do not determine, the multiplicity of flows of connection which can exist between the constituent elements, as they do in the elements themselves.[28]

Recently, Preston-Dunlop and Sanchez-Colberg[29] have been addressing the issues which surround the open work in their writings. Significantly, Preston-Dunlop and Sanchez-Colberg's work is grounded in a Foucauldian approach to dance analysis.[30] As far back as 1992 Sanchez-Colberg, quoting Foucault, argued for the importance of recognising in any analysis of dance the subject's general history (career), which comprises

> *series, divisions, limits, differences of level, shifts, chronological specificities, particular forms of rehandling, possible types of relation* (Foucault, 1977, p.10),

and the discontinuity and inexhaustibility of the subject. She further argued that a dance has not only an overt structure (the 'dance-object'), but also a covert structure which is

> *an intricate network of cultural, political, social, psychological and ideological structures which are inextricably bound to the totality of the dance inasmuch as they help to define its existence and specificity.* (Sanchez-Colberg, 1991, p.12)

She did not, however, elaborate on this in any depth in this work. In my research, I extrapolated from her insights, using Deleuze and Guattari's theories concerning the nature of events (1987) to examine the suggestion that the processes through which open works are instantiated, are of at least as much importance as their material features in establishing the identity of the open work. This then became ineliminably the sine qua non of my choreographic research.

As a theorising artist, I found that the model offered by Deleuze and Guattari, which is grounded in the work of process philosopher Henri Bergson, because it emphasises an open becoming over being and closure, was more in accord with the nature of open works, as I understood it, than those models which emphasise being over becoming. In open works it was clear that the thinking in the work, the thinking of the work, is active, multi-directional, polyvalent. It privileges, rather than merely acknowledges, process.

Deleuze and Guattari offered a particularly productive framework through which to view the ontological status of the open dance work. Their work introduces many ideas which are consonant with the particularity of the open work. In direct

---

[26] The 'work of the work' is, Benjamin argues, subject to change over time. Margolis (1995) similarly suggests that the 'nature' of a work is not fixed.

[27] Although many post-structuralist thinkers would eschew the term 'work' preferring Barthes' texte instead, the designation texte does not exclude artists' production from a claim to workhood. Indeed Barthes argues cogently that Work and Text are coexistent, symbiotic inasmuch as it is futile to try to separate out works and texts materially. (1977, p. 156)

[28] Under a Deleuzian model the concepts underpinning the work constitute elements of a kind.

[29] Sanchez-Colberg has also adopted the open work as a choreographic framework for her professional practice, Futur/Perfekt.

[30] Developed by Sanchez-Colberg in 1992 as an approach to an analysis of tanztheater.

contrast with the theories of identity discussed earlier, Deleuze and Guattari do not attempt to formulate identity conditions for the entity, the idea, the concept. Rather they

> *go beyond experience to the conditions which account for things, states of things and their mixtures given to experience (Boundas, 1999, p.87).*

Open works are, if you like, more like 'conditions' which account for the work, than products.

nomad thought

Deleuze and Guattari focus on the ways in which entities and events are actualised as forms of expression, and on the nature of the unformed 'states' from which they emerge, not on entities as objects, or bounded events. Their ontology is specifically an ontology "…not of static beings, but of dynamic becomings" (Murphy, 1998, p. 213). As such, it accommodates the specificity of the mode of being of open works, which are in and of themselves dynamic 'becomings'. The conceptual framework under which they operate supports my earlier descriptions of what is important in the context of the open work. Their ontology of the Event,[31] and understanding of the nature of entities such as artworks, is grounded in what they call 'nomad' thought (Deleuze and Guattari, 1987). Characterised by its structure as "a system of co-ordinates, dynamics, orientations" (Marks, 1998 p. 44), its movement is not linear, but

> *flexible and nomadic, transversal and non-hierarchical: this thought is able to move between "formations" and forge linkages and connections between different systems of knowledge-formation*
> *(Kaufman, 1998, p.5).[32]*

Deleuze and Guattari contrast nomad thought with 'representational' thought (which gives rise to an ontology of substance), wherein concepts have a symmetrical relation to the external objects to which they are applied, and operate on a principle of analogy and resemblance. The 'space' of representational thought is stable,

> *confined to a horizontal plane, to preset paths between fixed and identifiable points (Massumi, 1996, p.6).*

Nomad thought, conversely, is characterised by its multidirectionality. Rather than exhibiting a symmetrical relation to its objects, it privileges mobile, shifting pathways and interconnections between a network of concepts, events, objects and singularities. It does not aim to categorise the world into discrete components, as does representational thought, nor seek to pin down and define a concept or thing by virtue of the components from which it is constructed. Rather, it seeks to articulate the nature of the syntheses between elements which are exhibited in the actualised event or entity, without restraining their potential for endless reconfigurations into other forms. It acknowledges that entities are in process, and thus always subject to modulation as other systems act upon them. For this reason, any analysis grounded in nomad thought, rather than aiming to fix an image of the world or the things it defines, or propose an essential nature, sums up sets of intersecting disparate circumstances, whilst always leaving these provisional descriptions open to modification.

In that nomad thought is

> ...a mobile, bifurcating series of lines [which] is always an open system, with multiple exits and entrances (Marks, 1998, p.45),[33]

a system which simultaneously is engaged in

> ...the act of charting out a pathway and opening of that pathway to chance encounters (Kaufman, 1998, p.6),

it is in closer accord with the 'nature' of the open work than the theories discussed earlier. Indeed, the open work could be considered to be in and of itself a miniature system of nomad thought. Each work has a particularity, but that particularity is as much to do with the system which gives rise to its instantiations as the instantiations themselves.

Thus Deleuze and Guattari emphasise that it is the character of the process through which entities are actualised which is important for understanding their nature, not the series of instantiations which constitute their 'career'.[34] For Deleuze and Guattari an entity

> ...is not defined by the form that determines it, nor as a determinate substance or subject, nor the functions it fulfils. [It] is defined only by... the sum total of the material elements belonging to it under given relations of movement and rest and the sum total of the intensive affects it is capable of at a given power or degree of potential
> (Deleuze and Guattari, 1987, p.260).

This constitutes a germane characterisation of open works which are not merely identifiable through their observable material constituents. Rather the open work constitutes the "sum total" of these (including those not determined by the originating author) under "given relations of movement and rest".

---

[31] Deleuze and Guattari's use the term Event in a very specific way. They do not mean an occurrence, a concrete expression of a state of affairs which is articulated in the world as a material entity or as a temporally bounded occurrence (and 'event'). Rather, their Event has a double structure. It is not only the occurrence, which is "the effect of an infinetely long process of selection [which]determines that these two [or more] things of all things meet in a way at this time and place" (Massumi, 1996, p. 11), but is also the fluid, dynamic field from which such occurrencies emerge. The dynamic field (the Deleuzian "Event") has a distinct mode of being separate from the occurrence.

[32] Significantly, nomad thought is "not confined to philosophy [rather] it is a kind of philosophy that comes in many forms. Filmmakers and painters [and by extension artists from all disciplines] are philosophical thinkers to the extent thta they explore the potentials of their mediums and break away from beaten paths." (Massumi, 1996, p. 6)

[33] Marks' description of nomad thought has an overt resonance with Bartes' notion of the structure of a Text as a galaxy of signifiers with multiple entrances.

[34] 'Career' is a term used by Margolis in place of 'nature'. He argues that the nature of a work need not be invariant, rather "existing things may constitute or manifest singular careers in spite of possessing (through the length of those careers) 'inconstant' natures." (1995a, p. 138). In this he is aligned more with Deleuze and Guattari than with his own earlier writings. (Margolis, 1980; 1981).

Its 'workhood', lies in this, not in its material formulations.[35]

In their analysis of events and entities, Deleuze and Guattari clearly identify two types of entities, one represented by objects, the other by fluctuating 'states' or 'events' (for example, seasons, hours, dates, lives). Whilst the second has no material form it is susceptible to individuation. The individuality of a life, a day, a season, a growing, a decreasing, a transformation (all of which are immaterial events), however, differs substantially from that of a thing, or a subject. 'States', or immaterial events, are processes, not entities, per se. As a result

> the individuation of a life (or event) is not the same as the individuation of the subject that leads it (ibid., p.261).

They are subject not to a mode of individuation which relies solely on the presence of properties, as are material objects, but to one which

> consists entirely of relations of movement and rest between molecules or particles, capacities to affect and be affected (ibid.).

However, a third kind of entity might be proposed, one which is neither object nor entirely open process, but is a supple fluid entity which lies somewhere between a stable structure and an entirely open field, or plane, of undetermined elements. An open work which has composed boundaries prior to its actualisation exemplifies an entity of this kind. Like a Deleuzian entity (or event) an open work is composed of

> an extery milieu of membranes and limits, an annexed milieu of energy sources and action-perceptions (Deleuze and Guattari, 1987, p. 313).

As such it is a mobile structure, which has been built up from a multiplicity of interconnecting elements.

Deleuze and Guattari's argument is that entities/events do not constitute only the form/s they take, but also the pre-stratified plane from which those forms are generated. This too accords with the nature of the open work. This unorganised web of matter, flows and intensities is referred to as a 'plane of consistency' or plane of composition.[36] Like the radically open work the plane of consistency is not a formation, but a mobile

> unformed, unorganised, nonstratified or destratified body and all its flows (ibid., p. 43)

subject to continuous variation as events and strata are brought to bear on it. It is not, however, entirely molecular. It has

> a minimum of strata, a minimum of forms and functions, a minimal subject from which to extract materials, affects, assemblages[37] (ibid., p.270).

As such it seems to describe the open work with some accuracy. Further, the events which emerge from this plane, as either entities or occurrences, are the result of an accumulation of a variety of interactions with and within the plane. They may be the result of accidental collisions between previously unconnected strata which give rise to new forms of expression, or the result of conceptual frameworks (or systems of thought) which are brought to bear on the materials from which an event is constructed. The concepts brought to bear on an entity are as constitutive of that entity as its material elements. They are, in short, part of what the entity is, part of its 'nature', inasmuch as they are one of the media through which the un-, or at the very least under-organised network of matter, flows and intensities from which the entity or event emerges, are captured. Because the concepts brought to bear on an entity, including those concerning its nature, change over time, what we consider to be the 'nature' of the work is thus open to change.

In the case of open art works the plane of composition is the state-in-between the unformed mass of molecular elements from which entities and events are composed, and the bounded forms (that is, the entities, occurrences) which result from the synthesis of those elements. Radically open dance works exist as an active, fluid semi-bounded plane, which gives rise to a multiplicity of bounded forms. However, although the plane of composition of the open work has boundaries, those boundaries are always subject to being breached, and extended, as new linkages are made with other, until then unconnected, elements or strata, or planes of composition. The later productions of Intimate Memories constituted just such an extension of boundaries, inasmuch as they led to transformations which modified the mode of being of the 'work' not merely as a production, but also as a plane of composition.

entity-as-event

Inasmuch as open works constitute an unorganised multiplicity of elements or singularities, intensities,[38] events, concepts, and strata (or organising systems) which are susceptible to 'capture', they encapsulate Deleuze and Guattari's conception of the entity-as-event. Like the event they are formalised, or brought to expression, by a process of territorialisation (or 'stratification'),[39] that is, by the imposition of various systems of organisation on their constituent, under-formed elements. The activation of the process of territorialisation

---

[35] The 'thisness', or haeccity, to use a Deleuzian term, of a work is pre- and non-expressive, pre-perception, pre-semiotic. It is the unnamed, the unnameable, aspect of a work, that which is impossible to grasp and to articulate.

[36] Deleuze uses different terms for this concept in his writings. In his earlier works he used the term 'field of individuation' to refer to this concept (Deleuze, 1994). The 'plane of immanence' is invoked in discussions of the Idea, in What is Philosophy? (Deleuze and Guattari, 1994); the plane of consistency and 'Body without Organs' are used in A Thousand Plateaus (1987). Body without Organs' is invoked in particular with relation to discussions which refer directly to human beings and/or animals (ibid., pp. 149 - 166).The term 'plane of composition' is invoked in reference to works of art.

[37] The Deleuzian assemblage is more than merely an assembled collection of units. It also constitutes the active mechanisms through which the units are related. These mechanisms range between open, destratifying mechanisms, and the stratifying mechanisms which bring the relations between the elements of an assemblage to some kind of resting point, or form. All Deleuzian assemblages operate through a dialectic between the two. There are no entirely closed assemblages, and no entirely open assemblages. Rather, different assemblages emphasise one pole or another.

[38] The invisible relationships between forces which lead to the production of degrees of intensity in various qualities.

[39] Described as the 'plane of organisation and development' (Deleuze and Guattari, 1987, p. 265).

provides matter with forms, imprisons intensities into systems of
redundancy and organises small or large molecules into molar aggregates.
The strata range from the energetic to the social and cultural, [and]
function like acts and apparatuses of capture.
(Ansell Pearson, 1999, p. 153).

Directorial intervention in an open dance work is a form of
territorialisation that codes the fluid work system, captures, or
directs its flows and intensities in a particular fashion, and in
doing so synthesises elements and singularities in one of the
multiplicity of formulations through which they could be
brought into play. The director throws a 'net', or more
accurately several intersecting nets, over the work. These trace a
temporary pattern of links between the web of singularities,
intensities and concepts from which the work is constituted and
thus allow for it to be arranged into a particular configuration,
or form of expression. In the formation of any directorial
articulation of the work, several such systems of organisation
(that is, strata) may be active simultaneously, each modulating
the other as the work comes, temporarily, to some form of
'being' or expression.[40] Each production of an open work thus
constitutes a different, multi-level system of capture, and
patterns of synthesis. As each director (or in an improvisation,
group of performers) throws a different 'net' over, and activates
different stratas on the under-determined plane of composition,
new syntheses are formulated and applied, and new
perspectives on the work offered.

As such, an open dance work is a genuine Deleuzian
'becoming-object'- a continuous multiplicity which is multi-
dimensional, and open-ended, an assemblage of heterogeneous
elements with no centre of unification, no single focus.[41]
However, it does not simply 'become' something, and thus
reduce to becoming an object, an event, a state of affairs; rather,
it is a 'becoming' in and of itself. Constantly in variation, it is
not merely characterised by, but constitutes

the variations and dimensions that are immanent to it (ibid., p. 157).

Insofar as it can be said to exist at all, it exists as a site for
transformation. Thus an open dance work, as a work,
constitutes only the potential singularities, potential intensities
and the potential lines of connection which (can) exist between
them. In its raw state, like a continuous multiplicity, the work is
unformed, its elements open to continual reconfiguration as it
encounters and interacts with internal and external forces or
ideas to form new assemblages.

It became increasingly clear to me that open dance works find a
theoretical home in the work of Deleuze and Guattari. As
works, they foreground the dynamic nature of nomad thought,
rather than any representational frame which might have guided
their making. They proceed by a multidirectional process of
synthesis, and are always open to new modes of
territorialisation. An open work, like nomad thought is not

dance and the performative

*an instrument of reproduction but rather one of construction - it is not a
contained tracing of something larger, but is at all points constantly
inflecting [it] - the map constantly redrawn and reconnected, but its
functions are multiple (Kaufman, 1998, p. 5).*

Composing a work which encourages the construction of new
images, or new worlds, from a set of given materials, implies
that the aim is to allow those who engage with it

*to engage in a continuous variation of variables, instead of extracting
constants from them (ibid.).*

Interestingly, during the course of the research process my
theoretical dialogue with Deleuze and Guattari led me to extend
the remit of my choreographic research. If the open work, as a
work, is an embodiment of a thought which is always in the
process of being formed, and is compositionally an open
network of several constantly interacting planes of composition,
then it seemed that the logical extension of my choreographic
research into the open work was to develop works which
exploited the constant variation that characterises open works to
an even greater degree. Improvisation would have been an
obvious direction to pursue. However, my thoughts were
moving in another direction. A new genre of dance practice,
one which exploited the fast developing family of non-linear
digital software, was beginning to make an appearance in dance
at this time. The radical non-linearity of the interactive
programmes used by digital artists offered a particularly
appropriate environment in which to further my choreographic
interrogation of the open work.

**extending the mode of
choreographic research**

Interactive artworks are often described as 'machine systems' by
interactive artists (Penny, 1987). Deleuze and Guattari too make
extensive use of the metaphor of the machine in their writings.
('Machinic assemblages', 'machinic becomings', 'desire
machines', 'war machines' all make their appearance in
<u>A Thousand Plateaus</u> (1987)). For Deleuze and Guattari the
machinic assemblage exhibits

*lines of articulation or segmentarity, strata and territories; but also lines of
flight, movements of deterritorialisation and destratification (ibid., p. 4).*

It both composes and de-composes unified totalities,
*causing asignifying particles or pure intensities to pass or circulate, and
attributing to itself subjects that it leaves with nothing more than a name as
a trace of an intensity (ibid.).*

Interactive installations epitomise the machinic assemblage, and
not merely because they are an artistic 'machine system'. As
works, like the Deleuzian 'machine', they are asignifying. It is

**interactive installations
as event**

---

[40] I use the term 'being' here in the sense of the actualisation of one of the many modes of being to which the work is
susceptible.

[41] Boundas (1996, p. 83) suggests that a continuous multiplicity is better understood in terms of 'the multiplier' or the
'multiplying', than in terms of 'multiplicities'.

only when territorialised, when their constituent elements have been 'captured' by a network of connections and/or concepts imposed by interactors, that the work assumes a 'meaning',

becomes a thought, becomes an 'expression'. Each interactive installation, as a work, is a fluid construction, which contains a floating body of elements, forms and strata, and has

> relative limits within which it selects, perceives, captures, more or less consistently, its margin of deviation (Massumi, 1996, p. 57-8).

The 'work' is only semi-articulated in the shifting, fluid, unformed collection of elements, intensities and unrealised lines of connection from which it is constituted. Further, an interactive installation in action is not

> tied to a mental design but to an abstract design. Its number of dimensions continually increase as what happens happens (ibid.).

It is "a plane of proliferation" but this proliferation has nothing to do with an evolution, the development of a form... It is an involution in which form is constantly being dissolved, freeing lines and speeds (Deleuze and Guattari, 1987, p. 266-7).

In short, it is "a supple individual": its [elements] are correlated but not rigidly so. It has boundaries, but fluctuating ones

> [it is] a threshold leading from one state [the unformed] to another (ibid.).

As such it encapsulates the Deleuzian concept of the Event.

symbiotic relation of practice and theory

These ideas developed by Deleuze and Guattari began to permeate my choreographic activities, and gradually my enquiry into the ontology of flux led me towards the mode of choreographic practice in which I am currently engaged - the development of performative interactive digital environments.

These installations actualise Deleuze and Guattari's ideas in 'real-time'; that is, during, not prior to the work-event. Significantly, the early stages of this strand of research were conducted concurrently with my examination of the ontology of the Event. As that research progressed, questions raised by my theoretical deliberations informed, and even dictated, the direction of my choreographic research, leading me further into the domain of open-ended systems. At the same time, the questions raised by my choreographic research continually led to a refocusing of my theoretical investigation.

Interactive installations constitute unorganised collections of visual and/or sonic images and/or text materials. These are embedded in a complex web of potential connections (located in the programming) through which the interactor can organise elements in time and/or space by constructing the pattern of pathways between them in real-time (that is, during the interactive engagement). Structurally, the interactive installation comprises a multiplicity of fluid planes, each of which constitutes a mini-interactive system in its own right.[42]

ontology of interactive installations

These independent systems (which variously deliver visual, sonic or other forms of imagery, and/or constitute the fluid structure of potential connections between planes) intersect as the network of systems can only be brought into play by the behaviour of the interactors. As such, interactive installations are reactualisations of the Deleuzian plane of consistency, and any interactive engagement a real-time process of alternating territorialisations and deterritorialisations through which fleeting assemblages and affects are continually produced and destroyed.

Crucially, interactive installation works are instantiated as work-events by the behaviour of interactors as they engage with the events generated by the installation in response to their presence and/or their behaviour. Indeed, a central artistic intention of the interactive installation is that the work offers the viewer the opportunity to organise the material form of any work-event in response to their spontaneous imaginative response to the work. They are invited to create a world, rather than merely being provided with a constructed world upon which their imagination can play. Thus interacting viewers actually arrange the work's structure (e.g. temporal progression, spatial configuration and balance) in real-time,[43] responding to the new structures as they emerge, and thus generate a work-event which is in constant variation. In consequence, the viewer's role in the interactive art work is literally that of

> coupling [the] systems according to their plurality (Barthes description of the text, 1975, p. 11),

---

[42] It also constitutes a Deleuzian 'multiplicity'; that is, it is an assemblage of heterogeneous elements with no centre of unification. It has no single focus: it is multi-dimensional, and open-ended.

[43] 'Real-time' is a term used extensively in interactive arts practice to indicate that interventions taking place at the time of interaction activate a response in the environment.

of not only passing, intersecting, articulating, releasing meanings, but also of constructing the (temporary) configurations which articulate those meanings. As such, they become co-authors of the work-event, but not co-author of the work.

interactors' role Performative interactive artworks, which are the specific focus of my choreographic research, go a step beyond allowing the interactor to co-author work-events. Performative installations are designed to explicitly account for the interactors' role within the work-event (Saltz ,1997, p119) and thus to give rise to informal performances. That is, the interactive behaviour of the interactors, which is necessarily spontaneous, and the interactors themselves become an integral part of the actualised aesthetic object, not merely a trigger through which the work is actualised. It thus, in Deleuzian terms, becomes a contributing plane of composition in its own right, and at the same time an independent stratum in the work as a work-event. Such works are generally immersive interactive installation environments which operate through spatial interactivity.[44] The latter requires that the interactor physically immerses himself in the environment to give it life and allows his behaviour to become an integral element of the work in action. The interactor's behaviour becomes a visible plane of imagery in the work-event, although in contrast to a performance event, that behaviour is not the main focus of the work. As such, the audience becomes performer. This extends the Barthean/Foucauldian conception of the relationship between reader and work as taking place in the mind of the reader as she engages with it, to an incorporation of the physical presence of the reader into the work in real-time and real-space.

In addition, performative interactive installations make explicit during each of the work-events which emerge from them the principles under-pinning open works. The imagery from which they are constituted is generally activated by casual viewers (although performances can be devised with the installations) and thus are out of the direct control of the originating artist/s.[45] The movement of the installation imagery is, however, the result of a symbiotic, spontaneous *dialogue* between the interactor and the open-ended system, not the result only of the interactors' behaviour. That is, as the interactor engages with the work in response to the imagery and ambience it generates, the work responds to the actions of the interactor. This generates a different ambience, and thus different response in the interactor, to which the installation responds. Neither is 'in control', (in this way it resembles a conversation). The author/s do not therefore entirely 'disappear'. Rather both reader and artwork become implicated in the formation of the 'work-events' through which the latter is actualised.

Performative interactive installations are then 'becoming objects', which comprise a multiplicity of open-ended non-linear systems (visual, sonic, choreographic,[46]) which are in themselves complex multi-planed systems. Every new interaction which is generated by the action of any one of the systems from which the work is composed, reconfigures not only that system, but also its companion systems. As a result the composite systems are maintained in a perpetual state of movement and variation, both within and between systems, when the work is in a state of (inter)action. However, they revert to being a pure 'plane of consistency' when the work is idle.

This strand of my choreographic research is still in its infancy. To date, I have collaborated on two interactive installations,[47] Passing Phases (1996-1999) and Halo (1998), which explored the notion of the performative as a feature of interactive installations.

Passing Phases[48] is a multi-user interactive installation which features a series of images featuring close-ups of parts of the body. It explores the multiplicity of meanings which can be deduced from a single gesture. The gestures are displayed on seven computer monitors, which are placed on plinths arranged in a circle in a carpeted space. The images are of eyes staring out from the monitor, of mouths moving in silent speech, of hands and feet performing small gestures, each of which has an implicit emotional content. Each image has a looped fragment of sound attached to it, with some images sharing a single sound source.[49] The images were filmed so as to emphasise their corporeality. Many gestures involve touch, all involve a sense of intimacy. Fragments of the longer gestures were isolated and 'looped', creating independent repetitive gestures. The result is a sense of 'nervousness', which contrasts with the fluid sensuousness of the longer gestures from which they were extracted. Consequently, at one level Passing Phases explores the multiplicity of meanings which can be gleaned from a single gesture if features of the movement are modified, and in this sense is a continuation of the themes explored in Intimate Memories. At another level, however, it explores the seductiveness of the human body, even when presented as a digital representation.[50]

The individual gestures are stored as a 'string' of images which can be accessed at any point by the interactive programme, each monitor accessing that 'string' independently in accord with

---

[44] Spatial interactivity requires that the interactor uses full body movement to initiate events in the installation, rather than uses tools such as the touch screen, mouse, or joystick. The interactive interface generally comprises an invisible architecture of hotspots in a physical space.

[45] The degree to which control is relinquished depends to some extent upon the degree of freedom and control built into the interactive system. However, interactors' intentions are impossible to anticipate, and thus constitute a 'wild card' in the intentional frame devised by the artist/s.

[46] The 'choreographic' system might be pre-authored, or it might constitute the performative behaviour exhibited by individual interactors and groups of interactors as they interact with the installation.

[47] A third is being developed at the time of writing.

[48] Created in collaboration with Tim Diggins, Garry Hill and Nye Parry.

[49] The sounds were derived from the spoken word, then treated electronically.

[50] At yet another level, that of practical scholarship, it investigates the nature of the dialogue between multiple interactors and complex interactive environments.

instructions from the computer which is running the interactive programme. Consequently, the piece is made up of seven strands of the same material which is accessed independently, and at different points in the 'string', by each monitor. The effect to the interactors is of images moving from one screen to another, appearing, disappearing and reappearing first here, then there, now in front of them, now caught only out of the corner of their eyes. The physical sense is of being surrounded by scattered images, by eyes, by mouths, by gesturing hands and feet, each exuding a trace of an emotion, a barely expressed feeling.

The appearance and disappearance of the images and the composite rhythm of their movement across the screens is initiated by the behaviour of the participants in the space, both as individuals and as a group,[51] the interactive programme being triggered by pressure pads under the carpet. These react when stepped on by participants (who are asked to remove their shoes to enhance the sense of body and touch). The interactive programme responds with its own set of behaviours to the movement of the interactors. Two networks of behaviour thus intersect and modulate and/or disrupt each others' emerging systems of behaviour. As this is an 'open' installation, which interactors can wander into as and when they like, any 'work-event'[52] has no pre-determined beginning or end, for viewers continually enter and exit the environment.

Passing Phases is necessarily performative, inasmuch as the installation only comes to being as a result of the actions of the interactors. However, it did not fulfil its potential as a performative installation inasmuch as the interactors' behaviour remained that of spectators, rather than being explicitly accounted for by the installation. The intention of the installation was that the work would generate dance-like patterns of spatial behaviour as the interactors turned, paused, walked, slowed down, speeded up, as they moved back and forth in the space to view the images, and that interactors would gradually evolve a co-operative system of behaviour in the installation. This did not happen, due in part to the complexity of the interactive programme, and the subtlety of the interface,[53] which made it difficult for interactors to evolve appropriate systems of behaviour. There was, as a consequence, little sense that the interactors' spatial behaviours were guided explicitly by the installation. Thus, although interactors' responses to the installation indicated that it generated a satisfying aesthetic experience, the work was never realised as a performative installation. Any dialogue which occurred between interactors and installation remained accidental, which meant that the balance of the relationship was still between *viewer* and installation, rather than interactor and installation.

Halo   The second work, Halo (an interactive installation by digital artist Simon Biggs upon which I collaborated as a choreographer) from my perspective re-addresses the issues involved in the nature of the dialogue between viewer and interactive installation which had not been resolved in Passing

<u>Phases</u>. <u>Halo</u> was the result of a collaboration between Biggs, myself and composer Stuart Jones. Its starting point was derived from illustrations for Dante's <u>Divine Comedy</u> by Boticelli and William Blake, and from William Blake's illustrated book <u>The Marriage of Heaven and Hell</u>.

The work features eighteen, independently interactive, life-size digitised video images of naked human figures. These are projected onto two massive screens (nine figures on each screen), which are set opposite each other in the installation space. The figures respond to the movement of the viewers in the space between the screens, 'flying' above the viewers heads,

Sarah Rubidge and Simon Biggs, <u>Halo</u> *still image*

falling to earth or rising to the upper reaches of the screens, as the interactors move towards and away from the screens,[54] walking back and forth at ground level, pausing and staring, and following the viewers as they move from left to right, or vice versa, according to the location of the viewers in the space. The choreographic component of <u>Halo</u> includes both the movements choreographed for the figures and the structuring of the figures' interactive behaviours. As such the 'choreography' of the installation was shared between digital artist and choreographer.[55] As choreographer I composed the

[51] The computers responded to the pattern of spectator behaviour, noting the distribution of spectators on the 'map' of the pressure pads (e.g. clusters of spectators in one part of the space, an equal distribution of individual or groups of spectators in the space). The interactive programme organised the composite behaviour of the images in response to these spatial distributions, e.g. an image remained on the screen when a cluster of people were close to the screen, or disappeared when the balance of the distribution of the people in the space changed.

[52] In an interactive installation the work-event has no given beginning or end - or only to the extent that the first person to enter the empty installation space constitutes the start of the work-event, and the departure of a solo interactor constitutes the end of the event. In between the moments any number of interactors may have entered and left the installation space. A 'work-event' could last as little as one minute, or as long as three hours.

[53] See note 48.

[54] When interactors cross an invisible line in the space moving towards the screen the figures on that screen fall to earth, walk or stand. When interactors move away from the screen the figures rise to the heights of the screen and their upright stance is transformed into a fluid horizontal 'flying' motion.

[55] The choreographer was responsible for the development of the movement imagery, and consequently for the overarching structure of the screen-based imagery, and the generation of the two 'worlds' of the intallation space ('heaven' and 'earth').

movement material performed by the digitised figures. This comprised fragments of movement material which were designed specifically to be open to configuration into a number of apparently organic movement sequences. Consequently I generated the overarching spatial features of the motion of the images in space (vertical motion, and motion towards and way from the viewers.) The images were explicitly designed to generate the conditions a dynamic proto-social engagement between the interactors and virtual figures, inasmuch as the virtual figures advanced towards the interactors at an oblique angle, retreated from them, turned their backs on them, stared directly out at them. The sound environment constituted sets of sounds (derived from the vowels and consonants of Blake's text) which were treated electronically. The sounds for the flying figures appeared melodic, those for the earthbound figures seems like multi-layered murmurs, whispers and groans.

Simon Biggs was responsible for the architecture of the interactive systems,[56] and for the instructions which generate

Sarah Rubidge and Simon Biggs, Halo *still image*

the temporal organisation of the fragments of images and their large-scale spatial progressions. The interactive system constitutes a network structure which allows the choreographic fragments to be synthesised into a variety of organic phrases of movement, and allows the digitised figures to interact both with each other and with viewers in the space. Each digitised figure is programmed as an independent 'object' which is both independently interactive and configured to react to the other figures to generate group behaviours (in much the same way as each interacting viewer reacts independently to the figures on the screen but also relates to his or her fellow interactors in such a way as to contribute to a composite group behaviour). The overall effect is that of a complex network of interactions between and across two sets of performers, one virtual and one live, and the generation of a range of atmospheres in the installation space, from the quiet and meditative to the noisy buzz of social interactions.

Both <u>Halo</u> and <u>Passing Phases</u>, when in action, can be seen as actualisations of the constantly shifting processes of territorialisation and deterritorialisation which underpin Deleuzian 'events'. At the same time they are interrogations of theories concerning the role of the viewer in forming up the work. Because each installation is composed of several planes of composition, which are programmed to interact with each other, and each interactor constitutes a single plane of composition (through their individual responses to the installation and their fellow interactors) yet is part of a larger plane of composition (the interactors as group), the 'reader' cannot structure the event according to his or her own interpretation. Rather, they must engage in a motional dialogue not only with the installation, but also with their fellow interactors. Further, because the dialogue in both cases is a spontaneous dialogue, with interactors and installation responding spontaneously to events as they coalesce and dissolve, there is no way that the form of the work-event can be predicted, and no moment when a form of expression is composed. Rather, the work in action articulates not a form of expression, but the thinking of the work in action. It is this that is articulated in the work-event.

I am currently developing further frameworks for multi-user performative interactive installations frameworks in collaboration with other artists. These, it is hoped, will explicitly encourage interactors to engage with a multistranded interactive installation in semi-organised group interaction (that is to engage in a spontaneous group improvisation). The aim is that, as each individual interactor develops their own system of capture, they will develop it in response not only to the installation environment, but also to the motion of their fellow interactors. In this way a self-organising system will emerge in the installation, which both is performative, and in collaboration with the installation, constitutes an informal improvised performance event in its own right.

In this paper my central goal has been to provide an example of a practice-based research project which constituted a constant dialogue between theory and practice, and which subsequently led to developments both in the theoretical issues the project addressed, and in the choreographic practices which had given rise to the questions addressed in the theoretical enquiry. The choreographic enquiry brought into question certain aspects of dance theory which had frequently been adopted as philosophemes by dance theorists, an investigation of which advanced my approach to issues of identity in dance significantly. During the project, the theoretical enquiry deepened my

**practice as
interrogation of theory**

---

56 This structured phrases of movement from movement fragments, the internal behaviours of the figures, and the responses of the figures to the interactors.

understanding of open works as a mode of artistic expression, and facilitated my choreographic approach to generating such works, indeed led to a fruitful line of choreographic research, and several new works with questions to ask.

selected bibliography

Ansell Pearson, K. (1999). *Germinal Life: Difference and Repetition in Deleuze.* London, New York: Routledge.

Armelagos, A. & Sirridge, M. (1977). The Ins and Outs of Dance: Expression as an Aspect of Style. *Journal of Aesthetics and Art Criticism* 26.

Armelagos, A. & Sirridge, M. (1978). The Identity Crisis in Dance. *Journal of Aesthetics and Art Criticism* 37(2).

Armelagos, A. & Sirridge, M. (1984). Personal Style and Performance Prerogatives. In M. Sheets-Johnstone (Ed.), *Illuminating Dance* (pp.85-100). Lewisburg: Bucknell University Press.

Ascott, R. (1995). *The A-Z of Interactivity.* Leonardo Electronic Almanac, 3.

Banes, S. (1983). *Democracy's Body: Judson Dance Theatre, 1962 - 1964.* Ann Arbor: U.M.I Press.

Barthes, R. (1977). The Death of the Author. *In Image - Music - Text.* London: Fontana/Collins.

Barthes, R. (1977). From Work to Text. *In Image - Music - Text.* London: Fontana/Collins.

Benjamin, A. (1994). *Object Painting.* London: Academy Editions.

Bergson, H. (1911). *Matter and Memory* trans. N. M Paul & W.S. Palmer. London: George Allen & Unwin.

Boundas, C. V. (1996). In Ansell Pearson, K. (1999). *Germinal Life: Difference and Repetition in Deleuze.* London, New York: Routledge.

Brown, E. (1966). *On Form.* Darmstadter Beitrage zur Neuen Musik, 10.

Bunuel, L. (Ed.). (1987). *Trisha Brown.* Paris: Editions Boug.

Deleuze, G. (1994 (1968). *Difference and Repetition.* (Paul Patton, Trans.). London: The Athlone Press.

Deleuze, G. & F. Guattari. (1987). *A Thousand Plateaus: Capitalism and Schizophrenia.* (Brian Massumi, Trans.). Minneapolis London: University of Minnesota Press.

Deleuze, G. & F. Guattari. (1994.) *What is Philosophy?.* (H. Tomlinson and G. Burchill, Trans.). Verso.

Derrida, J. (1978). *Writing and Difference.* Chicago: University of Chicago Press.

Foucault, M. (1969). What is an Author? In J. Harari (Ed.), *Textual Strategies: Perspectives in Post-Structuralist Criticism.* London: Methuen & Co.

Foucault, M. (1972). *The Archaeology of Knowledge.* (Sheridan Smith, A M, Trans.). London: Routledge.

Goodman, N. (1976). *Languages of Art* (2nd ed.). Indianapolis/Cambridge: Hackett Publishing Company Ltd.

Ingarden, R. (1989). *Ontology of the Work of Art* (Raymond Meyer with John T Goldthwait, Trans.). Athens: University of Ohio Press.

Iser, W. (1989). *Prospecting: From Reader Response to Literary Anthropology.* Baltimore & London: John Hopkins University Press.

Kaufman, E. &. K., Kevin John (Ed.) (1998). *Deleuze and Guattari: New Mappings in Politics, Philosophy and Culture.* Minneapolis, London: University of Minnesota Press.

Kemp, S. (1996). "Reading Difficulties" in P. Campbell (ed.), *Analysing Performance.* Manchester: Manchester University Press.

Kurtz, M. (1992). *Stockhausen: A Biography* (Toop, Richard, Trans.). London, Boston: Faber & Faber.

Landow, G. P. (1997). *Hypertext: The Convergence of Contemporary Critical Theory and Technology* (revised edn.). Baltimore: John Hopkins University Press.

Locke, J. (1690). *Essay Concerning Human Understanding*

Margolis, J. (1977). The Ontological Peculiarity of Works of Art. *Journal of Aesthetics and Art Criticism,* 36.

Margolis, J. (1980). *Art and Philosophy.* Brighton, England: Harvester Press.

Margolis, J. (1981). The Autographic Nature of Dance. *Journal of Aesthetics and Art Criticism,* 39(4).

Margolis, J. (1995a). *Historied Thought, Constructed World: A Conceptual Primer for the Turn of the Millennium.* Berkeley and Los Angeles: University of California Press.

Marks, J. (1998). *Gilles Deleuze: Vitalism and Multiplicity*. London, Sterlling Virginia: Pluto Press.

Massumi, B. (1996). *A User's Guide to Capitalism and Schizonphrenia: Deviations from Deleuze and Guattari*. Cambridge, Mass. London: MIT Press.

McFee, G. (1994). Was that Swan Lake I saw you at last night? Dance-Identity and Understanding. *Dance Research*, XII(1).

Moulthrop, S. (1994). "Rhizome and Resistance: Hypertext and The Dreams of a New Culture" in G. Landow (ed.), *Hypertext Theory*, Baltimore and London: John Hopkins University Press.

Murphy, T. (1998). Quantum Ontology: A Virtual Mechanics of Becoming. In E. &. K. Kaufman Kevin John (Ed.), *Deleuze and Guattari: New Mappings in Politics, Philosophy and Culture* Minneapolis, London: University of Minnesota Press.

Norris, C. (1991). *Deconstruction: Theory and Practice*. (Revised Edition ed.). London, New York: Routledge.

Pavis, P. (1982). *Languages of the Stage*. New York: Performing Arts Journal Publications.

Penny, S. (1995). *Critical Issues in Electronic Media*. In HYPERLINK http://mitpress.mit.edu/e journals/LEA/lea_toc.html

Penny, S. (1996). *From A to D and back again: The Emerging Aesthetics of Interactive Art*. Leonardo Electronic Almanac, 4(4), http://mitpress.mit.edu/e- journals/LEA/lea_toc.html.

Rubidge, S. (1998). Embodying Theory. In I. Bramley (Ed.), *Dance Theatre Journal*. London: Laban Centre.

Rubidge, S. (2000). Identity and The Open Work. In S. Jordan (Ed.), *Preservation Politics*. London.

Saltz, D. (1997). The Art of Interaction: Interactivity, Performativity, and Computers. *Journal of Aesthetics and Art Criticism*, 55(2).

Sanchez-Colberg, A. (1991). *German Tanztheater: Traditions and Contradictions: A Choreological Documentation of Tanztheater from its Roots in Ausdruckstanz to the Present*. Unpublished Ph.D. thesis, Laban Centre/City University.

Sparshott, F. (1995). *A Measured Pace*. Buffalo London: University of Toronto Press.

Thom, P. (1993). *For an Audience: A Philosophy of the Performing Arts*. Philadelphia: Temple University Press.

van Camp, J. (1981). *Philosophical Problems of Dance Criticism*. Unpublished Ph.D. Thesis, Temple University, Philadelphia.

Waldrop, M. M. (1994). *Complexity*. Harmondsworth: Penguin.

Wollheim, R. (1978). Are the Criteria of Identity that Hold for a Work of Art in the Different Arts. Aesthetically Relevant?. *Ratio*, 20.

Wollheim, R. (1980). *Art and its Objects* (2nd ed.). Cambridge: Cambridge University Press.

Wollheim, R. (1987). *Painting as Art*. London: Thames and Hudson.

Wolterstorff, N. (1980). *Worlds and Works of Art*. Oxford: Clarendon Press.

Futur/Perfekt
Sanchez-Colberg
Theatre enCorps
Max Thielmann

chapter 9

Futur/Perfekt: re-locating performance... or a dance about everything and the kitchen sink

Ana Sanchez-Colberg

I have long, indeed for years, played with the idea of setting out a sphere of life - bios - graphically on a map

Walter Benjamin (1997, p.295).

introduction: setting the framework

Futur/Perfekt is an international performance event launched in 1998 by the British-based dance theatre company Theatre enCorps. The project consisted of a series of exchanges and collaborations amongst companies engaged in dance-theatre. The nature of the project, a single creative process spanning three years, aimed at opening up to question the now conventionalised assumptions and codified structures of practice and reflection which have defined the way we engage with dance as makers, performers and spectators. Intrinsic to the project was the need to continue to address the prevailing gap between practice and critical reflection. Futur/Perfekt is a performance capsule that contains contributions from dancers, designers and audience (albeit in different proportions) and in which the different elements of the performance capsule are layered as the event accumulates new objects, persons, traces of its own history and travels through its performance calendar that at the time of writing has stretched over four continents and nine cities resulting in a variety of outcomes (lectures, conferences, collaborative workshops, community projects).

identity in performance

The idea for Futur/Perfekt started in 1997 in the midst of another creative process and, inevitably, fuelled by issues arising from it. The project Now We Are No Longer Who We Were Then..." was devised as an alternative performance of Cocteau's Jeune Homme et la Morte, taking as its sources all the archival bits and pieces which have survived. Recurrent themes, which I now recognise permeate all my work - memory, personal histories, the process of becoming historical subjects - were present. Like, Alice, Alice, Alice...Are You a Child or A Teetotter (1989) and Family Portraits (1993), the work was generated through a condensation of the different time zones of the narrative within a singular spatial context. This spatio-temporal density was used as a device to raise questions about the way we perceive and create narrative within the context of performance and the fluidity of the notion of identity within it. In Alice... all characters, White Queen, Red Queen, Cat, were different ages of Alice's character, in interaction with each other within one space. Similarly in Family Portraits, the single living-room environment in which the couple interacted served as an arena where different versions of a never-fully-revealed-story get told, retold, edited, magnified and forgotten. In En Viva Voz (1996), the idea of identity was linked to a moving stage set that progressively re-contextualised the movement material whilst, alternatively, the dancers also effected change upon the space. In Now We Are No Longer... these two strands converged. Conceptually, the Young Man and the Young Girl met, in an atemporal space inhabited by their older selves - their dead other - the selves they never became. Around them, the walls of the stage space opened, collapsed, condensed, constantly changing the context of the action, whilst video images which seemed to bleed from the walls, referred to other spaces, and other selves. Therefore, the main thrust was a concern with the way in which spaces (and time within those spaces) define particular modes of being.

The process of Now we are no longer... was taking place within the first wave of the "millennium phenomenon". The conjunction of those two circumstances - a small scale, highly personal endeavour, within the context of other larger lottery supported, public, global-reaching projects - opened up an explosion of questions: about the role of memory in our personal history, how that history is contained within our bodies, about the relevance of dance in the new millennium, about dance and bodily expression within a technocratic vision of the future, about whether or not bodies could actually disappear. Central to the questioning was a concern with the now accepted yet so little contested view of the disappearance of the body due to methodologies that advocate the phantasmagoric nature of bodily representations without a more complex consideration of the t/here-ness of the body and that t/here-ness in relation to possible representations. The dialogue with myself concurred with an acute awareness that the face of the map of London was drastically changing. The riverbank was being transformed into Millennium Mile. Everywhere new spaces were being created, which were forcing, inviting, challenging us - the users, dwellers, and inhabitants of the city - to explore alternative ways of being in those spaces and thus act as tangible forces in the shaping of that metropolitan landscape. I was interested in what seems to be a new flexibility in what used to be fixed spaces. Old, historical locations, which used to have demarcated areas of 'go', 'no go', and of fixed determined use, were being transformed into architecture of the ephemeral, still of grand scale, but allowing for a malleability of interaction between bodies, users, dwellers, inhabitants, and the micro-spaces, sites and localities contained with it.

Therefore, the project began to formulate a series of research problematics, research that was both artistic and theoretical and, therefore, choreological. There was a central exploration of the relationship between contexts for performance and the contents that define and are conversely defined as dancerly within those contexts. In an inversion of conventional approaches to dance that tend to define the dancerly on the basis of kinetic features, I began to toy with the possibility that contemporary dance performance may be defined by contexts that are negotiated as being dancerly. This then allows for a consideration of the features within to be defined as dance elements (or rather strands within a choreological perspective).

Futur/Perfekt *Max Thielmann*

In Futur/Perfekt it is the notion of space in all its variables (and the relationship of space as a context to the body) that defines the **kinetic aspects** of the performance (not limited, however, to body-kinetics, but also movement of language, artifacts, set design, music etc, but more of this later). A second focus stemmed from the concern that, notwithstanding the agreed body-based focus of dance (that we have all argued gives dance its specificity), dancer scholarship, with some exceptions, continues to be dominated by theories of linguistics and readerships, perhaps now of cultural vision and gaze construction. These have imposed, one could argue, 'from outside', a particular discourse upon the way we reflect on dance practice. Through Futur/Perfekt I wish to discuss, expand, extend recent debates on how the body 'matters' (as a verb) in performance and how the body matter (as a concrete being) affects that process. In many ways, I see Futur/Perfekt as a performance event, but also as a creative laboratory of continuous testing of hypotheses through practical experimentation and not about creating a singular cultural product that needs to be reproduced and retailed. There is a third and final concern, that arises from the project's international network of collaborations, and that is an exploration of the relationship between globalisation and ethnicity as it pertains to the concept of dance-theatre, one that has raised questions nationally and internationally about the politics of support and funding that govern and legitimise dance practice. However, this lies outside the scope of the present study.

Futur/Perfekt *Liam Muir*

repositories of knowledge, enactment, agency

These concerns with the relationship between identity, spaces and localities - the artifacts which remain as traces of that interaction (the stuff that history is made of), personal landscapes, cityscapes and transportation through them, about the material and immaterial forces that affect any creative process and the effect they have in the way we engage with our art form as makers, performers and spectators - affected various aspects of the conception of the work. Futur/Perfekt began as a model for a flexible space of interaction, where the codes and rules that have conventionally delineated particular ways of framing performance (and therefore understood it as a product) are questioned. Futur/Perfekt is concerned with perspective, positioning and location, about traces in landscapes, about topographical and archaeological searches through strata of histories contained within our bodies in relation to the spaces we create and then inhabit, mundanely and artistically. In Futur/Perfekt, bodies and spaces are **repositories of knowledge** that activate particular responses according to particular frames. Futur/Perfekt aims to expand any discussion of embodiment in dance to include a consideration of **enactment**[1] as a pro-active process of **agency.**

This essay is another outcome of the project. As previously mentioned, I am entering this discussion with theory and practice from the perspective of a dance artist, both as performer and choreographer, who fortunately or unfortunately, has found a context for her work or at least a significant amount of that work - within the realm of academia. It is perhaps this circumstance that gives rise to a particular feature of this essay; that is, the inherent tension between the personal and political 'I' engaged in the creative process of the making and the more abstract and abstracted formal 'I' that engages with the theoretical canon that cuts across, propels and at times contradicts the artistic voice. They are one and the same, yet very different aspects of this *me*. This perhaps extends the choreological tripartite perspective to its most extreme deduction, as this essay attempts to encapsulate three different perspectives of making, performing and appreciating co-existing within the singular author.

dance performance as an event:
the conceptual framework expanded

Given <u>Futur/Perfekt's</u> concern with the interrelated processes of making, performing and reception, an approach is required which can articulate how these particular perspectives are negotiated and practised within each instance of the event. <u>Futur/Perfekt</u> began as creative research for a framework that could account for the complex web of energies - participatory economies within the theatre - which define the work. I have been experimenting with a model that takes a **multi-modal approach** to both the creation and reflection of/through practice. Such an approach presupposes that 'theoretising from practice' allows for the co-existence of diverse conceptual perspectives (and methods) within a single discussion. Consequently, the approach proposes that what are irreconcilable theoretical perspectives that cannot co-exits within abstracted theoretical models, can indeed co-exist at the level of practice, and most certainly at the moment of performance.

multi-modal approach

---

[1] I suggest that any consideration of embodiment needs to include the notion of enactment as a subprocess of it. For the purpose of this essay, embodiment is the sum-total/gestalt of knowledges and conditions that support our corporeality. Embodiment simultaneously 'contains' all dimensions of our corporeality. I refer to enactment as the process of cognition-perception-action through which one distils a particular set of actions/projections into the world from the total possibilities contained within our embodied corporeality. For example as a dancer, I am trained in a variety of ways of generating material, but faced with a particular task, I will discriminate bringing from the total pool of knowledge available, that which seems to 'respond-correspond' to the challenge of the task. Therefore, I am able to shift from dancing emphasising form (as when executing particular vocabularies from particular styles) to emphasising progress of flow moving auricularly as in more postmodern styles. I am also suggesting this is related to different kinds of kinetic behaviour on stage. For example, dancers in a work by Bausch may, in response to the question, 'What moves us', generate a series of mundane phrases of behaviour whilst in the next scene the same question can lead to the repetition of more formal material. I suggest that each response comes from 'different' sources of knowledge about themselves as subjects in general and as subjects in performance specifically, and inevitably refers to the link between these various knowledges embodied within each. In the case of tanztheater, given its concern with the performers' experience as source of the event, this is further I suggest, linked to the issue of performer's persona. The performer who acts on stage is not 'masking' an absent true self (as Goffmann would have it). For example, take the case of a dancer in a piece by Pina Bausch, Dominique Mercy. On stage he is and isn't Dominique Mercy. He is the Dominique Mercy that we identify as Dominique in Bausch's piece but we understand that behaviour to be particular to the context of Bausch's work. It may hold some relevance to the Dominique that operates and lives outside of Bausch's work. Moreover, there may be other 'dimensions of Dominique' different from the Dominique on stage. One does not cancel the other, one does not obscure, mask or is a 'mirror' of the other. One context brings forth one, another context the other. Each informs the other, limits and expands it. All, (although I know I am speaking on behalf of Dominique), equally real. This, I suggest, is linked to De Certeau's concept of the 'ruse' and 'tactics' within his theory of practice (<u>De Certeau</u> 1998). I propose that this is linked to Lefebvre's practico sensorial realm (Lefebvre, 1991, p.200).

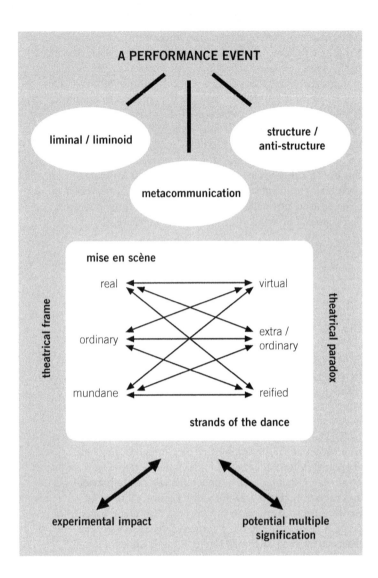

A PERFORMANCE EVENT

liminal / liminoid

structure / anti-structure

metacommunication

mise en scène

theatrical frame

real ⟷ virtual

ordinary ⟷ extra / ordinary

mundane ⟷ reified

theatrical paradox

strands of the dance

experimental impact

potential multiple signification

transaction, metacommunication, liminoid space

I propose that in its concern with the creation of a particularly experiential encounter amongst those participating in the event - whether as makers, performers or spectators - Futur/Perfekt is located within the realm of the performative. In identifying this performance qualifier I am highlighting the **transactional nature of the event;** its concern with proposing a particular context in which a particular kind of human exchange (social and individual) can take place. It is this context that will then determine the content of the event. Therefore, the overarching idea unifying the production belongs to the realm of Bateson's **metacommunication**[2] - the transaction of social, psychological and ideological frames through which participants engage in the making of belief rather than make believe. Moreover, within the frame of knowledge identified as performance, there is a common premise that considers that the event is an/other/alternative domain of human experience, that operates within a **liminoid space;**[3] one of ambiguities, subversive, in a space/time dimension related to, but operating differently from, conventionalised frames of the real.

The manipulation of **frames**[4] - the boundaries that delineate particular entities and differentiate one from the other - is central to the project. The notion of framing operates in various ways. Frames identify boundaries: where is the boundary that separates the theatre elements (text, dramatic interludes) from the dance ones (gesture, formal movement)? What is the line between dancerly movement and the everyday? Where is the line that separates the dancer from the dance? The dancer from other performers on stage? The maker from the spectator? The performer from the maker? What differentiates choreography from dramaturgy - movement of the bodies from movement of the space? Frames also serve to bring particular aspects into focus, not unlike the Brechtian **V-Effekt**, in a manner in which the familiar becomes unfamiliar and therefore opened to revision. Frames are that which highlight the various strata of Futur/Perfekt's corporeality. In as much as these liminal frames are established, not to mirror society but to provide a framework for action, Futur/Perfekt engages with what Sutton-Smith defines as **anti-structure**[5]. This concept identifies the ludic nature of any activity that, rather than integrating humans to a preformed social structure (the world as is), "involves the potentiating of novelty, flexibility, autonomy and communitas"[6] (the world becoming).

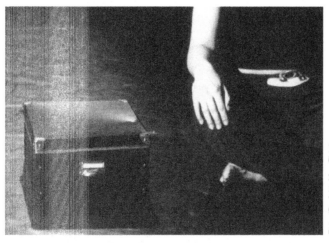

Futur/Perfekt *Max Thielmann*

I propose that these three concepts - metacommunication, liminality and anti-structure - are crucial to understanding the various theatrical paradoxes that sustain Futur/Perfekt. Within this frame, the elements and participants are constantly negotiating participation (via various perceptive channels) within the event, operating within a continuum between:

[2] The concept of metacommunication is discussed in Bateson, Gregory (1972) and also in Sutton-Smith, (1979).

[3] See Turner, Victor (1982, pp.20, 60).

[4] See Goffman, Erving (1974).

[5] Sutton Smith develops the notion of ludic dialectic based on Turner's idea of the dialectic between structure/anti structure within cultural processes. See Brian Sutton Smith (1979) and Turner (1974, p.298).

[6] originally, Sutton Smith (1979) quoted in Sutton Smith (1984).

• the **real** (stage space, props, bodies, sound) « the **virtual**/the **imaginary** (past memories, past cities, the scene just gone by that will be remembered later) **AS SOURCES.**

• the **ordinary** (this is something I know, have encountered, eg. bus tickets, expired credit cards) « the **extraordinary** (the I don't know, can't recognise as pertaining to my frame of reference, I believe it to exist but I don't possess it as a skill or knowledge, objects kept on collection, taken on a tour, conventional rubbish made into the scenery of the work) **AS CONTEXTS.**

• the **mundane** (gestures of everyday, words I recognised, objects left on stage, boxes) « the **reified** (but the gesture is exaggerated, the music too loud, the speech blurred, the boxes are hanging, the dancer never dances, the memory becomes a movement void of any personal significance, German language, Finnish, which I may or may not understand, a personal object is abstracted, made into scenery) **AS TREATMENTS.**

The oscillation between (and across) these generates the theatrical tension within the mise-en-scène necessary to sustain each instance of the event as well as establishing a tension between the micro-environments of each instance of <u>Futur/Perfekt</u> and the macro-project in its entire three years duration. The experimental model that guided the choreographic investigation can be thought of as :

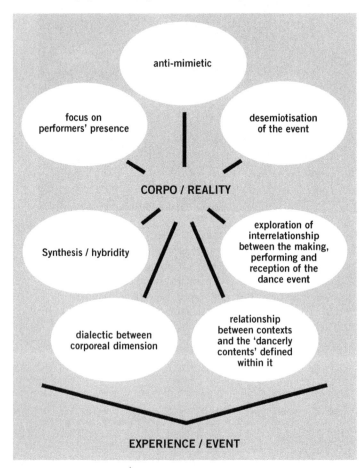

It places at the centre of the production, a concern with physicality, what I have termed the **body-matter(s)** from which all other nexial connections arise. I purposely refer to body, not performer, to problematise issues concerning embodiment, corporeality, inter-subjectivity as they pertain to performance. This decision was supported by various considerations. In contemporary performance practice, the concept of performer locates the identity of the dancer as executant, the active agent of the event. The conceptual model that gave rise to <u>Futur/Perfekt</u> questions this bias by proposing that the whole event is based on agency of all participants (albeit engaging in different kinds of activities through distinct and related processes). Moreover, performer carries a 'proscenium bias' that <u>Futur/Perfekt</u> wants to leave behind. The concept of body taken from a phenomenological context proposes a consideration of human bodies who, at the moment of performance, do more than perform and are **material, tool, subject and source** within a singular event.

body matters, material, tool, subject, source

<u>Futur/Perfekt</u>:
experiencing: the body/movement nexus

> the body serves both as a point of departure and a destination... but what body precisely are we talking about?
>
> Lefebvre (1991, p.194).

As previously stated, the project began with questions focusing on the nature of the body as the subject of and the subject in performance. These guided the way in which choreographic tasks emerged. The stage of research and development started with two dancers, one choreographer, one theatre director, and an empty stage space. Given the thematic interest in the process of memory/history "inscribed in the body", we took a memory of a past place (not a memory of a past event) as the first trigger for choreographic investigation. This choice had particular implications: in focusing on the memory of a place, I was wanting to encourage dancers to explore physical states of being in the process of remembering that space. It was not about representing the bygone space in the present time or about representing how one felt 'about' that memory. Rather, the memory acted as a trigger to begin a process of experiencing 'now'.

There is, nonetheless, a sense of evocation of that other/absent place, but it is not a transitive this-for-that mimetic operation (as in conventional semiotic equations) but more a coexisting of evolving **embodied layers,** at the moment of performance. For example: in the first day of rehearsals, I asked Adam Murby and Ivana Ostrowski to engage in breaking down the

embodied layers, blueprint, positioning, process of remembering

Futur/Perfekt Paul Houghton

constitutive layers of sensorial information contained in the memory. We called the first improvisation **'the blueprint'**, using the architectural drawing as a working metaphor. Each dancer chose a 'door' to the memory and from that **positioning** began to trace the boundaries/ dimensions of the memory site in the rehearsal space. However, because I wanted the improvisation to be more than just a formal/structural exercise, I insisted that the tracing had to betray the **process of remembering.**

attention, projection, intention, focus, dramaturgical content

This had an implication on the eukinetic features of the movement material and manifested: a rhythm of stops and gos, moments of total paralysis, of start again; the dynamics of the processes **of attention** (as dancers stop to try and remember), **projection** (looking across from where they are standing to another part of the space), **intention** (the direct and strong quality of movement once a decision has taken place), **focus** (actions are flexible and light when the thought is not fully formed, the focus changes as they 'see themselves performing'). The spectator's attention and perception (myself as a choreographer spectating) was constantly shifting from experiencing the dancers in space as mere formal figures, to seeing the space as a minimal area not yet shaped, to seeing a person actively moving, thinking, processing, succeeding and failing as s/he operated within that space, creating a spatio-temporal density. From the onset, the piece was created as a process where the different layers of the bodily material - kinetic, personal, sensorial, formal - co-existed, giving dynamic tension to the event. These layers shaped a **dramaturgical content** of the work without actually telling a story.

The evolving dramaturgy was further developed through simple manipulations: asking the dancers to go through the space but start from a different door, by the addition of another dancer, who served as spatial **harmonic contrapunct** and also as a **rupture** to whatever narrative closure might be evolving in response to the first solo figure's material. From the idea of the blueprint, six devising strategies were developed, and yet the dancers had only 'walked'; no dancerly movement vocabulary had as such evolved. The co-existence of what Lefebvre insists are diverse bodies inhabiting a single physicality was made manifest in the second stage of manipulations. I asked Adam and Ivana to work through the site 'inhabiting' the details of the 'terrain' - switching from the perspective of **me in the space** to **me as the space.**

harmonic contrapunct,
rupture,
'me in the space',
'me as space'

> There is an immediate relationship between the body and its space, between the body's deployment in space and its occupation of space. Before producing effects in the material realm (tools and objects), before producing itself by drawing nourishment from that realm, and before reproducing itself by generating other bodies, each living body is space and has its space: it produces itself in space and it also produces that space...
> (Lefebvre, 1991, p. 169).

We called this the two dimensional body-map, and generated fragments of phrases that traced visible and invisible walls, windows, the underneath spaces of tables, curtain laces, etc. It was at this stage that we began to develop more elaborate kinetic fragments that forced the dancer to switch (or traverse through) these diverse 'dimensions' and to become aware of the experiential changes that came about as a result of those switches. These journeys through dimensions offered more than a variety of sources for movement; they also had an effect on the dancers' consciousness, awareness, focus, attention, intention; and on how those, in turn, may affect future 'impressions' made on a potential spectator: from focus on surface (touching the space with the skin, hair, lips) to flesh (the implosive tension of torso and arms of a six foot dancer trying to squeeze into a three foot virtual space) to articulated movements (arms reach, slap, grab, touch) to action agency and locomotion (leg movements making the dancers locomote into space, actions evolved, jumping, turning, gliding...), to moments of existing as pure spatial volume during the moments of movement and music tacit on stage.

Just as the memory was grounding itself to the space of the now, I manipulated each dancer's cross of axes. Although in an actual gravitational space, dancers began to move through their memory site as if the floor kept shifting from underneath them, transforming the seemingly pedestrian movement into abstracted motion - located within the memory but not allowed the pleasure of closure/recognition within the actual space.

This was the beginning; the first floor map of a memory, traced along the empty space of Studio 7; the first opening of the space/time dimension called 'the work' in each and everyone's

transportation,
transformation

'here & now'. We had been given (German) funds to present the R&D in Berlin. So Berlin it was. The city at that moment in 1998 was transforming itself into the city of the future, whilst at the same time attempting to reconcile two spaces, divided by a wall no longer there but still there. What would normally have been just a touring decision for a prefixed performance product, actually affected the dramaturgy of the work. Each dancer's experimentations led to the delineation of different maps. These became journeys furthering the idea of a dramaturgy of spatial **transportation**[7] and **transformation**[8] based on locality, and not narrative as a conventional time-ordered story of events. Like a map, each choreographic cluster of movement was composed of the points/features of the space; however, the movement through it could be at any time shifted, re-located, re-placed. Interestingly, it is at the moment of encounter with the 'metaphoric Berlin' that the "personal/emotive" layers began to evolve and be integrated (after great negotiation) into the event.

Futur/Perfekt Max Thielmann

At times the body, which we have yet to explore, gets covered up, concealed from view, but then it reemerges - then it is as it were resuscitated. Does this suggest a connection between the history of the body and the history of a space? (Lefebvre, 1991, p.196).

text   Adam Murby, British male, had never been to Berlin and Ivana Ostrowski, female, originally from Berlin, insisted that she could not remember the city ("the past is gone you can't change it so who cares..." she once said in rehearsals). Adam's story seemed to be marked by an acceptance that material traces of his past - although rich in memories - had disappeared with the death of his parents and the loss of his childhood home. For him, the journey towards Berlin was one of acceptance of that which was inevitably lost. Berlin became a veritable city of future potential. For Ivana, the journey became one of rescue of a past lost to denial, and a future, also contained within the city of Berlin, that was to come with acceptance of that past. For the Berlin piece, we decided to extend the experimentation of body/space to include text. We had the opportunity to collaborate with Israeli director and playwright Noam Meiri in devising strategies to explore the textual aspects of the memory. The challenge lay in attempting to keep the textual components tied to the notion of space, locality. The dancers developed with Noam long sections of speech based on three questions: a memory past, the now, and the idea of 'imaginary' Berlin. After long debate, we agreed to leave the 'speeches' as discreet components (ie, not treated choreographically). This had interesting consequences. For the duration of the speeches the audience was given a significant amount of information that was wanting to convey fact. However, these facts, albeit communicating semiotically, served as another rupture of the physical dramaturgy whilst, paradoxically, propelling it.

Futur/Perfekt *Paul Houghton*

The speeches were spoken in native tongue. For the East Berlin audience, the event (within a dance festival) started with an eleven minute speech, in English, of an England/London that for Adam is 'real' but for many of them remained 'imaginary' and for others inaccessible (it transpired in conversations with management that many of the audience members were not English speakers). So the event's spatio/temporal beginnings were not synchronic or stable. Adam's speech was of real events in his house in Leicester but the concrete objects of the speech were virtual presences encapsulated in the images of the text. It could be argued that it was a speech about ordinary events, ordinarily conveyed yet presented within an extraordinary context (a dance piece). For many the scene was reified

semiotic content, sensorial impact

---

7 I am borrowing from Schechner's discussion of the concept in <u>Performance Theory</u> pp. 166, 184. The notion of transformation involves the 'new becomings' (as an actor 'takes on' a role). However, I am linking this to the previous discussion of enactment in which, rather than inhabiting an absent other, one is materialising through the enactment, particular knowledges. That knowledge for the performer (and I would also argue for the audience) is kinetic, visceral, textual, linguistic, sensorial, cultural, cognitive and experiential.

8 Again, I am borrowing from Schechner and Turner. The act of performance requires a transportation from the real to the liminal. This transportation can be actual (going to the theatre, participating in a processional event, etc) but also virtual (as the transportation from real to liminal that happens via NVC cues of focus, projection). For example, street performers in Covent Garden: through a complex interaction with the passers by, a performance frame is established and negotiated through an amalgam of NVC cues (focus, volume, orientation) as well as by the types of activities performed (getting ready, tracing a playing area on the ground, blowing a whistle and calling for everyone's attention). This negotiated network transforms the audience in Covent Garden from shoppers to audience members in as much as they are transported from a shopping space to a performative one. I also propose that in the case of <u>Futur/Perfekt</u> when the performers displace themselves within the space whilst traversing through different corporeal dimensions (flesh, skin, bone, mass), tool-subject, source, material the transportation motion through the strata creates a series of kinetic transformations of the resulting perceived images. It is this series of transformations/transportations that constitute the dramaturgical content of the piece.

because, unable to understand the English, the scene was abstracted into a series of sounds and movements that did not carry their **semiotic content,** yet were full of **sensorial impact.** It could be further argued that those unable to understand 'the words', may or may have not been 'in the performance', or that, unable to understand the words, were focusing on Adam's moving figure, or perhaps they 'entered' when Ivana's speech in German took place, which allowed the German speakers in, but may have still left the 'dance audience' out since she spoke, not unlike a Beckett figure, in almost complete stillness. Language was not only information; language was also an issue of space, a boundary positioning the participants in, out, at the margins of the event evolving. Therefore, language was a key in the preliminary negotiation that established the rules of operation of the evening (in this case of disruption, of sensorial information, of spatio-temporal relation, of semiotic meanings). Language contained the negative moments of silence and stillness where/when, given the intimacy of the space, you could hear the performers breathe as if the event's existence insisted through the dancers' physicality. For me, all these negotiated tensions, perhaps unresolved, became the so-called 'content' of the evolving dramaturgy of <u>Futur/Perfekt</u> on September 18-20, 1998 in Pfefferberg, Berlin. It was a dramaturgy of having been there, experienced.

symmetrical inversion

On stage the various versions of the journey were never presented at the same time. Time/space dimensions were constantly intermixed and juxtaposed to create a sense of ambiguity (whose story is being told now, where are we, who is the speaker, who the protagonist?) that contributed to generate a palpable sense of Berlin as an ever-changing city landscape. An interesting structural development supported this ludic poetics of time and space. As previously stated, the 'dance' began with two very long speech scenes (text was the trace of the memory), but as the dance moved from past to present (and ended with an open future), words began to be replaced by a density of movement material (the here and now of the physical dimension, of the performer in the event-in-the-making). The **symmetrical inversion** gave internal cohesion to the components, albeit presented in fragmented episodes throughout the length of the piece.

> *What the map cuts up, the story cuts across...*
> *(de Certeau, 1998, pp.129).*

negative space

After the Berlin piece, we began to work on the London phase of the project: <u>Futur/Perfekt: London Calling</u>. Five dancers instead of two: Adam remained, but Ivana had left the project. I had decided that to be consistent to the idea of spaces and identity, material which belonged to a dancer within a particular locality was irreplaceable (ie, could not be taken on by another). In the absence of Ivana, the Berlin material became a prologue; an eleven minute capsule of the Berlin piece, which became a sort of prologue to <u>London Calling</u> and subsequent events. In <u>London Calling</u>, the more Ivana was absent the more powerful her presence was and, in fact, served as catalyst for the genesis of stage 2. Rachel Whiteread's **negative spaces** (the house in East London, to the chairs at the Sensation exhibition) come to mind. A duet became a solo. Another duet became speech, taking as its source fragments of remembered episodes belonging to the piece's collective past: of the sensation of having danced with Ivana (which sounded like the words of a lover saying farewell to a lost love), fragments of text she had said, fragments of text he had said, and also Adam's recollections of his extra-theatrical visit to Berlin, what happened to him in the actual Berlin during the series of performances there...

Futur/Perfekt Max Thielmann

Outside all of the cabs are the same colour. Not black but cream. I should have known, they're all be Mercedes. She said "Bobo", a pet name for her brother Boris, but I wasn't allowed to call him that. 'Links oder rechts' I got myself thinking. Wo kann ich verkaufen Volkornsbrot?... She said that was crap. "On, off, on, off, books, boring books, fenster," she said that. Over a 'Wernersgrune', he said that I should turn left and go straight past Karlstad to Leopoldplatz. She said, "Halo Mutti" und she kissed Bobo in the Nase. "Wo ist Papa", she said he was standing in the crowd. She said there was a quick embrace a cold embrace. "Wie gehts Papa...?"

Stille.

Upstairs in a big flat, he felt like a foreigner. Listening to The Verve he started to reinvent himself. He said flowers, she said, "Ach, für Mich?". In the sky she mentioned the "Tegelsee". He asked what it meant to her.

Stille.

Adam Murby, Pfefferberg/Tacheles, Berlin, September 1998

This has become a choreographic strategy: language sections are mostly in the past tense, speech sections tend to be telegraphic, itemising elements of the memory, lists that bypass syntax and therefore narrative. Language flows from presence, the words only describe material facts in space, where they are in relation to space and locality:

> Una habitación en lo más alto de la casa, con papá somos cuatro...
> Pantalones, calconcillos, underwear, men's underwear, socks...
> (Domingo Bermúdez, London Calling).

Lacan, Lefebvre, lateralisation, location, flesh

In <u>London Calling</u>, spatial metaphors continued to guide the process into movement material. Each cast member had a personal history, and, more significantly, <u>Futur/Perfekt</u> as an event now had a collective memory. We had a space past (Berlin) and also a place in the present (London), with the possibilities of future journeys (also defined in terms of spatial displacement, not of the passing of time). The idea of creating a spatial now at the moment of performance that insists on opening a space 'here & now' took me to question various assumptions about the way dance works, and about the now uncontested assumption that the body engaging in movement on stage, like language, operates as a code, and is therefore bound to norms of semiotics, interpretation, mimesis, representation and reproduction. The assumptions are carried by the pervading metaphor of theatre as mirror, given contemporaneity in the work of Lacan[9] and postmodern theories of cultural reproduction (that, moreover, assume that all culture(s) operates in a capitalist framework). The experiential data that has evolved from <u>Futur/Perfekt</u> has led

<u>Futur/Perfekt</u> *Max Thielmann*

me to question the Lacanian methodologies that privilege the visual-linguistic in the creation of identity. In another outcome of the project called <u>Bodies Matter</u>, presented at the Performance Studies Conference in Mainz, March 22nd 2001, I suggested the ways in which <u>Futur/Perfekt</u> offered a critique of Lacan whilst supporting Lefebvre's spatial/rhythmical analysis. Lacanian methods collapse the subject in two dimensions: the body is for and of an-other, itself an image and an illusion in which body is relegated to a surface reality. In London Calling, dancers recall a space in their minds, which leads to the execution of a series of actions that take place 'here and now' (made materially present through/in their physicality; the physicality at that moment being real neurons, fibres, muscle, etc at work). Therefore, Futur/Perfekt constitutes a system of operations, not a system of representation. Furthermore, Futur/Perfekt devising strategies are located within location and lateralisation[10] processes that Lefebvre argues are a precondition of the territory before signs and signifiers are added. The solo material was based on moving from here to there, as was the group work; solos were made to coincide, interrupt each other; the impact of two bodies meeting created new material; there was hardly ever any choreographed unison (which would imply a passive inscription of the body). There were two moments of shared unison material; a point that I had to concede to the dancers who felt that it was 'exhausting' not to have some resolution along the way. They were the 'London Quartet' in which dancers did take on the movement of another dancer who had to leave the project early on because of long term illness. This was a taking on of vocabulary, but in a manner that sustains the conceptual framework of the work. It was not an imposition of someone's vocabulary code on the dancers. Rather, it was the physical memory of an absence that could only be 'recollected' in the enactment that made the trace material. The other is the almost final Quartet: we call it the 'happy quartet' (that dancers insist audiences need - that is there but nags me as choreographer every time I see it, but - they would walk out if I took it out). I have found ways of conceptually validating its existence. However, I tend to bring in an epilogue that ungrounds it, usually a more theatrical scene taking us back to the raw body.

Moreover, the material of Futur/Perfekt comes from the uncoded systems of sensory stimulus - sound, smell, auricular perceptions - as we displace ourselves through social space and within our personal space. In Futur/Perfekt these non-symbolic fleshy systems are the starting point and also part of the active body engaged in a complex bodyspacemovement nexus that cuts across the metaphoric bodies of discourse. Futur/Perfekt proposes that this intersection creates an unresolved dynamic tension at the moment of performance. The tension is not necessarily about fragmentation: fissures are not gaps but traces of motility (in the same way that atom particles as they move are not creating a series of vacuums but streams of motion). Futur/Perfekt suggests that the split body of discourse may be integrated in practice.

[9] 1 anticipate that many will detect a contradiction. On the one hand I am using Lefebvre to argue against Lacan, but I also find affinities with de Certeau (who has Lacanian background). At this stage of the ongoing research, I suggest that in de Certeau's discussion of space in the city, which many have equaled to Lacan's discussion of language and the real, the bodily aspect of the relationship between city and space aligns him to Lefebvre if one considers the narrative of actions that are a result of tactical displacement within the city and how those differ from the discursive telling of the story that is later told. This is an ongoing aspect of the research which has not yet found final form in my thinking.

[10] Lefebvre (1991, pp.199-200).

Futur/Perfekt:
experimenting with space[11], and sound

> How many maps in the descriptive or geographical sense might
> be needed to deal exhaustibly with a given space, to code and
> decode all its meanings and contents?

> Lefebvre (1991, p.85).

**reversibility
of roles**

The way in which Futur/Perfekt could disrupt the visual-
linguistic was further experimented with in the collaborations
with musicians, playwrights and designers that have joined the
project at various stages. The notion of space provided a
common ground for the collaboration with designer Emma
Robson, and composers Steve Williams, Phil Durant and Pedro
Gomez-Egaña. In all instances there was a slight **reversibility of
roles.** For example, in working with Emma Robson who joined
the project in 2000 as designer, I was focusing on space
(a place) whilst Emma was thinking in terms of movement (the
design becoming). However, shared concerns with allowing the
work to be a place of becomings unified and dissolved any
possible contradiction in the shared intentions of the
collaborators. In particular, Emma was keen to reverse common
assumptions about the nature of choreography and design;
however, cross-fertilisation, cross reference, spillage and
bleeding from one discourse to another were inevitable. Our
common aim was to formulate a single 'multi-modal'
framework for performance; not, as traditionally understood,
two or more different discourses coming together and
interacting (i.e. as happens in site-specific work where the
dancers either come in and inhabit a space already created, or
designers and choreographers work independently and then
allow the elements to co-exist). The questions of how to create
this multi-modal framework underpinned our collaboration
(which also included the performers and composers in the work).

**becoming space
scenographic
perspective**

Emma was particularly interested in a radical revision of what
constitutes the material contribution of the designer: of finding
extreme possibilities in which the designer may not contribute
an actual material element. Emma wanted to contribute new
elements within the discursive/strategic frame from what was
already there, affecting therefore, the new, the next. Emma was
concerned that the contribution of the designer is usually
measured in terms of things on stage, whether this is as
minimal as surface treatments with light or whether the stage is
filled with three-dimensional structures such as furniture, props
and large screens. Emma was interested in what might happen
if the designer started rethinking her potential contribution to a
work; rather than filling the stage with material stuff, to
concentrate on creating new possibilities for what already exists
(as happened with what Emma inherited from Futur/Perfekt),
and create new thoughts for these objects. With Futur/Perfekt

Futur/Perfekt Max Thielmann

there was a real possibility for her to work in this way, because Futur/Perfekt already existed. When Emma became involved, there had already been two years of events that had taken place in Berlin, Winchester, Chichester, London, Phoenix and Puerto Rico and there was an embryonic set. I had mentioned that so far I felt dissatisfied with the way in which the set components were integrated: I felt that the various set elements (boxes, objects collected, placing of the boxes on stage) were not being stretched to their full potential given the work's premise. Emma was motivated by the notion of a **becoming space,** a space that would be continually giving out information: how to allow the space to become, to disclose, to give up to perception, to be integral to content, to be able to impart information about the nature of Futur/Perfekt, the contrasts, ambiguities and fluctuations of the work. This was the challenge. Emma approached these questions from a **scenographic perspective:** how does the space in which the dance takes place contribute to the mediation between past, present and future? How is the layering of spaces, as the dance continues through its travelogue, to be made materially concrete at any given time: in the texture, the surfaces, in the structures present in space, in the clothes worn by the dancers, by the objects present? How can we discover new strategies and a more initiatory role for the designer/scenographer in collaborating to create the performance event? How can the scenographer become intrinsic to the making of meaning of the performance event?

---

[11] Previous version of the discussion between Emma Robson and myself appeared in Dance Theatre Journal, December 2000, 'Futur/Perfekt: Becoming Space'.

In order to achieve our joint aim it was necessary for the scenographic space to:

---

intervene in the action

---

be performative

---

deny the traditional opposition in theatre between set and action, animate/inanimate accessory and essential, scenographic space and performer-time

---

make present the production process in the resulting performance(s), drawing attention to itself as the deconstruction of its process

---

be part of an incessant, unstable space/composition, always in the process of undoing and re-forming itself.

---

modify itself unceasingly - and that this modification of the scenographic action will become part of the action/text of the performance

---

Above all the scenographic space must not:

---

be a given beforehand

---

constitute a static contextual frame for the performance

---

mise en scène
mise en boîte

The identity of the Futur Perfekt project as a performance time capsule meant that at each performance, a new box arrived and each audience member was invited to put something into it. So the boxes were integral to the performance. Emma wanted to provide a space for the boxes to belong within the space of the performance and also create a logic for the way in which they arrived in the space and the way in which they inhabited it. Within the performance of Futur/Perfekt the boxes were about containing remnants, memories of past performances, places encountered, chance events, dreams and nightmares. For Emma, the boxes became a kind of condensed **mise en scène** or as she coined it, a **mise en boîte,** that contained the traces of previous moments, chance encounters and events. In an extreme example of the malleability of all elements of the event, a lighting design from a previous performance of Futur/Perfekt (hanging bulbs) was scrapped and put in a box, its presence still resonant in the space, but now deposited, stored, classified and shelved. However, it was still used, albeit differently, as a source of light at one point in the performance.

Emma came up with the idea of a storage system, an archive of these mise en boîtes. Within Futur/Perfekt, the mise en boîtes were moments, glimpses of past or future encounters. Not unlike the original personal memory, the boxes act as a collected memory of previous events that will trigger the event's present stage. The treatment of the boxes extended further the temporal/spatial ambiguity explored in the relationship between body and movement. She suggested the boxes should float in the space, not be anchored to the ground. The boxes would be both 'here and now' (they occupy a particular space, concretely) but by not being fixed to the ground suggested a future potential relocation whilst containing elements from very precise past instances.

Futur/Perfekt *Max Thielmann*

This worked especially well with the Futur/Perfekt collaboration with Brudderman & Papp (Vienna) at the Lilian Baylis Theatre in May 2000. For that encounter, the project had embraced the centenary celebrations of Freud's Interpretation of Dreams since the collaboration between the two companies was being supported by the Dreamscapes Festival. The columns of floating boxes had clear links here. Emma took her inspiration from the painting Träumen (Dreams), by Karl-Horst Hödicke, (1989). In this painting disembodied heads of dreamers floated through a deep blue space, their faces lobster pink, their lips scarlet. They appeared as jewels, precious and contained. Emma decided to take this colour scheme into the mise-en-scène of the performance. The horizontal shelving within the columns was painted the same intense blue and the new boxes were painted in the pinky-orange of the faces in the painting. This entrance of colour reflected changes in the identity of the piece. As colours entered we began to differentiate between the old piece of the 20th century (very black minimal design), from Futur/Perfekt as it enters 2000 with colour bleeding through, cutting through the darkness. The transformation and transportation inferred in the metaphor "from darkness to light" affected various other elements of the dramaturgy. It gave us a metaphor to understand the journey from dream to physicality, from the inner landscape of dreams to the visible landscape of the performer on stage. The statement, which came of a scenographic decision, became a working metaphor for movement material as well as for the development of text.

dance and the performative

mise en boîte
mise en scène

The arrival of the boxes for this cluster of performances was given more significance than in previous events (where the boxes had been already in the space when the audience came in). Because the new boxes were distinguished from those of past performances by their vivid colour, it seemed logical to demand an arrival into the space that was particular to them. We decided to fly them into the space: Emma tied them up as parcels, which each performer received and unwrapped. As a way of feeding the conceptual framework for that event, Emma researched into the Freudian symbolism of a box. This gave us some sources to manipulate aspects of the dance structure: the opening of each box as a way of letting the dream out, a process which became stage business, unwrapped each box as an introduction to their time on. Freud suggests that wrapping may symbolise a desire to conceal feelings from yourself or from others or a sense of shame or guilt or inadequacy or longing for the warmth of love. In all cases, he suggests that the first thing to do is to remove the wrappings or to uncover that part of you which needs attention. During the Vienna performance, Jemima Hoadley opened the first 'dream box', inhaling a breath of air which then led her to motion and from there to recounting a recurrent dream of skiing. This recounting became an amusing and touching story, partly because it demonstrated with honesty and vulnerability that perhaps the unwrapping of the boxes indicated that in this space and for this duration nothing would be concealed; everything would be played out from the private and painful to the amusing and ridiculous, from darkness to light.

The biggest challenge was to lose the proscenium within the proscenium and disrupt the visual-linguistic dominance of its codes. All the spaces that Futur/Perfekt has been rehearsed and performed in have been either definite proscenium spaces or sites whose hard architectural features have predisposed the user to work within proscenium rules. In the creation of the environment for the event performance, we tried to create various areas of focus within the proscenium (through the suspension of the hanging columns of boxes, and the objects which begin to occupy the shelves) so that the tendency to perceive the proscenium as a window, a singular mirror into another world, was disrupted through a proliferation of micro-spaces within the macro-space of the proscenium. There were experiments to decentralise the focus, disrupt the visual-linguistic narrative through the exploration of spatial asymmetry, varying degrees of spatial density and emptiness, and create marginal spaces of action that competed against the 'central space', not only visually but also through other senses, as noise and sounds cut through from margin to centre.

These concerns were further explored in the Colombian collaboration with Ballet Experimental Contemporáneo in July 2000, following a first encounter in April that year. Emma took her experimentation with 'reversibility' further and experimented with the manipulation of the objects collected within the action, expanding their use beyond displaying them on the shelves. The aim was to allow the manipulation of objects through the space to invoke the journeys that had taken place so far. In many ways the objects now became the points of the compass anchoring the event, although they were physical traces of now absent bodies of events past that insisted on cutting into the event now. The final Colombia performance took place in a non-theatre space (Studio 8 at the Laban Centre London). The columns of boxes framed a space of performance within which Futur/Perfekt took place. In a sense, they contained the action and watched over the action. In the Colombian phase Futur/Perfekt: Entre Mito, Sueño y Realidad, Emma became more involved with trying to make the objects within the boxes take on more of an active narrative in the space. We wanted a moment of chaos in the performance, and spent some time with the performers working on a section where the objects are taken from their boxes and placed in the space, sometimes placed with speed, sometimes with deliberate care. We created a logic and rules for how this occurred. As a result, the objects became significant as performers breaking free from their archives to give us glimpses of previous locations and events.

Futur/Perfekt performance video still

A space exits when one takes into consideration vectors of direction, velocities and time variables. Thus space is composed of intersections of mobile elements. In a sense actuated by the ensemble of movements deployed within it (de Certeau, 1998, p.145).

The collaboration with the various composers who have joined in at different phases of the project shared many of the concerns and strategies of the collaboration with Emma. For the research and development that led to the Berlin phase, I used material that had been devised from previous collaborations with

**accummulation,
distortion,
contamination,
acquisition**

composer Steve Williams. Steve had been involved with the company's work since <u>Portraits</u> in 1993 and shared with me an interest in the physicalisation and spatialisation of the theatrical mise en scène (he is also a lighting designer, web designer). In pre-research to <u>Futur/Perfekt</u> (without dancers) Steve and I had done some recording experimentation using sounds coming from a memory source to create sound landscapes. I provided written texts from personal journals (about lost love). Steve worked on a memory of his childhood on the family farm in Spain (that still exists). We manipulated the sources in a variety of ways. For example, we 'physicalised' the journal entries by recording them as speech, but using only the inhale/exhale patterns, the sounds made by me licking my lips whilst reading, of the clicks of my tongue. It was not a textual translation, from memory to words, but the creation of a trace from the results of an action, generated by that memory, the effects of a

<u>Futur/Perfekt</u> performance video still

memory-event. The text was hidden behind the layers of bodily sounds: only few words - 'to begin again', 'unable' - cut through the noises: the body/flesh desemiotises language through action, not repression (the horror of the Lacanian traumatised flesh). On his part, Steve collected sounds from the actual farm (he went to visit during a pause in the R&D). These were manipulated to create 'music' that was interrupted every now and then by the sounds of cars passing, of a dog barking, of flames flicking, of a man walking down gravel pulling his zipper down and pissing. This score, itself a capsule from the R&D, was used (as a necessary inheritance) by the first team of performers that were involved in 'the Berlin piece'. It was an internal test of possible strategies of **accumulation** (new material developed because the question 'where am I now' always leads to new responses, there are new boxes every night, new objects are given in), **distortion** (the treatment of the journal entries), **contamination** (having to deal with music not composed specifically for the material as I experienced it in the process of 'remembering'), **acquisition**[12] (new performers come in for discreet period, so we end up with new materials not planned, eg. the speeches developed with Noam), that later defined the main system of generation that activated the macro-project. What was dramaturgically interesting were the points where Steve's mise en son found moments of synchronicity with the evolving dramaturgy of <u>Futur/Perfekt</u>. By the time we reach <u>London Calling</u>, the sound of the dog-barking in Spain had been linked to the memories of Adam in Berlin ("in the distance I heard a dog bark"). Later, a single bark interrupted a new vocal composition.

A very different collaboration took place with Phil Durant. Phil, brave man, came into the process of <u>Futur/Perfekt: London Calling</u> three weeks before the expected launch date. Phil saw a significant amount of the 'work' 'finished' before he started to compose. However, he not only composed for the movement already made, but created a sound landscape: his sound landscape of London that gave new impetus to the dancer's material just as we thought it was 'closed for now'. Whereas Steve's material was technically produced but remained quite textural and organic in mood, Phil's personal version of London was all technology: fabricated, prefabricated, full of constant repetition that seemed to drive the idea of 'London', of going from A to B and ending up lost in Z. Moreover, Phil worked on the idea of metaphorically organising the events as 'twenty four hours in London'. The individual stories (not composed to represent) acquired significance in terms of location within a episodic macro-structure of 'evening commuting', 'at home', '4am in Soho', 'daybreak in the city' that gave us a necessary internal cohesion, but was not a direct message 'intended' for an audience. In no way were we intending to describe or 'represent' 'a day in the life of London'.

For the Vienna project we did not have a new musical collaborator but rather found 'new thoughts' (as Emma would say) for the now 'collected' material; an open work experimentation of what goes with what, sections that had been originated to Steve's material were now performed to Phil's, for example. We collaborated with actress/playwright Birte Bruddermann in the composition of more textual elements that became the new source of soundscape for this event. As previously mentioned, the Vienna phase was taking place during the centenary celebrations of Freud's <u>Interpretation of Dreams</u> supported by the Dreamscapes Festival. Birte (who was also a non-dancing performer in the piece) researched Freud the man, his work, and the city of Vienna. Through Birte's speech section, Freud became an invisible 8th performer: not unlike Ivana, the more he was not there (but references are made about him) the more effect he had on the development of the work. Birte created a series of scenes that, as in the Berlin piece, undercut the dancerly material. She was never Freud, but Freud was made present in her opening speech where she tells us she has been reading Freud and cannot understand him: she goes

---

12 See Ana Sanchez-Colberg (1999). In the essay I discussed the historical processes of accumulation, distortion, contamination and acquisition with reference to the project.

on to another scene where she tells us about Vienna, describing the city, as she goes with her boyfriend to visit Freud's house, then she gives us a lesson in Freudian dream theory. In the closing speech - delivered as fast as she could echoing the verbal release associated to Freudian therapy - she finally tells us what connects London and Vienna, Freud and us, the dreams within ourselves to Futur/Perfekt...

Futur/Perfekt performance video still

Going from darkness to light, from war to freedom, Vienna to London. Cancer to Cancer. Darkness to light. From thoughts to release. From river to river. Light in a moment of explosion like my friend who took the gun and put it to her head. This one single moment of release. Leaving everything behind to become... light and stillness.

Death bringing birth. Vienna to London. Cars. Colours. Images changing. Faces. Streets. Sounds. Connections. Problems. Thoughts. From Bergasse. Leaving behind friends, places, clothes, tables, glasses. If now they burn the books soon they will burn people. From fire to tranquility. From language to language. From tradition to death. Cancer Pain. Pain. Pain. Losing all illusion. Disillusioning dreams.

Laster verlieren. From horses to buses. Maronimann. Grasen. Kaffeehäuser. From right to left. Gemütlich Langsam zum 3/4 Takt.

Birte Brudermann in Futur/Perfekt: Dreamt, Dream...Still Dreaming, London 2000.

The most recent collaboration was with composer Pedro Gomez-Egaña, for both the Colombian collaboration in July 2000 and what we called the consolidation (the story so far) phase in London May 2001. Pedro was instantly inspired by Emma's idea of reversibility. As a composer he had been working with creating performance scores based on the visible rhythms and the accidental noises created by bodies moving in a space. So he was well in tune with the idea of a physicality in the music score. For the first event in July, Pedro wanted to include a 'live-music' component. Overnight we found our cast enlarged to include Pedro, playing violin 'live' and three performers/singers who created a series of intervening scenes with voice/sound/text. The effect of the larger cast, coupled with Emma's intention of populating the space with the objects, led to a transformation of the event. The Colombians took over, transforming the post-modern sparsity of previous events into a tropically baroque landscape. Pedro extended some of his working methodologies for the next collaboration Futur/Perfekt: There & Back that took place May 1st-5th 2001 at the Blue Elephant Theatre in London. Not unlike Emma, Pedro worked kinetically with the performers, transforming a previous theatrical scene in which dancers talked about the 'map of their rooms' into a chorus of silent kinetic rhythms.

In keeping with the idea of the 'story' so far, Pedro took on the challenge of not only creating new material for the piece but maintained that the final score had to have four sources: the 'old' (sections of music that through use now belonged to particular sections of movement: we speak of Adam's dog, of Hely Jarvinen and Domingo Bermudez's music, of the music 'of the happy quartet') the totally 'new' (with no precedent), the almost new (reworking of material from the July encounter which was recorded in this instance) and the hardest one **'the alias'** (material that had to betray its transformation from Berlin to present). The notion of 'alias' came about from very specific circumstances. Between London and Phoenix we underwent a change of cast. Joana Simas and Konrad Gabriel left the project and Jemima Hoadley and Mark Glover took over. However, whereas from Berlin to London, new members created new material, the changeover took place four days before going to the USA so we had to pass on/take on material.

alias

To be conceptually consistent, I decided that we had to devise strategies that indicated that this material was 'not mine' but 'his/hers' in 'whose place I am standing'. These reverberated across the strands. Speeches spoken by Joana, now retold by Jemima, began with "she said". Material that had not been clearly videoed was taken out and Jemima and Mark 'filled in the gap' by responding to the material that survived. Mark, who is taller than Konrad, started many of the movements by squeezing himself into 'position', indicating that he was inhabiting a space constructed by another. When we arrived at There & Back, Joana returned to the project. Rather than eliminating surplus material, I decided to betray even further the doubling that had taken place. This became known as the 'alias', material that linked Joana's and Jemima's histories within the event. Joana's material had the original music from London Calling. Jemima's material - that had used that music but has since become her own work - had, therefore, no score. Pedro took on the challenge to create material that echoed Joana's (which had been composed by Phil) but then moved to be very much Pedro's own. In another instance of aliases and transformations, Hely decided to shorten her solo, not for aesthetic reasons but because the memory that led to that solo journey was, to quote her, 'no longer relevant'. Pedro created a score in which words of that no longer relevant journey (originally spoken in Finnish and never translated: I still don't 'know' the 'facts' of her speech) were juxtaposed to the sounds of the material that remained. Pedro, Hely and I agreed to have one of Domingo's speeches take place simultaneously. Two scenes that used to follow each other now took place synchronically.

Futur/Perfekt: process & product:
history is to memory as memory is to
performance... or performance as history of the
memory or the memory of a history?

> Memory is not an instrument for exploring the past but its
> theatre. It is the medium of past experience, as the ground is
> the medium in which dead cities lie interred. He who seeks to
> approach his own buried past must conduct himself like a man
> digging. This confers the tone and bearing of genuine
> reminiscences. He must not be afraid to return again and again
> to the same matter; to scatter it as one scatters earth, to turn it
> over as one turns over soil. For the matter itself is only a
> deposit, a stratum, which yields only to the most meticulous
> examination what constitutes the real treasure hidden within
> the earth; the images, severed from all earlier associations, that
> stand - like precious fragments or torsos in a collector's gallery
> - in the prosaic rooms of our later understanding...

> Walter Benjamin (1997, p.314).

The above quotation - found sometime last year, once the
project had been going on for two years - resonated with me in
many ways. It seemed to summarise not only the dynamics of
memory and history in general, but those processes in relation
to Futur/Perfekt specifically. This further corroborated my
intuitive proposal of a link between notions of history, memory
and the body, as source and trace of those two related processes.
In doing so, Futur/Perfekt questioned the validity of theories of
language to sustain a reflection of performance within larger
historical, social, personal knowledges and practices. It also
validated - personally and critically - the way in which the
project has questioned the idea of 'performance as metaphor'
and substituted it for the idea of 'performance as memory' (as
crucial to 'knowledge' at the moment of performance, not
performance 'about' memory).

Futur/Perfekt adds a twist. Let memory not be considered only
as a mental act, let memory inhabit the realm of the corporeal
(thoughts and actions). Let this corporeality in its human form
be that which bridges any temporal gap and consequently
instils the objects of the past with present significance; the 'later
understanding' that Bejamin refers to. The performers give
personal significance to their growing history tied to the history
of the project. Moreover, the audience of each instalment bridge
the work's own series as they give a trace of their own history
to propel the project on to the next. The body switches from
being the negative "gap that we ourselves are..." to a notion of
the body as having positive valence containing both the mental
and affective; not as opposites within a continuum, but as
dynamic attributes within a network (from the psychological to

the vegetable to the mineral, the physical to the psychical, the verbal to the bodily) that constitute the corporeal existence of <u>Futur/Perfekt</u> as a human phenomenon in this world.

<u>Futur/Perfekt</u> proposes a possible relationship between the idea of history (as a content of events) and the philosophy of history (as a debate of contexts and rationales) to the process of performance. <u>Futur/Perfekt</u>, the incomplete future tense describing an action that will have passed somewhere in an undefined future... the tense of the 'will have become'... as the central temporal structure of any performance event. On the basis of this process of thinking the work has been devised. Not as a piece, but as an event which will tell its own story as it reflects on the process of its own historicing. A work that explores the relationship between the process of performance, its arbitrary/circumstancial/intentional and non-intentional products (and byproducts) and their relationship to the making, performance and perception of this process; a piece that will generate its own traces; a piece which reveals its internal mechanisms of making and, by doing so, argues against the now common oversimplifications and generalisations which have been used to define what makes a piece 'work'; a piece full of thought and analysis in the making, but which does not stop from operating on the intuitive, the chaotic; a piece that sets a journey for all those involved, with agreed outcomes but with an explorative attitude towards the routes to be taken.

Futur/Perfekt objects collected in performance (Colombia)

Alter, J. (1990). *A Socio-Semiotic Theory of Theatre.* Philadelphia: University of Pennsylvania Press.

Bateson, G. (1972). *Steps to An Ecology of the Mind.* New York: Ballantine.

Benjamin W. (1997). A Berlin Chronicle in *One Way Street and Other Writings.*
(trans: Edmund Jephcott and Kingsley Shorter). London: Verso.

Csordas, Thomas J. (1994). *Embodiment and Experience.* Cambridge: Cambridge University Press.

de Certeau, M. (1998). *The practice of everyday life.* Berkeley: University ofCalifornia Press.

Garner Jr, Stanton B. (1989). *The Absent Voice: Narrative Comprehension in the Theatre.* Urbana:
University of Illinois Press.

Garner Jr, Stanton B. (1994). *Bodied Spaces: Phenomenology and Performance in Contemporary Drama.*
Ithaca: Cornell University Press.

Goffman, E. (1974). *Frame Analysis.* New York: Harper & Row.

Huizinga, J. (1955). *Homo Ludens: A Study of Play Element in Culture.* London: Beacon Press.

Laban, R. (1966). *Choreutics (ed Ullmann).* London: Macdonald & Evans.

Lacan, J. (1977). *Ecrits. A Selection.* London: Tavistock.

Lefebvre, H. (1991). *The Production of Space.* (trans. Nicholson-Smith). Oxford: Blackwell.

Melrose, S. (1994). *Towards a Semiotics of the Dramatic Text.* London: MacMillan.

Merleau-Ponty, M. (1962). *The Phenomenology of Perception.* (trans. Colin Smith). London: Routledge.

Sanchez-Colberg, A. (1992). *Traditions and Contradictions: A Choreological Documentation of Tanztheater
from its Roots in Ausdruckstanz to Present.* Laban Centre London. PhD Dissertation.

Sanchez-Colberg, A. (1996). Altered States and Subliminal Spaces: Charting the Road Towards A Physical
Theatre. *Performance Research* 1(2).

Sanchez-Colberg, A. (1998). Space is the Place: A Reconsideration of Laban's Theory of Space in
Contemporary Choreography. *Proceedings Continents in Movement,* Lisbon: Portugal.

Sanchez-Colberg, A. (1999). 'Futur/Perfekt: Archival Flesh (On Memory, Bodies, Performance and History),
Society for Dance Research, *Exploding Perceptions Conference,* October 1999, Conference Proceedings.

Schechner, R. (1988). *Performance Theory.* London: Routledge.

Sutton-Smith, B. (1979). *The Dialectics of Play.* Schorndorf: Verlag Karl Hoffman.

States, Bert O. (1985). *Great Reckonings in Little Rooms: On the Phenomenology of Theatre.*
Berkeley/London: University of California Press.

Turner, V. (1982). *From Ritual to Theatre: The Human Seriousness of Play.* New York: Performing Arts
Journal Books.

Turner, V. (1974). *Drama, Fields and Metaphors.* Ithaca: Cornell University Press.

Vazquez, J. (1986). *Lenguaje, Verdad y Mundo: Modelo Fenomenologico para el Analisis Semantico.*
Barcelona: Antropos.

Die Grünen Clowns
Laban
Kammertanzbühne Laban
Anon

chapter 10
issues in revivals and re-creations: a choreological enquiry
Valerie Preston-Dunlop

The problem I faced in attempting to recapture some of the repertoire of the Kammertanzbühne Laban (Chamber Dance Theatre Laban) [1] was: how do I reach a repertoire that is, to all intents and purposes, lost ? There exists almost no film footage, only occasional fragments taken in rehearsal under poor circumstances at a time when film was in any case primitive. There exist no notated scores because the Kammertanz that I hoped to locate was functioning between 1922 and 1928 in the years just before Laban completed his notation system.

Rudolf Laban, Green Clowns *Toni Nandi*

If the identity of the dances I wanted to find lay in their surface form, it would have been a hopeless task to attempt reconstructions on the slender evidence available. What nagged in my mind was my personal knowledge as a student and co-worker with Laban (altogether a twelve year association) that his work was not about surface form but about content, tightly

---

[1] The Kammertanzbühne Laban functioned in Hamburg from 1922 moving to Berlin (via Würzburg) in 1926. It continued until 1929, latterly directed by Dussia Bereska until she left Laban for Paris when he became Director of Movement for the Prussian State Theatres, resident at the state opera house at Unter den Linden in Berlin.

structured improvisation, and copious use of the contributions of the dancers in his rehearsals.

The issues arising centred on questions of this sort: does the identity of a work lie in the processes by which it is made as well as in its final surface form ?

remounting a
stable work

That question contains a problem concept of 'final surface form'. Does a dance ever have a final surface form? Is there a finished product, taking into account that a dance, as a performance art, will be performed more than once? Inevitably, it will be slightly different on each performance, with new casts bringing in their own interpretations, in different venues where spacing and visual context are peculiar to that venue. A work in repertory balances between forces that attempt to stabilise it and forces that, by their very nature, inevitably keep it in dynamic flux.

Notated scores offer a stable record of the work as it existed when the score was written. Watching David Bintley rehearsing the première of <u>The Snow Queen</u> (1992) for Birmingham Royal Ballet, I observed the choreologist with pencil and eraser in hand, finalising his score as Bintley found himself able to say: 'that is what I want'.

Watching him continue the next day, Bintley referred to the choreologist who reminded him that the movement he had settled on was like this, not like that. The piece became firmly embedded in the bodily performance of the dancer creating the role with Bintley but even more firmly fixed by the marks on paper of the Benesh score. The score was then referred to as 'the bible' of the work as, I believe, are all scores in the company.

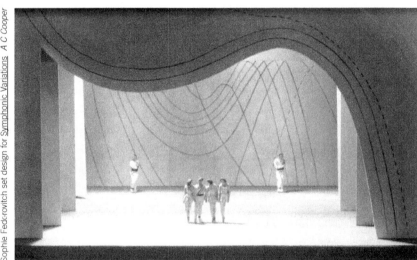

Sophie Fedorovitch set design for <u>Symphonic Variations</u>   *A C Cooper*

During the same period, Ashton's <u>Symphonic Variations</u> (1946) and Jooss's <u>The Green Table</u> (1932) were also in rehearsal, both works being recorded in notation: Ashton's in Benesh, Jooss' in Labanotation. Judith Maelor Thomas undertook the preliminary mounting from the score of <u>Symphonic Variations</u> concentrating totally on getting the steps right :

> *"chassée step step"*, *"and-a-li-ft"*, *"1, 2, you're turning 3 and a 4"*,
> *"step assemblé"*, *"saut de basque"*, *"just tombé on it and piqué"*,
> *"downstage with the right leg"*, *"on the open leg"*.
> (quoted in Preston-Dunlop, 1995, p. 213).

and on the spacing:

> *"use your tram lines"*, *"get back to your slot"*, *"straight across the back"*,
> *"a shallow diagonal"*, *"go in to your partner"*, *"don't kill the centre
> couple"* (ibid.).

Michael Somes, an original soloist in the work, supervised the
final coaching, getting at the qualities not in the score but in
the work :

> *"Be absolutely there... the position has got to register immediately"* (ibid.).

This way of working, superlatively efficient for a work of ballet
whose identity lies in its surface form, was not available to me
for the Kammertanz, nor would it have reflected how Laban
worked with his dancers.

Both Somes and Maelor Thomas were concerned from the **directorial**
beginning with the reception of the work. It must look right.
What should register for the audience and what should be
fleeting had to be in place. Els Grelinger worked with a
different directorial issue. She discussed with me her writing of
the score, and mounting from it, of Charles Weidman's
Lynchtown (1936)

> *"You have to set the steps, the movements, pathways and groupings of the
> work but also provide the motivation out of which the original dance emerged"*.
> (Els Grelinger, interview, 1994).

Original motivation comes in all sorts - kinetic and dramatic. In
the case of Lynchtown, Weidman's work derived from the grim
horror of a barbaric lynching in a southern state, an appalling
incident that he witnessed as a child and never forgot. Walter
Terry describes the feelings and actions that Weidman
embodied and which Grelinger had to arouse for the
remounting.

> Lynch Town (sic) strikes home, it strikes at the very being of the
> American, for the trembling evil of the lynchers themselves and the evil of
> the onlookers who share vicariously in the horrible thrill seem to vibrate
> across the footlights and attack the complacency of those who sit in the
> safety of the theater (Terry, 1956, p. 110).

Here the score is written to give the main actions and essential
stylistic features of Weidman's work while not cluttering the
score with detail of the first dancers' interpretation. What the
work needs to succeed are motivated, personal responses to the
monstrous event. Each 'onlooker', 'listener' and 'whisperer'
approaches the broken prostrate figure, curious, appalled,
gleeful, vicious. Here is a mounting that leaves room for the

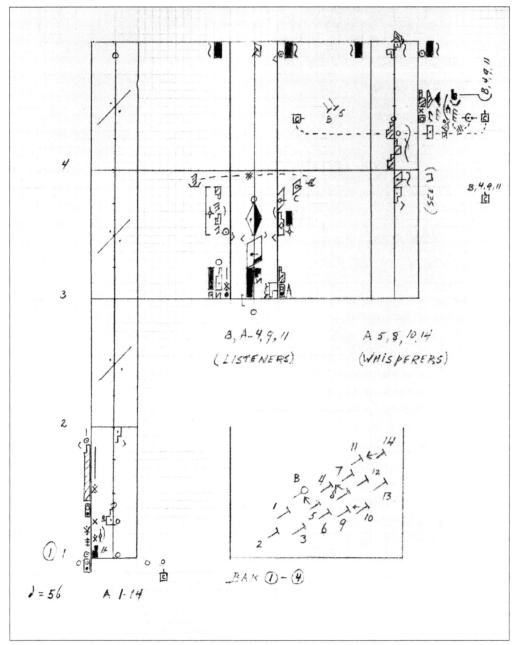

Lynchtown, Charles Weidman

director to use her skills to elicit meaningful performances from each participant, in order to get the ether from stage to the auditorium to 'vibrate', as Terry described.

To get at the Kammertanz at all I had to discover the motivation for the dances listed in the repertoire and that meant going beyond drama into kinetic motivation and across decades to motivations of the 1920s. Grelinger recounts reading widely on the lynch culture to grasp the repellent reality of racial bestiality. I did the same to get at the turmoil of post-war Weimar Germany.

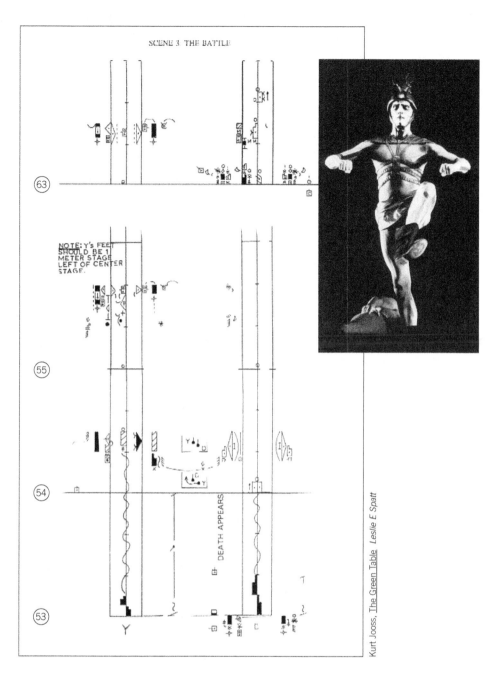

Kurt Jooss, <u>The Green Table</u> *Leslie E Spatt*

Kurt Jooss had been a Laban dancer in that culture, between 1921 and 1924. Something of his early experiences could still be traced in his own master work. Anna Markard undertook the rehearsals and coaching for the Birmingham Royal Ballet's remounting of <u>The Green Table</u>. Because the vocabulary of Jooss was not a ballet vocabulary, her verbal language was quite different from that of Maelor Thomas. She was mounting a 1932 dance drama on a ballet company so she had to wean the dancers away from their customary way of thinking. Being aware of the audience, always, is necessary in balletic works, as Michael Somes demonstrated. Not so in Jooss' work. Markard needed the company to:

identify with the role honestly... don't qualify the movement for the audience... you have to commit yourself to the movement...... don't ornament (Preston-Dunlop, 1995, p. 213).

By 1932 Jooss had developed his own choreographic way but had retained many Labanesque qualities to his work, essentially finding the kinetic motivation of a role. Markard asks for commitment to the movement. The dramatic events on stage emerge from that. Laban qualities are not necessarily to be found in the surface form of Jooss' dances, which were much tidier than Laban's. Jooss had introduced ballet-based steps for the legs which are nowhere to be found in the scraps of film of the Kammertanz works. Certainly, honesty with a role, committing yourself to the movement and not to the audience, were essential to an ausdrucktänzerin.

the Kammertanz as performative

Laban saw his company as different in nature from a ballet company. Writing about it in Germany in 1935 he said:

> *Ours was the first and only specialist dance-theatre, the first and also probably the last in Europe for some time to come, for we have travelling dance-groups but no resident dance-theatres...... A considerable number of subscribers came to visit our regular performances* (Laban, 1975, p. 106).

Two significant concepts emerge. The first is the introduction by Laban of the term dance-theatre. He is not combining two arts, dance and theatre, but treating dance as a theatrical art form - that is, performative, one that essentially sets out to engage its audience in a two-way process. The second concept is that of regular audience members, the same people who came again and again. The company could not function as dance companies do now, taking months to create one work, which to survive has a short season and then tours. Laban set out to engage his audience regularly with a varied repertoire. He continued:

> *Familiar characters came into being, who were welcomed by the audience like old acquaintances just as in medieval theatre. There were for example, the jester, the juggler, obstinacy, rage, playfulness, the dandy, the tyrant, death and many others* (ibid.).

To put together such a varied programme on a regular basis was a task that needed new thinking. Sharing responsibility and co-authorship were Laban's solutions, so that the creativity and time required were not shouldered entirely by himself:

> *A wealth of short dance works were produced with her [Dussia Bereska] both participating and directing* (ibid.).

The performances included solos which were made by the company members on each other, with Laban, Bereska, Jooss and Gertrud Loeszer directing. Other solutions were both audacious and pragmatic:

> We even performed the same dances in different costumes, sometimes in a
> historical and at others a timeless way so that we would not simply be
> guided by our taste but also by reactions of the audiences, whom after all
> we wanted to attract in the first place (ibid.).

Costumes here are seen as changeable, as part of the dynamic
flux of the Kammertanz dances. They are unfinished on-going
fleeting events.

When Nicholas Beriozoff mounted Michel Fokine's
Schéhérazade (1910) on the newly formed Festival Ballet (now
The English National Ballet) for the opening of the Royal
Festival Hall in 1952, the original Léon Bakst costumes were
copied in an attempt at authenticity, although the
documentation shows that Bakst himself made several versions
of the designs after the first performance. There was no
question of mounting the work with a new visual concept.
There may well have been reference to an audience's need to
have something festive to celebrate. That was what the Festival
of Britain was intended to give the British public, who were
emerging from the severe austerity of wartime conditions and
post-war rationing. Schéhérazade is colourful and energetic.
Being an out-of-work dancer at the time, I was employed to
paint the stripes on the trousers for the corps de ballet. Yard
upon yard of cotton material was dyed to match exactly Bakst's
design. Through the day and night I hand painted the stripes, in
paints specially mixed to match Bakst's image. There was no
compromise. Schéhérazade, so far as Beriozoff was concerned,
was a finished product to be reproduced.

Peter Williams wrote of the performances of the work at the
Stoll Theatre preceding the Royal Festival Hall season:

> Nicholas Beriosoff has most faithfully revived the work and he himself
> gives a brilliant performance of the waddling stupid old Eunuch.
> Unfortunately this type of narrative ballet no longer holds its power - it no
> longer shocks, the colours are not exotic, the choreographic mechanism is
> too obvious (Williams, 1952).

The question has to be asked: does the identity of Schéhérazade
lie in the form that Beriosoff so diligently revived or does it lie
in a more complex mix?

The work continued in the company's repertory for in 1962
J[ohn] P[ercival] castigated the artistic directors for adding a
long "would-be soviet style" pas de deux with lifts and jumps
and "much realistic erotic pantomine" which he judged to be
an "atrocity". C[live] B[arnes] put it:

> I am not sure what one can do nowadays about Schéhérazade except
> perhaps refrain (Barnes, 1962).

Nattiez (1990) would suggest that the identity lies in the
poietic, trace and esthesic levels of content; that is, in the
making procedures, and in the work's actual fabric, and in the

spectators' response. One has to ask, to whom or to what is it worth being faithful?

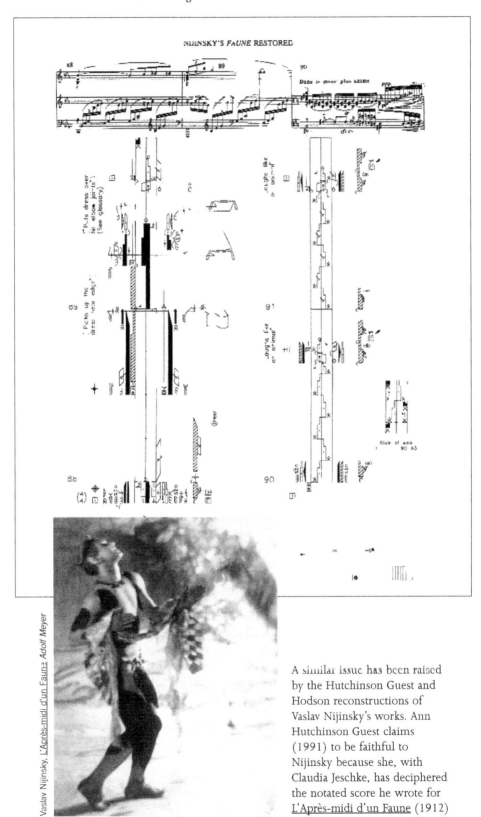

Vaslav Nijinsky, L'Après-midi d'un Faune *Adolf Meyer*

A similar issue has been raised by the Hutchinson Guest and Hodson reconstructions of Vaslav Nijinsky's works. Ann Hutchinson Guest claims (1991) to be faithful to Nijinsky because she, with Claudia Jeschke, has deciphered the notated score he wrote for L'Après-midi d'un Faune (1912) and supported the resulting information with contextual evidence. In that respect, she is treating the dance as if it were an object, where the score is treated as the object's identity. Rightly, Hutchinson Guest points to the many "memory-based" versions of the work, spurius in their authenticity. The notation scholarship she exhibits is profound. Whether this scholarship has enabled her to find the event or not depends on the view taken as to whether a dance is a performative work, interactive with its spectators, and in flux, or a completed art object. She has found Nijinsky's surface form and narrative intentions (as recorded in his notation) but that is not the whole picture of the event. What about the processes of making, the kinetic intention and the audience's culture-influenced perception? Should they matter in a revival / reconstruction / re-creation or not ? Hutchinson Guest makes it clear that her aim was to restore a work in its original form against a scenario of other less authentic attempts. Its reception and its making processes were marginal to her research.

The investigation of the Kammertanz Laban repertoire proved the dances to be of another kind. I both could and could not restore Laban's repertoire to its original form. What I had to find were not products but unfinished on-going fleeting works whose surface form was, by its nature, changeable. My faithfulness had to be to changeability, since Laban's works were not completed art objects. In the event, several re-creations of the Kammertanz have taken place, in which different casts, different movement material, different costumes have been the rule.[2] That multiplicity was essential to remain authentic to dance works in flux.

Millicent Hodson claims authenticity for her extensive research into Le Sacre de Printemps (1913). In her preface to the reconstructed 'score' she discusses a range of background information surrounding the work (Hodson, 1996). She mentions how Sacre became lost, the personality problems in the Ballets Russes surrounding Nijinsky, critical responses to the première, behind the scenes reasons for allowing Sacre to disappear, the short term deliberate oblivion of Nijinsky, and the evidence she worked on. She does not discuss Sacre in relation to the ontology of reconstruction of a performative work of dance theatre. She works within the parameters that finding as exact a replication of the 'steps' as she can is her prime responsibility. Like Hutchinson Guest she treats the work as an object completed at its première. Much ballet repertoire is so treated, including Symphonic Variations and The Green Table.

Such a position may do justice to the event. Or it may not. Both Faune and Sacre caused a scandal in their time. Neither caused a scandal in their 1990's rebirth. From a choreological perspective the question arises: if these directors had treated dance as a performative art would their revival have been different? The directors appear not to take into account that a performative

performative issues

---

[2] Video recordings of each performance of the Kammertanz are in the Laban Collection in the Laban Centre London's Library.

piece of theatre engages an audience and that that engagement has repercussions that are embodied in the work's form. Such an event is a phenomenal and semiotic double figure-of-eight weaving between the making, performing and receiving people. That was clearly Laban's view of his works. For the Kammertanz re-creations I had to take the double figure-of-eight into account. Works that he regarded as comic I had to make comic, those that were ornamental had to be so, for those that he regarded as grotesque I had to find a grotesque image for today (after investigating what "grotesque" meant for him at that time).

Was Beriosoff faithful to the performative event of <u>Schéhérazade</u> in 1910 at the Théâtre National de L'Opéra? Peter Williams wrote that the dance caused a furore because of its voluptuousness and

> retained its magic until Diaghilev's death in 1929. Revived by the de Basil and Blum companies during the thirties it had little to offer except during a short season at the Alhambra Theatre in 1936, when Fokine himself supervised the production for the Rene Blum Company.
> (Williams, 1952).

Presumably, Fokine did not feel the need to be faithful to the form of the première but rather to his 1936 public. Whatever alterations he put in place, or whatever change in the motivation of his dancers he conjured, the magic returned. One can only conclude that Fokine did not regard his work/s as final products, or completed art objects.[3]

living work or completed object

Sarah Rubidge discussed these issues in her article 'Reconstruction and its Problems', developing Roger Copeland's argument of the previous year 'Revival and Reconstruction'. (In <u>Dance Theatre Journal</u>, Vol. 12, no. 1 and Vol 11, no. 3.) Copeland had discussed the radical revisions of the ballet repertoire, with <u>Nutcracker</u> by Mark Morris as <u>Hardnut</u>, and <u>Giselle</u> by Mats Ek as examples. Rubidge considered the lack of revisions of early modern dance works. She questioned whether the value of these works was purely historical or whether they had artistic value in themselves and were therefore worth seeing as works in their own right. Revisions, if done, are undertaken by treating dances

> not as historical documents, although they might also serve that purpose, but as living works of art, subject to the interplay between dance director and the dance work (Rubidge, 1995).

Here, Rubidge points to two significant concepts: seeing the work as a living work and not as a completed historical object, and, the nature of the interplay which is crucial.

The 'dance work' includes everything in the performative event - all parties, including the culture in which the original work was made and the culture of the time when the revision is undertaken. Matthew Bourne paid attention to these for the court scene in his revision of <u>Swan Lake</u> (1995). The references to princesses and royal personages were given a definite Windsor flavour at a time when the dysfunctionality of the House of Windsor was topical.

> The original version [of a dance work]becomes part of the history of dance [as a score or as a video recording] not its sole identifying determinant. The records allow for what Jonathan Miller calls an "afterlife" (Miller, 1986), a life which emerges from a dialogue between the director and the work and which, while it acknowledges the originators, is not dependent on their perceptions and visions (Rubidge, ibid.).

Huchinson Guest and Hodson have supplied important quasi-historical documentation of the works that they researched, not revisions.[4] Rubidge's discussion leads beyond revision, towards the concept of a dance being considered as an open work. An open work is seen as one that was never made to be a completed work but one that contained an irreversible 'kernel' which must always be present in any instantiation. Identification of the kernel is a primary requirement. Just what that might be - surface forms, structures that hold the work together, or changeability itself - constitutes a major topic, debated in Rubidge's doctoral work. (Rubidge, 2001). Instantiations of an open work kernel become, then, the responsibility of the director of each instantiation.

Are the Kammertanz works open works? Did Laban ever believe that they were completed art objects? Did he want other people to produce them, re-create them in their own style with another surface form? It seems likely that he did in one instance for he encouraged two choreographers to do just that with his dance drama Gaukelei (1923) made with his larger company

directorial dialogue with the Kammertanz

Aurel Milloss, Gaukelei *Anon*

Kurt Jooss, Gaukelei *Anon*

---

[3] Clement Crisp (Financial Times 08.01.02) scorns a recent 're-reading' of Schéhérazade under the heading "how not to". Given in Paris it was "offered as plotless scenes colour coded for day, night, dusk, Marrakesh and an orgy". He likened the movement to "a child's idea of dance......" the child having probably seen "a snatch of an unsuitable video...", the women's clothing "layered in variously extravagant fabrics, and looking like spendthrift dragqueens". In the same evening and by the same company (Paris Opera) Jerome Robbins' complete modernisation of Faune as Afternoon of a Faun (1953) which takes place in a dance studio on a hot afternoon, was performed "flawlessly", and preceded by a performance of "Nijinsky's original", "looking a masterpiece and a modern one at that".

[4] I qualify their documents as quasi because the original performances are irrevocably lost.

Tanzbühne Laban. Jooss created his version in 1930 in the Essen city thetatre and Aurel Milloss his in 1935 in the Düsseldorf opera house. No doubt for Laban, this was another experiment, for none of his peers were treating their works as open. He was at the time choreographer at the state opera house in Berlin. There, as everywhere, operas were revived with new productions as a normal occurrence. However, an opera is not regarded as an open work but one where the line is rigorously drawn between the composer's work, registered for posterity in its score, and its production, which is available for change.

If I were to treat the Kammertanz dances as open works, I could make any or many instantiations of them, provided that I could identify what the original kernel was. A person with no Laban experience could equally create a valid instantiation. While that would constitute an interesting piece of research it is not what I needed to do.

The purpose of my research was to remain closer to Laban's methods. I was concerned with following Laban's own processes of dance making and artistic criteria in order to give insight into a way of working that was radical in its time. I had to re-create, not revive, or reconstruct or newly instantiate. Such a process, I claim, is of historical interest distinct from, but no less valuable than, the revival of surface form. Both process and product constitute identity, re-creations of which constitute two distinct modes of authenticity.

Returning to the Kammertanz repertoire, I discuss here the movement material and the evidence that could be found of its generation and use.

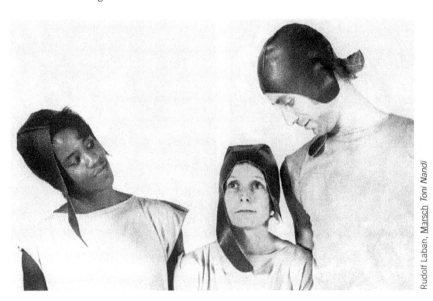

Rudolf Laban, Marsch *Toni Nandi*

recovered data The programme for the season of 1924 was divided into short works that were Ornamental, Ecstatic, Rhythmic, Grotesque, Stylistic[5], and longer dance poems, dance dramas and dance comedies. Reminding himself years later of the inventive sources for these works Laban wrote of some being 'representations of inner stirrings', others being 'a feeling for form and a delight in line'. They included 'mime dances characterising city experiences,' which

> were built up out of affirmtive nods, negative shakings of the head, defensive movements of the hands, beckoning waves, arms opening in surprise and similar everyday movements (Laban, 1975).

In an interview with choreographer Aurel Milloss in his Rome apartment in 1990, he recalled having seen the Tanzbühne Laban in Konstanz in 1926, and being overwhelmed by their production. In particular, he was struck by Laban's performance of the grotesque solo <u>Marotte</u> (Obsessed). This solo is a mime dance, made up of the behavioural material Laban described. Milloss recalled that the piece was structured in rondo form with a recurring motif consisting of a churning circular gesture of the dancer's arm, externalising a churning inner state. Between the repetitions were all manner of 'obsessive'

Rudolf Laban, *Marotte* *Toni Nandi*

movement motifs. The work was without music but was not silent, various actions causing body sounds and cries.

From my days as a student I recalled Laban working with fellow student Ronnie Curran on a solo entitled <u>The Obsessed</u>. We had no idea at the time that it was a re-creation of <u>Marotte</u> but in retrospect it is now obvious to me that it was. Curran was asked to find obsessive motifs and Laban worked with him in typical expressionist mode to get him to intensify them and find their organicism. Note: rather than coach Curran to get what he as choreographer wanted, Laban worked with him to enable him to find the performance for himself and thereby create the role as personal property. Again and again, Curran repeated his movement fragments until they grew, in size and intensity, into a crisis of tension from which he fell back into his chosen recurring motif, in ABACADA structure. In re-creating <u>Marotte</u>,

objective and subjective data

---

5 The Stylistic dances were based on national folk dance material which, being an international group of dancers, they could teach each other and develop. Having no knowledge of authentic folk dance I did not attempt to refind them.

I combined the churning motif seen by Milloss with other obsessive material found by the dancer, searching for movement that would create body sounds; in this case the thumping of the man's elbow on the ground as he fell, still churning, a cry as he shied away from an hallucination, a repeated slap as he attempted to brush himself clean of imagined dirt. Each gesture repeats and grows organically as the solo lurches from one intense crisis to another. Curran was bare-chested, vulnerable; so was my marotte.

The Ecstatic dances were based on themes of spirituality, religious prayer exercises and dervish dance materials. In <u>A Life for Dance</u> Laban describes his encounters with the Moslem lay brothers 'and their endless turnings', during his youthful visits to his father's military manœuvres in Herzigovina. (Laban, 1975, p. 50 et seq.) To re-create the <u>Ecstatische Zweimännertanz</u> (ecstatic duo for men) I collected Laban's references to spirituality which abound in his writings and recalled the unusual history classes that he gave us as students. There were no history books, no resources beyond Arbeau's <u>Orchésographie</u> and Curt Sachs's <u>World History of the Dance</u>.

Laban taught history practically through eukinetics and choreutics starting with the rhythmical pounding of the earth in so-called primitive dance, moving on next to ancient Egyptian ritual. Here Laban used his Rosicrucian knowledge of the geometric base of Egyptian religious culture.[6] The tetrahedron, or pyramid, was the perfect three-dimensional form around which Laban learned that the prayer movements of the ritual were structured. These movements we danced, self-accompanied by bells, cymbal and gong, arching and bowing, accenting from the shoulders to eternity through angular arms. He recalled the prayer gestures encountered in his youth in Sarajevo and Constantinople, and the trance-like revolving of the Dervishes. He taught the timelessness that trance states induce and the control of dynamic intention so that a spell-like state might be reached.

Sylvia Bodmer, Kammertänzerin in Hamburg 1921 - 23, and teacher with Laban in Britain, created dance studies for The Manchester Dance Circle, one of which was ecstatic and based on the tetrahedral orientation in space. When reconstructing her studies, and filming them under her guidance and that of her co-artistic director Enid Platt,[7] Bodmer's discussions with Laban on the spiritual content of crystals were recounted. All of this data informed my re-creation of an ecstatic dance for two men. Its original surface form was lost but I knew its likely content and Laban's methods of getting a lived creative performance of a duo from his dancers.

In contrast, for a comic duo for men <u>Bizarrezweimännertanz</u> I referred to costume designs first seen on Kurt Jooss and to chaotic movements from a film fragment of him while a student dancer. These acted as a stabilizing force for an improvisation. I had seen Laban improvise a ludicrous stalking mock battle with Ewan McColl, co-director with Joan Littlewood of Theatre Workshop.[8] The original performers in the 1924 bizarre duo were Laban, then forty five, and a younger company member. I cast two men with a similar age discrepancy. It proved to be hilarious.

Three ornamental dances were re-created. The resources for Orchidée were a fragment of film of Dussia Bereska, seated bare-breasted with transparent loose trousers over shiny (gold? silver?) knickers of the kind seen in many of the photographs of the dances. The dance was

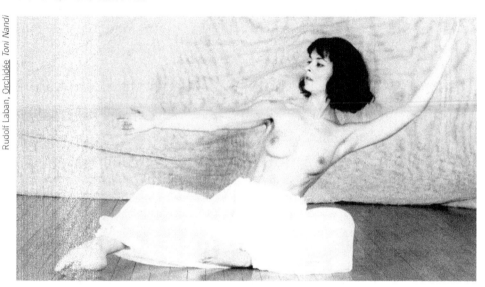

Rudolf Laban, Orchidée Toni Nandi

......*a solo by our leading dancer which became well known and which was almost a symbol of of the spirit of our theatre. It was called The Orchid, a composition of the most subtle arm and finger movements which got its name because it seemed to express the inner life of a bizarre flower in the process of unfolding (Laban, 1975, p. 107).*

Arm and finger movements were the basic form, but exotic, not behavioural, and of a bizarre flower. Laban's hand and arm movements were well known. John Hodgson quotes from an interview with Kurt Jooss on Laban's own performance:

'He had marvellous hands' Jooss later declared. ' It was as if fire came from them when they were in motion' (Hodgson, 2001, p. 94).

The film fragment of Bereska gave a starting point for the re-creation directed by collaborative choreographer

6 Rosicrucianism is a spiritual quest-based learning sect which Laban joined in his student days. See Preston-Dunlop's biography of him, (1998a).

7 In The Laban Tradition : Sylvia Bodmer, (video), Laban Centre (1986).

8 That event was Laban's 70th birthday celebration in Manchester, a wild party cum performative event, in which all manner of spontaneous 'performances' took place.

Dorothy Madden. She developed the motifs referring to the exercises in hand and arm intricacy given by Laban to his students, as part of choreutic studies.

Krystall and Rosetten were two ornamental solos judged to have movement material from Laban's space harmony sequences, based as they are on crystal forms. Two contrasting forms were chosen for these solos, an axis scale, its labile and its stable form, for the Krystall and the volutes of the A-scale combined with movements from a transversal 7-ring sequence for Rosetten.[9]

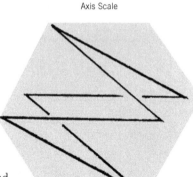

Axis Scale

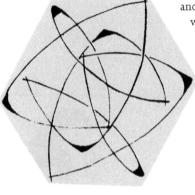

'A' Scale Volutes

The movements are sharp and straight sculpted forms in the kinesphere for Krystall contrasted by curves overlapping each other harmonically, like the petals of a rose for the other. Lisa Ullmann was a master at composing a dance study from a choreutic scale or a ring and I referred to her method for these two ornamental fragments. These three solos I decided to present twice in each performance, with different dancers and different costume, as Laban described. In this way the performances spanned the aesthetic of pre- and post- 1924, the year of the New Objectivity in Weimar culture epitomised in the arts by the stringent lines of the Bauhaus.

Zeitgeist A unique feature of the Kammertanz dancers was their group spirit. They did everything together from making costumes to searching for food.

> Even the smallest detail of the scenery, every operation, every note, every step and all the necessary arrangements were animated by our collective artistic determination (Laban, 1975).

The group, of both sexes, had an age range from Laban at 40 plus, through mature men such as Albrecht Knust, who had been at the battle front throughout the 1914 - 18 war, to young women and men, including Kurt Jooss and Sylvia Bodmer, who were beginning a career in dance. Their first eight weeks together in 1922 took place 'in a meadow' (Preston-Dunlop, 1986), training and rehearsing in the open air. Dancing like that with feet feeling the ground, bare limbs and midriff sensing the wind and the sun, with the sky over head, has an effect on a dancer. It brings about a strong sense of corporeal relatedness to nature, the cosmos, each other, simplicity, fundamentals. These people shared their dancing, their living space, their meagre belongings and food. The result was an extraordinary sense of community, resulting in an ability to improvise together, to respond, to react, to support, to intervene, to enter into a self made liminal space where the magic of theatre could be made. To re-create the Kammertanz works I had to engender something of this spirit. So we too danced outside, in little clothing and bare feet and improvised together in rhythmical silence, and shared our resources.

Laban's use of music, or rather absence of it, is in stark contrast to the music for the other works discussed here. Noël Goodwin, writing in 1988 of <u>Symphonic Variations</u>, discussed the audience's perception of the César Frank music for the dance. It is a concerto. It gives the audience a great deal to absorb:

revivals and music

> not only the two (ear and eye) attention modes but a third, the solo instrument (Goodwin, 1988).

Louis Horst, discussing the musician/choreographer relationship, was of the view that sound should not overwhelm the senses in a dance performance:

> Music should be transparent, open and spacious, so that the audience can see the dance through it (Horst, 1969).

Laban was more radical. Writing to Susanne Perrottet in 1912:

> Dance is - for me - its own art. [I must] create, determine entirely alone the laws of dance, an art which is often merely an accompaniment to music.[10]

It is well documented that Laban set out to remove dance from music, an act that he saw as essential as a first step to enabling dance and music (or sound) to be autonomous arts capable of being used by choreographers and composers in all manner of ways, as equals. Laban's Kammertanz works include examples of his experiments in dance freed from the domination of music. He goes on in the same letter to Perrottet to say that a creative dance person finds music a grave limitation. Throughout his career, Laban did not use music for his dances that was written for any other purpose than for dance, if he used it at all.

> Besides silent dances we performed works to the accompaniment of gong, drum and flute, or to simple music. All our music was composed expressly for our dances. Dance always came first...... [for <u>Above and Below</u>] we composed the music at the same time as the dances and suddenly one day, during a rehearsal, the musical motif for the moon was born. Our leading lady [Dussia Bereska] who performed the moon was dancing with such elan and expression that all the members of the cast spontaneously hummed and whistled a melody which became the accompaniment (Laban, 1975).

[9] Diagrams of these choreuic forms can be found in Laban, (1996); and in Preston-Dunlop, (1984).

[10] The original letter is in French. A German translation is published in Wolfenberger, (1990).

Following in Laban's footsteps Jooss' long term musical director F.C.Cohen wrote the score for <u>The Green Table</u>, giving the eukinetic and dramatic qualities of the choreography a sonorous atmosphere but never directing the movement action. Jooss, originally a music student, did not need music to organise his movement but he knew he could increase his audience's appreciation of his work if he included atmospheric and rhythmical sound.

sound in <u>Green Clowns</u>

Sound was an issue in the re-creation of <u>Green Clowns</u> (<u>Die Grünen Clowns</u>) The work has a variety of sound sources. It is a suite of dances that explores social comment sometimes seriously and sometimes ironically. The work appears fragmentally over a period of years under various titles, in 1928 being given at the Second Dancers' Congress in Essen, co-directed by Dussia Bereska. In that performance it had six parts. I was unable to recognise enough sources to re-create two of the sections, so settled for a four-part suite.

It opens with <u>Maschine</u>, an exploration of a theme close to Laban's concerns, the machine's domination of Man. The conveyor belt had just been invented and was profoundly feared, as Charlie Chaplin portrays in his film <u>Modern Times</u> (1936). Adda Heynssen was one of Laban's musician colleagues. Her piano piece <u>Machine Rhythmns</u>, published in Great Britain in the 1940s for the machine dances being created by students, was its accompaniment. Dorothy Madden assisted me with this work. She found extremely uncomfortable movement material, kneeling in a continuous tactile line, to embody the erlebnis aspect of the man/machine apprehension, the incessant musical rhythm dominating the tempo. The factory overseer looms over the crouching figures, suggesting a precursor to the Death figure in <u>The Green Table</u>. The dancers felt their individuality crushed through the de-personalised unison material as well as signifying through it

<u>Krieg</u> (War) was punctuated by sound generated by the masked dancers as they interacted with each other with increasingly belligerent dynamic. Breath and vocal cries gradually rent the air. Rapid group interchanges took place. The group movements and group forms were found in the notation for groups added by Albrecht Knust to Laban's notation to enable him to write canons, circling and wheeling, leading and following, common in Laban's choral works for amateur movement choirs. <u>Krieg</u> develops into a procession of the dead and dying for which

slightly different photographs provided the motivation while leaving the form somewhat open. We looked at how each person could have created that image and with what feeling, what kinetic intention. The dancers' sighs created the sound as they collapsed, weakened, subsiding in the procession.

<u>Green Clowns</u> ends with <u>Club der Sonderlinge</u> (<u>Club of the Eccentrics</u>). Slurping licks, snarling bites, tickling pokes, smacking kisses are interspersed with idiosyncratic striding, wobbling, jostling behaviour, shouting at the audience. Laban's description of his experimental 'dynamic materialisation' <u>Nacht</u> (1927) contains similar elements. Created the year before the <u>Green Clowns</u> performance and a full evening's work, Laban bemoaned the lack of appreciation of it by the more conservative members of his audience who walked out.

---

[11] To date nine re-creations have been made, several with Laban Centre faculty, alumni and students, one with Helsinki's Theatre Academy dancers, another in Kinki University in Osaka.

[12] See video, <u>Valerie Preston-Dunlop presents Recreations of Laban Dances 1923 - 28</u> (1992).

Gertrud Snell, one of the dancers, described the exhiliration of the performers who thought <u>Nacht</u> "a fantastic, avant-garde, propaganda piece"(Preston-Dunlop, 1998a, p.133). <u>Club</u> certainly uses the spirit of <u>Nacht</u>.

the spirit of the work

What is the spirit of an event? What does it mean to get into the spirit of something? Clark Moustakas discusses such an experiential process as 'heuristic research':

> *the process of internal search through which one discovers the nature and meaning of experience...... The self of the researcher is present throughout the process and, while understanding the phenomena with increasing depth the researcher also experiences growing self awareness and self knowledge. Heuristic processes incorporate creative self-processes and self-discoveries. (Moustakas, 1994, p. 8).*

To get into the Kammertanz spirit during the original practical research was a gradual heuristic process, every hour of an intensive creative workshop - rehearsal - performance[11], as participants turned themselves from contemporary dancers into co-authoring ausdruckstänzern and tänzerinnen, thereby discovering more about their own creative and performative preferences and abilities. The 'spirit' of the Kammertanz, of <u>Symphonic Variations</u>, of <u>Faune</u>, of <u>Sacre</u>, of <u>The Green Table</u>, of <u>Swan Lake</u> is what has to be found so that the interplay of director and dance in any revisitation can be a genuine interplay rather than an imposition of directorial preferences. Laban's dances were fundamentally an experiment in Weimar performative dance theatre. To interact with those experiments my collaborators and I engaged with the range of primary sources available to us through a choreological perspective coloured by our prior experiences and intense curiosity.[12]

Rudolf Laban, <u>Green Clowns</u> *Toni Nardi*

Frederic Ashton	Symphonic Variations	Sadlers Wells Ballet	1946
David Bintley	The Snow Queen	Birmingham Royal Ballet	1992
Matthew Bourne	Swan Lake	Adventures in Motion Pictures	1995
Michel Fokine	Schéhérazade	Ballets Russes	1910
Kurt Jooss	The Green Table (Die Grüne Tische)	Folkwangbühne Essen	1932
	Gaukelei	Folkwangbühne Essen	1930
Rudolf Laban	Gaukelei	Tanzbühne Laban,	1923
	Orchidée	Bereska	1923
	Oben und Unten	Kammertanzbühne Laban	1923
	Marotte	Kammertanzbühne Laban	1924
	Krystall	Kammertanzbühne Laban	1924
	Rosetten	Kammertanzbühne Laban	1924
	Bizarrezweimännertanz	Kammertanzbühne Laban	1924
	Ecstatische Zweimännertanz	Kammertanzbühne Laban	1924
	Die Grünen Clowns	Kammertanzbühne Laban	1928
Aurel Milloss	Gaukelei	Stadt Oper Düsseldorf	1935
Vaslav Nijinsky	L' Après-midi d'un Faune	Ballets Russes	1912
	Le Sacre du Printemps	Ballets Russes	1913
Jerome Robbins	Afternoon of a Faun	New York City Ballet	1953
Charles Weidman	Lynchtown	Humphrey Weidman Group	1936

B[arnes]. C. (1962). Harem Scandals, *Dance and Dancers,* Vol 13 (4).
Benesh, R. & J. (1969). *An Introduction to Benesh Movement Notation.* New York: Dance Horizons.
Copeland, R. (1994). Revival and Reconstruction. *Dance Theatre Journal,* Vol 11, no. 3.
Crisp, C. (2002). How Not To, How To. *Financial Times,* 08/01/02.
Goodwin, N. (1988). Ashton and the music of dance - three way partnership, *Dance and Dancers,* Nov-Dec, pp.17-19.
Hodgson, J. (2001). *Mastering Movement: the life and work of Rudolf Laban.* London, Methuen.
Hodson, M. (1996). *Nijinski's Crime against Grace: Reconstruction Score of the Original Choreography for Le Sacre de Printemps.* Stuyvesant: Pendragon Press.
Horst, L. (1969). Symposium on composer/choreographer, *Dance Perspectives,* No. 38.
Hutchinson Guest, A. (ed) (1991). *Nijinsky's Faune Restored.* London: Gordon and Breach.
Laban, R. (1935). 1975 (trans. Ullmann, L.) *A Life for Dance.* London: Macdonald & Evans
Miller, J. (1986). *Subsequent Performances.* London: Faber & Faber.
Moustakas, C. (1994). *Phenomenal Research Methods.* London: Sage Publications.
Preston-Dunlop, V. (1984). *Point of Departure: the dancer's space.* Verve Publishing.
Preston-Dunlop, V. (1986). video. *In The Laban Tradition: Sylvia Bodmer.* Laban Centre.
Preston-Dunlop, V. (1992). video. *Recreation of Laban Dances 1923 - 28.* Verve Publishing.
Preston-Dunlop, V. (1995). *Dance Words.* London: Harwood Academic.
Preston-Dunlop, V. (1998a). *Rudolf Laban: An Extraordinary Life.* London: Dance Books.
Rubidge, S. (1995). Reconstruction and its Problems. *Dance Theatre Journal,* Vol 12, no. 1.
Rubidge, S. (2001). *Identity in Flux: A Theoretical and Choreographic Enquiry into the identity of the Open Work, unpublished PhD thesis.* Laban Centre London.
Terry, W. (1956). *The Dance in America.* New York: Harper and Brothers.
Williams, P. (1952). Shéhérazade, *Dance and Dancers,* Vol III, No 6 p.15.
Wolfenberger, G. (1989). *Susanne Perrottet: Eine Bewegtes Leben.* Bern: Benteli Verlag.

Documents in The Laban Collection. Laban Centre London

Kunst der Fuge
Amanda Miller
Ballet Freiburg Pretty Ugly
Klaus Fröhlich

chapter 11
multiple embodiment of ballet and the dancer's cultural agency
Paula Salosaari

When I began the research on multiple embodiment of the vocabulary in ballet class (Salosaari, 2001), I took for granted the view that the dance artist creates through a four-stranded dance medium consisting of the performer, the movement, the space or the visual setting and the sound or the aural elements of the dance (Adshead, 1988; Sanchez-Colberg, 1992; Preston-Dunlop, 1998). However, my understanding of the dancer-movement nexus was shallow, looking at it rather from the outside in terms of how the dancer's appearance, gender or ethnicity or perhaps her projecting personality affected the dance. In reality, I still looked upon the dancer as an instrument or material for the dance, performing fixed and fully predetermined movement material. I did not really see the dancer as an aesthetically experiencing and acting person, nor had I envisaged the consequences this could have for the dance.

My research, though acknowledging the connection between the outside and inside views in dance (Preston-Dunlop, 1989), paid attention more to the dancers' experiences than to the outward appearance of the dance. Listening to and analysing the dancers' experiences of intentional performance changed my viewpoint from seeing a mechanical dancer performing fixed dance material to understanding that the dancer embodies the movement in an individual way in each live performance. When the dancers engaged with and intended the dance with structural images, their phenomenal experiences of the dance changed. These experiences gave rise to revelations of performance possibilities and thereby to creative renewal of the ballet vocabulary. The dancers ceased to be simply material to be moulded. Their experiences of the motivation of the artistic content in the dance and their ability to create new embodiments of it, empowered them to a response and agency in performance to the ballet culture. This agency is based on the dancer belonging to and 'knowing in her bones' the tradition she is working in.

In the dancers' experiences, the new performance possibilities emerge from their engagement with the dance when it transcends in lived performance. These experiences are therefore not reflected, objective or logical choices made during performance. They emerge from pre-reflective lived experience as spontaneous and indeterminate revelations. The revelations bring with them aesthetic feelings and are thereby justified by their makers as valid insights.

the concept of multiple embodiment

The concept of multiple embodiment was defined as a result of the research. It is based on the understanding of the ballet vocabulary as a qualitatively open form pregnant with potential content, and of the dancer as able to experience, reveal and act on this content in multiple ways, making individual movement choices and thereby developing artistic judgement of dance qualities. When a dancer performs an arabesque, she repeats a traditional fixed form. However, in each performance of that arabesque there can be something in the dancer's experience of it that is fresh and new, something that transcends the dance material as the dancer has known it before. Something happens that could be called creative. Every performance of an arabesque, or any other movement of the vocabulary, is to some extent individual while at the same time representing the known form. The intention in teaching multiple embodiment in classical ballet is to enhance this flux - the individual contribution of the dancer, her creativity - rather than hiding it behind the need to reproduce the tradition.

The performer/movement nexus then began to consist for me of the person owning the movement by embodying and phenomenally experiencing it and being thereby informed by the experience. Here was a nexus that made deeper sense. It is a nexus that highlights the ballet class in flux rather than safeguarding conventions by transferring fixed forms and aesthetic principles from one generation to another. It is a nexus that eventually has consequences to ballet as art, and that raises the status of the ballet dancer from a skilled technician to a developing artist, a cultural agent of change.

My research can then be looked at from the standpoint of how to understand and promote the classical vocabulary in a qualitatively open-ended way and to educate the dancers in a way that gives them the opportunity to develop and enhance their agency as active members of the evolving ballet/dance culture.

practical nature of the research

As a dance practitioner, a ballet teacher, I had gradually begun to experience ballet teaching as partially problematic. After many years of training and teaching I had started to feel that I was not able to develop myself and my students broadly enough in a ballet class. Specifically, the problem seemed to be the fixed nature of the vocabulary to be learned and the hierarchic teacher-centred manner of delivering it to the students. Having tried to expand my skills in contemporary dance classes, I finally defined the problem in my research: "I would utilise my learned codified ballet technique in an environment of repetition and reproduction and forget about being creative, or improvising and producing my own dance movements, or, I would be inventive cutting myself off from ballet. Combining the two was not an option" (Salosaari, 2001, pp. 11-12). My gradual growth in awareness of the mismatch in ballet class between teaching technical skills and artistic learning in an open-ended way caused what Jarvis calls 'disjuncture' in my own practice. Disjuncture makes the practitioner aware of a problem and therefore precedes change (Jarvis, 1999, pp. 66-68). Finding a solution to the posed problem has been a personal journey towards change in my own teaching. Out of necessity the research has also been practical/ practice-based.

Salosaari workshop

To begin to solve the problem I arranged practical ballet workshops in which I introduced changes to the traditional manner of teaching. The workshops were undertaken by three different groups of dancers and students; fourth (and final) year dance students specialising in becoming dance teachers at The Theatre Academy in Helsinki; nine to fourteen year old dance students at The Finnish National Opera Ballet School: and a group of active independent dance artists (dancers and teachers). The independent dance artists group came together for the longest period of time (14 weekly sessions) and were also the most articulate on their experiences in class. Therefore they became my main informants in the research, although all groups have contributed to the data.

tools to multiple embodiment

divergent production, a basis for multiple solutions

In the research, the means to empower the dancer to become an agent of change were discussed on the basis of opening out the vocabulary to multiple performance solutions which the dancers explored. They took responsibility for their individually chosen solutions. In educational terms, teaching was changed from being reproduction of the given vocabulary to divergent production in which many solutions to the same task were possible. Mosston and Ashworth (1994) have discussed a spectrum of possible teaching styles for the teaching and learning of different kinds of movement skills. The spectrum is divided into two groups according to whether the styles in it facilitate teaching known phenomena or whether they invite creative solutions from the learner. Two styles, one from each group, were of specific interest in the research.

In a ballet class, almost without exception, the teacher presents the movement form to be learned, students repeat it as closely as possible, and afterwards the teacher provides feedback based on the teacher's criteria of excellence. These behaviours define the ballet teaching style as command style (ibid.). Their aim is also clear, fast learning and safeguarding of the traditional vocabulary and aesthetics. Because the aim in my research was to enhance the dancers' creative responses, an open-ended teaching and learning style was needed. Such is the 'divergent production style' (ibid.) in which the learning outcomes are open to divergent answers. Rather than offering a fixed model to be reproduced, the teacher in this style designs tasks that invite multiple answers. I entered the practical research with this change of teaching style in mind. The results of the research showed the consequences of the change to the learners/dancers.

The research indicated how a reproductive style can be opened out in terms of the dancers' experience by offering images for the dancer to intend and motivate their dance with. When dancers explored the same movement sequence with different images, they produced new and unexpected ways of performing, their own spontaneity surprising them. A dancer might give the dance a new kind of impulse, feelings of countertension might emerge or perhaps security of performance and an increased sense of balance appeared. That which at first glance may seem reproduction can be opened out to creative experiential solutions.

The fact that these solutions were unexpected and could not be anticipated changed the hierarchic teacher-learner roles in the ballet class. The ownership of knowledge was divided between the teacher and the students. The dancer's phenomenal experience, as will be explained later in 'revelations', is a response from the dancer's whole person and artistic background, convincing the performer and bringing with it strong aesthetic feeling. This inner response justifies the new to the dancer. Therefore, it is a way for the dancer to own the movement, create it anew each time. This ownership may result in the dancer questioning a teacher's information as appropriate. A teacher's anatomical correction may have little to do with the "owner's" immediate decisions. The dancers are invited to explore, test and possibly take further the tradition. They are invited to discover and recreate the vocabulary. If the experience contradicts with the given responses of the teacher, it can lead to further questioning and testing of the traditional way of conceiving of ballet.

The dancers' creativity was further challenged by open-ended tasks that called for interpreting the vocabulary or creating individual new dance material. The teacher's role was to provide the playground and tools for creative production.

Salosaari workshop

In the ballet workshops, the dancers' experiencing of the qualities in the classical vocabulary were enhanced by introducing structural images of the dance as tools to explore and create within the ballet context. The structural components of dance are constituents of the medium itself and therefore communicate the formal qualities of dance, including those inherent in the ballet vocabulary. They indicate what can be intended in formal dance material.

structural imagery, tools for multiple production

The images may be spatial components of the dance such as progression in space, projection into space, kinesphere planes and directions. Or they may be movement actions, such as transference of weight, twisting, balancing or over-balancing, gathering towards or scattering away from the centre. They may be the relationships of body parts playing with proximity and touch. They may be dynamic properties of the dance such as timing or flow in the movement and so on. By applying imagery into ballet the dancer can choose and change intention in the same dance material, thereby producing multiple embodiments of the same step (Preston-Dunlop, 1998).

The structural components were used in the ballet workshops, as images to intend the ballet vocabulary. Using images interchangeably gave the dancers means to have varying viewpoints on the same movement. Using imagery to intend the dance gradually expanded the dancers' array of potential performance qualities and thereby increased their versatility of artistic and technical skill.

In addition to opening out the qualities in one 'step' or combination into multiple performance solutions, using the structural images helps the dancer to pay attention to and reveal qualities underneath or behind a step. These hidden qualities may be regarded as deep structures of the dance, to use a linguistic term. The deep structure of an arabesque can be, among others, its projection into the surrounding space. Energy is radiating from the dancer's focus, hands and leg, perhaps chest, elongating the lines into the surrounding space. The dancer can have the same intention of projecting into space but give it a totally new embodiment, changing the surface form, still stating, "projection of energy into surrounding space".

This is how the images can serve as tools to movement exploration, interpretation and dance composition. With these tools the teacher can create tasks that ask for multiple solutions in a ballet class. Exploration opens out potential performance qualities. Interpretations are the dancers' choices of qualities revealed by exploration. Compositions of new movement material are dancers' new responses to the deep structures of the dance.

In this essay, I use as an example images of the dancers' kinesphere, the space immediately surrounding the dancer, which they mould by moving in it. I discuss the dancers' descriptions of their own experiences while they explored ballet with these kinesphere images.

illuminating the potential expressiveness of space in ballet

Only long after my basic training in ballet I became aware of the expressiveness of the space in and through which I danced. In adddition to knowing the eight numbered directions in the stage space (Kostrovitskaya & Pisarev,1978) and some awareness of presenting movement in a favourable angle to the audience, my understanding of space was intuitive rather than the kind of conscious engagement that for instance Preston-Dunlop speaks about:

> *there is a difference between feeling yourself dancing and feeling yourself dancing in and with the space. That is a difference to be discovered.* (Preston-Dunlop, 1998, p. 122).

The idea of a kinesphere was foreign to me. The basic directions were stressed by the teacher's comments like "lift up the body" or "leg behind". I built my largely intuitive understanding from these hints. With an open introduction to the kinesphere the dancer's understanding of the expressive potential of the space-in-the-body and the-body-in-space concepts (ibid. p.121) the dancer's engagement with space can be expanded. Kinesphere models map the space around the dancer giving it a virtual scaffolding for the dancer's reference (Laban, 1966).

The models of the kinesphere were first introduced to German dance by Rudolf Laban in 1926, and published in English in 1966, as part of choreutics, his analysis and practice of spatial form. The movement sphere is understood as having a centre and a surface and with the dancers' movements and focus radiating energy into space. Movement lines can be central, peripheral or cut across the kinesphere in-between its centre and surface.

mapping the kinesphere

The kinesphere maps structure the surrounding space, giving it directions, specific places, which when embodied become itineraries. Dance styles and choreographers embody space in various manners (Preston-Dunlop, 1998, p. 126). Ballet is

the octahedron map of the kinesphere

Salosaari

understood to conform to the octahedron kinesphere "map", which offers the central dimensions of up-down, right-left and forward-back. Ballet's verticality emphasises the down-up dimension and in principle its poses end in the six polar directions of this model. For instance, in an attitude the hands often are in directions up and to the side (either right or left), the head stating up, the leg behind stating back, the supporting leg stating down. Ballet makes exceptions to this classroom rule. Reality is not static. The dancers' comments in class demonstrated how a dancer's use of the model is flexible and imaginative. The image in the dancer's experience is dynamic rather than rigidly fixed. Her back may be slightly leaning forward, still stating up, the leg behind may be slightly higher than horizontal, the hands may curve forward from the absolute statement "right". However, the codified ballet vocabulary is built on verticality and the three-dimensional balance of the movement.

icosahedron map of the kinesphere

In the icosahedron map of the dancer's kinesphere the vertical, horizontal and forward-back dimensions open out into planes; the vertical opens to the door plane, the horizontal to the table plane and the forward-back dimension to the wheel plane. When a dancer stands in a wide second position with the arms opened high to to the sides she is embodying the door plane. A ballet dancer bending forward from the hips in port de bras may for a moment state the table plane with the upper body and the arms. A dancer twisted from the upper body holding her hands in front and behind, as in Vaganova's fourth arabesque, is embodying the wheel plane with her upper body. The icosahedron maps fuller areas of space while adding twelve directions of possible orientation (the corners of the three planes). Using these, a dancer's movement can radiate outwards in oblique lines, to complement the basic six octahedral directions.

the cube map of the kinesphere

It is difficult to imagine the movements of traditional ballet vocabulary embodying the cube model. The corners of the cube seem to state all the directions that are missing in ballet: high-right-forward, high-left-forward, high-right-back, high-left-back, deep-right-forward, deep-left-forward, deep-right-back, deep-left-back. The model tilts the vertical centre line into four diagonals that, if inscribed by the whole body, throw the moving person off-balance. This is unknown to the codified movements in the ballet vocabulary which state "I am upright, balanced and calm" rather than "I am risking a fall". By now these off-balance movements are already everyday in contemporary works of ballets such as Amanda Miller's or Ashley Page's, but they are seldom incorporated into the ballet classroom.

orientation in space

Spatial orientation can be complicated in the sense that it is possible to have different kinds of orientation in space. In the workshops we used two: directions according to the dancer's own body front, and, according to the axes of the stage space. In "body-front" orientation the dancer imagines himself or herself inhabiting the kinesphere in such a way that the sphere turns and moves with the dancer and the front is always conceived of as in front of the dancer. When the dancer turns facing upstage, the front is towards upstage in the dancer's mind's eye. In "stage space" orientation the kinesphere stays in place while the dancer moves inside it. The front is where the audience is situated or imagined to be. When the dancer turns, what is conceived of as front stays towards the audience. The kinesphere is then like an immobile box (the stage) in which the dancer finds his directions and spatial places.

Ballett Freiburg Pretty Ugly *Klaus Fröhlich*

exploration of ballet with spatial images

Kinesphere images were used to explore and interpret given dance material as well as to compose new dance combinations. These activities are described here as an example of the images introduced in the workshops. Many non-spatial images were used as well; for instance, those concerning the dynamics or actions or perhaps relationships in dance. Overall, I found it preferable to work with many kinds of images so that the dancers were not closing their performance into a specific way of experiencing in ballet, but were open to and capable of changing the emphasis in performance. The present discussion focuses on dancers' experiences while concentrating on different spatial models. It shows how the ballet dancer's understanding of the surrounding space could be enriched and how images benefitted the dancers' performance and offered ways to ballet-based co-authorship in class. In the following discussion we look at some of the dancers' comments during the work. The dancers' awareness was gradually expanded by offering one kinesphere model after another (octahedron, icosahedron and cube) as an image for ballet, in consecutive workshops. The following examples of student comments in class comprise the raw data of the research, which was analysed and thematised. Here it is presented to give an idea of the practical base of the

ballet workshops, raw material for the practical research

tuning in

Often the workshops were begun with tuning in to the image or theme used in the class. During tuning in, I introduced the theme of the class by verbal explanation or pictures, perhaps moving myself, to illustrate the images in question. After that introduction the dancers improvised with the image, finding their own movements to embody it. This acted as a holistic warm-up for the class; body-mind-aesthetic feeling in unity. During the tuning in period, dancers sometimes posed questions to clarify the image for themselves. The octahedron prompted a friendly exchange of questions.

Dancer 1:	Was this model made for ballet?
Dancer 2:	Is this kind of a joke - the legs and arms going to the side at different heights from two centres?
Dancer 3:	How about when the leg cannot be taken quite to the side?
Dancer 4:	What about if I need to take the leg up, it is not possible, is it?
Teacher:	Maybe not for me but for Sylvie Guillem it would be OK.
Dancer 5:	Are they places or directions?
Dancer 3:	When I think of two centres I feel that they are places but when I move I feel that they are directions.

Working in the icosahedron reminded the dancers of their previous knowledge of the form. During tuning in, the dancers used their imaginations to picture themselves in, to be surrounded by, the icosahedron form.

Dancer 1:	These are like planes used in anatomy.
Dancer 2:	It is difficult to figure in your mind the lines between the corners (on the surface of the model).

Dancer 3:	The front seems exciting, like that (indicates)
Teacher:	Now, let's just do ballet with this image in mind. Talk to me if there are problems and ask as soon as there is need to.
Dancer:	Could we repeat once more the planes? (Teacher shows once more the planes and directions explaining how they differ from cube directions.)
Dancer 4:	Is the idea to think more of the corner directions than the planes themselves?
Teacher:	Yes, I'm thinking more of the directions.
Dancer 4:	Does the direction to the side exist?
Teacher:	Let's concentrate on the directions in this image for the moment. The question is, what kind of effect does this image have? Of course the side direction exists, but our concentration is now in this image.

After the tuning in, dancers began to explore regular ballet barre and centre work with the day's image; first, the octahedron with its basic directions and inherent verticality. Although the images initiated individual comments from the dancers, the change of image seemed to result in common types of experiences. The octahedron prompted awareness of stance and multidirectionality. It caused the dancers to change positions and movement pathways. It enhanced the awareness of spatial areas as "supporting structures to go to while moving". The following is a short excerpt of discussion in class.

expanding the image of the movement sphere

Teacher:	You take the octahedron with you when you move, front is always in front of you. Let's dance and talk afterwards. There is no single right experience, there are lots of possibilities for individual experience. I am interested in the difference of moving as normally in a ballet class and now with this image. Is there a difference? If so, what is it like?
Dancer 1:	Difficult to do fast, need to go slowly.
Dancer 2:	I became aware of the centre as staying in place and periphery moving more and now the connection. Easier to connect different body part.

Dancer 3:	Fascinating experience, but different from D2. Directions everywhere: the hand on the barre, realised the need to keep elbow down, bending back there was something I was going to; easier; plié up and down and the widening sideways, more three-dimensional.
Dancer 4:	I felt a supporting structure in space, there was something also behind my back; safer; helped balance.

In the following workshop I introduced the icosahedron. My expectation was that it would not be very useful for a ballet dancer as the ballet poses are structured in the octahedral places/areas of space and directions. Much to my surprise, this became a class full of dancers' comments of new realisations of movement awareness and facilitation in class. Curves became more rounded, the planes supported the movement making it lighter and more secure.

T:	Any notions?
D1:	It was easier to do fourth port de bras because I was thinking of the plane (wheel); even if the end directions are front and back the whole movement is happening on the plane.
D2:	My only notion was that when in the port de bras I was thinking of the directions, I changed the movement a bit. For instance to the side, I was reaching more towards the door plane corner than bending as much as possible sideways. Also bending forwards was more rounded, going first to the high wheel plane corner and only then forwards.
D3:	It was agonising to think of the door plane and realise the controversy between clean open ballet positions totally open to the sides. I was thinking, do I open hands all the way sideways or leave them rounded slightly forwards. The same in grand plié. Reminded me of the Russian ballet school. Help!

. . . .

| D1: | I felt the wheel plane directions in the tilts (rond de jambe in plié while upper body is swaying forward and back). More so in front. There were two directions at once: the leg |

> behind and down and the forward up simultaneously. Behind less, because the body has to go first up from the hips and then curve behind without losing the statement down with the hips.

> D2: The rond on the floor was more full, as there were more directions; not just forward-side-back-side but forward-front corner-sideways-back corner;

> D3: I had a short table plane feeling in the port de bras; then it disappeared when I continued bending.

. . . .

> D1: The table plane supports the hands.

> D2: I tend to turn the body in battement tendu sideways. The feeling of the door plane helped me stay in place, even if I was not altogether on the plane. It was there to support me.

Changing the image of the kinesphere's centre is one principle in Forsythe's improvisation with dancers. It was interesting to notice that this change to the image happened intuitively with some dancers.

> D: When you look for the directions, somewhere you find them. Suddenly the chin was in table plane forward direction.

Dancers also differed in their favourite orientation in space.

> T: Any difference in body orientation or stage space orientation?

> D1: Stage orientation is much easier. In the body orientation, when I began to turn I lost all the directions, my mind was late.

> D2: Body (orientation) was easier for me. Even when I tried to keep the image in place, it began to turn with me.

multiple embodiment of the vocabulary

Exploration with kinesphere imagery initiated subtle changes in the dancers' performances of the same movement combination on repeated embodiments. Taking a port de bras from down through forward to up : Is the lifting up of the hands emphasising the verticality of the body so bringing the hand in a line slightly closer to the body or is it complementing the vertical line of the body by emphasising the rounded forward curve (octahedron image)? While opening the arm from front to side : Is the dancer aware of beginning and end directions or is she reaching towards other directions on the way? Or does the dancer illuminate the space alive with tension between the body and the hand? Is the dancer's intention to open out the space rather than moving the hands? Does the dancer contain the alongée-line inside her kinesphere or is she sending energy out into the surrounding space?

Salosaari workshop

Dancers discovered new performance choices through exploration with spatial imagery. Where a hand lift had been just a lift with perhaps accidental quality, or a quality as close to the teacher's suggestion as the dancer mastered, it became discovery and awareness of possibilities and therefore an exercise of personal choice and development of personal taste. The expansion of the array of performance possibilities also invited the dancers to explore their technical and artistic limits. It invited them to discover and develop new skills to embody dance qualities in more and more versatile ways.

In addition to qualitative performance alternatives, the deep structure as basis for composition stretched the embodiment possibilities. This is how classical ballet was multiply-embodied with the kinesphere images of the body and its movements.

dancers' experiences, from obstacles to revelations and stretching ballet's cultural borders

Overall, the dancers' experiences while multiply embodying ballet could be divided into three different kinds: obstacles to experiencing in a new way, revelations and stretching artistic limits. Intending with imagery and acting on it in embodiment was recognised by dancers as having the capacity to change their experiences of dancing from ones described as obstacles to experiencing in a new way to ones of personal revelations and change.

An obstacle was a momentary or more persistent inability to engage with the dance in an open-ended way; that is, to experience the movement in a new manner. In addition to some general resistance to change in a ballet class (governed by traditional aesthetics), some dancers were first tied by their persisting performance habits and the way they had learned to experience ballet. Ballet dancers are traditionally asked to verify their dancing through outside evaluation, mirrors and the teacher's corrections. The dancers were not always used to "listening" to their own experiences and communicating them to the group. During their years of training, dancers may also have created an habitual response to ballet which they were either unable (at first) or resistant to give up. For some dancers, feelings of artificiality and pretentiousness first obscured their senses until revelations began to happen. The two experiences excluded each other. It is not possible to feel artificial and at the same time be surprised by a new creative performance solution that feels artistically motivated.

obstacles

Revelations were experiences that in one way or another informed the dancers and facilitated performance in a way that felt significant to the dancer. Revelations were accompanied by aesthetic feeling. Dancers commented with words like 'soul in the performance', 'fascinating experience', ' dance-like', 'playful', among others. The revelations were characterised by spontaneity and indeterminacy. It was not possible to anticipate the dancer's reaction to the image at a certain time. Intention with an image guided but did not determine the dancer's experience and performance. The dancer had to embody the image and react to it corporeally. The same image could affect a different kind of experience with repeated explorations. Revelations appeared from the haze of immediate perception and lived experience, taking the dancer by surprise. Revelations heightened the dancers' awareness of their body and its movements and facilitated performance of the vocabulary.

revelations

Dancers might become aware of the need to change their position

I felt the need to turn the elbow down

or through feeling the twists in the body, adjust their positions, or release unnecessary tension in the body during dancing. Facilitation also appeared as a feeling of easiness, lightness or support. In many instances and with varying images - for instance, the planes in the icosahedral kinesphere model - dancers reported improved balance.

stretching ballet's borders

The open-ended use of the images invited the dancers, not only to be versatile in traditional performance qualities, but to experiment beyond the generally accepted way of performing in ballet. During an experiment a new way of performing could be found, which in one way or another created a tension between the established manner of performance and the new emerging one.

Giving the dancer freedom of choice in class is unusual behaviour in a ballet teacher. Implicitly, we tend to believe in one "right" or "correct" way of execution, that suggested by the teacher and backed up by the tradition as we understand it. Already the making of personal decisions in open interpretation had caused mixed feelings in the dancers. Dancers' nervous giggles in class indicated this tension when I suggested that an interpretation with the image could be different in the same movement when it is performed to the other side. Stretching the rules was experienced by some to be even more dangerous. Dancers differed in the amount of deviation from the established conventions that they could tolerate or enjoy. What was acceptable to one dancer made someone else feel uneasy.

interpretations and co-authoring in ballet class

The interpretational products in classes echoed the dancers' experiences. My aim as teacher was to promote open interpretation, one that varied according to the dancer or even different performances by the same dancer, each artistically intended. A form-breaking interpretation came about when the dancer creatively discovered new ways of performance that evolved from the tradition or when the dancers stretched their previous understanding of ballet.

The dancers' creative discovery and versatility in performing was further stretched through co-authoring tasks inviting them to create new dance material with the deep structures of ballet. Dancers were asked to mix ballet with their individual movements (mixing vocabularies), alter the traditional form in some fashion (altering) or give the movement a new surface form through its deep structure (open work). One of the altering tasks was based on the kinesphere model, changing ballet combinations from octahedron to icosahedron and cube form. The end results showed similarities in the change; the cube for instance throwing the octahedral balance overboard, flowing from one off-balance line to another. Within similarities, each task left leeway for dancers' individual solutions.

In the embodiment of dance, the dancer as a human being plays an important part. Often the dancer is considered to be the choreographer's material or instrument. Different mediums have different kinds of materials. It is different to be paint in a painting and to be a dancer in a dance. The paint does not experience what it is to be artistically meaningful - to be paint in a particular way in a painting. But a dancer does experience the meaningfulness of becoming in the dance and becoming the dance, as the dancers' comments in the workshops indicate. My explanation of the findings are informed by Csordas' (1994) vision of cultural flux as embodiment, transcendence beyond received cultural norms in experience and objectification; that is, shared cultural understanding, as well as to the dancers' experience of motivating their own culture of dance (Fiske, 1990).

interpreting the dancers' experiences and comments in workshops

The dancers' comments (including obstacles, revelations and stretching limits) exemplify their experiences of motivating variously their dance culture and its coded vocabulary. In this case the dance/ballet is seen as a culture, a community of persons creating and maintaining aesthetic norms and practices. Because the dancer embodies the dance in his body and with his senses, the embodiment is one of representing, and at the same time, living the evolving codes of the dance, semiotic and phenomenal at the same time.

The feeling of artificiality or pretentiousness while performing, a main obstacle, signifies a meaning that is firmly established in the tradition and repeated in such a way that it is not renewing itself. Revelations were described as indeterminate and spontaneous, bringing with them artistic motivation and informing the dancer about performance possibilities. Therefore they speak about codes-in-the-making, creativity and strong motivation. The feeling of stretching limits signifies the dancer's new potential in performance that is artistically motivated. However, in terms of the cultural environment participants suspect that change may not be readily accepted. Stretching limits breaks established norms. The dancer has to decide whether to push the culture forward or to yield to the conventions.

ballet class in flux

The principle of multiple embodiment understands ballet as evolving through representation and transcendence, with the dancer in the key position of the activity, experiencing and evaluating the change. Ballet teaching through multiple embodiment is seen as forwarding an evolving tradition rather than, as is often said, simply forwarding an existing tradition. Forwarding an evolving tradition means that the teaching and learning activities provide opportunity for the dancer's agency. In multiple embodiment, illuminating the qualities in the vocabulary open-endedly and promoting personal choice and discovery leave freedom for the dancer to explore within this opportunity. The change or renewal the dancing person initiates and communicates through his performance is dependent on his or her physical skills and artistic values and boundaries. Therefore, by acting in the culture the dancer not only evolves the art form, but at the same time tests, risks and stretches his/her artistic identity and person. The evolution of the culture and the construction of self are concurrent processes depending on each other (Csordas, 1994).

Exploration can expand this construction of the cultural/artistic self. It tested both the dancers' physical versatility as well as artistic resilience. The performers' identities were constructed alongside the aesthetic choices they became aware of and made. The dancers acted on the basis of their own perception and cultural habits. Evaluation was intrinsic to the act in the way that the person was socially/culturally/corporeally informed. The dancers acted as agents with cultural awareness and individual taste in creating the dance.

When I began this research, I was aware of the need to see ballet as an evolving art form but did not guess that teaching ballet would reveal itself to me as a cultural phenomenon and itself as in the process of artistic evolution. In my mind, evolution was the business of the art somehow separated from the classroom. The cultural collisions that began to happen early on in the workshops finally woke me up to see reality in a new way. The signals may have seemed minor at first. Giggles on my "radical" behaviours in class, resistance of various kinds and questioning, dancers' joy or scruples when facing their own creativity. These signals grew in significance as I gave the participants the time to reveal themselves. While analysing and placing the emerging data in a cultural context with Csordas' cultural phenomenology, it became evident to me how the culture is actually evolving in a subtle way right there in the classroom before our eyes and ears, within the experiences that we as participants witnessed.

bibliography

Adshead, J. (Ed.) (1988). *Dance Analysis: Theory and Practice*. London: Dance Books.

Csordas, T. J. (1994). *The Sacred Self, A Cultural Phenomenology of Charismatic Healing*. Berkeley, Los Angeles, London: University of California Press.

Fiske, J. (1990). *Introduction to Communication Studies*. London and New York: Routledge.

Forsythe, W. (1999). *Improvisation Technologies. A tool for the Analytical Dance Eye*. ZKM digital arts edition.

Jarvis, P. (1999). *The Practitioner-Researcher, Developing Theory from Practice*. San Francisco, California: Jossey-Bass Publishers.

Kostrovitskaya, V. & Pisarev, A. (1978). *School of Classical dance*. Translated by J.Baker. Moscow: Progress Publishers.

Laban, R. (1966). *Choreutics*. Ed. by Lisa Ullman. London: Macdonald and Evans.

Laban, R. & Lawrence F.C. 1974 (1947). *Effort*. London: Macdonald and Evans.

Mosston, M. & Ashworth, S. 1994 (1966). *Teaching Physical Education*. USA: Merril Publishing Co.

Preston-Dunlop, V. (1989). *Choreological Studies: A Discussion Document*. Unpublished London: Laban Centre for Movement and Dance.

Preston-Dunlop, V. (1998). *Looking at Dances, A Choreological Perspective on Choreography*. London: Verve Publishing.

Preston-Dunlop, V. (1979). *Dance is a Language, Isn't it?* London: Laban Centre for Movement and Dance.

Salosaari, P. (2001). *Multiple Embodiment in Classical Ballet, Educating the Dancer as an Agent of Change in the Cultural Evolution of Ballet*. Acta Scenica 8. Helsinki: Theatre Academy.

Sanchez-Colberg, A. (1992). *German Tanztheatre: Traditions and Contradictions, A Choreological documentation from its Roots in Ausdruckstanz to the Present*. Unpublished Doctoral Dissertation. London: Laban Centre for Movement and Dance.

Watermotor
Trisha Brown
in performance
Lois Greenfield

chapter 12
a choreological analysis of Trisha Brown's <u>Accumulation with Talking plus Watermotor for Stephen</u>

Frank Werner

the aims

This analysis focuses on the examination of the dyad language/text - movement in Trisha Brown's choreography <u>Accumulation with Talking plus Watermotor for Stephen</u>, a solo dance in honour of Stephen Petronio, performed by the choreographer at the Joyce Theater in New York City on April 9, 1996. My emphasis, however, is not to illuminate what Brown means with this dance - her principle objective is clearly stated in the title of the piece: it is meant to be an homage to Stephen Petronio. Rather, I aim to elucidate how she creates meaning(s) through the integration of movement and language/text, i.e. through the differentiated, synchronic exploration of the relations between these two elements. Moreover, I propose that she achieves this without denying a historical, diachronic dimension of her work. Resulting from this fusion are a bundle of additional meanings which have this piece transcend the idea of a traditional homage.[1]

the methodology

The fact that Trisha Brown is talking while she is dancing[2] implies a further question: Why is she dancing while talking and not dancing to music? Does she consider talking as music, or would music be an unimportant, even obstructive element within this dance? Brown's use of talking while dancing deserves a closer look at her attitude towards music.

The umbrella principle of my analysis is the choreological concept of the strands of the dance medium, as set forth by Sanchez-Colberg (1992). This concept takes a holistic, discursive, macro-structural approach to the analysis of dance and aims to incorporate its synchronic and diachronic aspects. Therefore, it

---

[1] "Homage is an expression of high regard, often a ceremonial tribute that conveys allegiance or professional respect" (Morris, 1981, p.632).

[2] In this essay, the terms 'talking/sound' and 'dancing/movement' are used interchangeably, according to the usage of these terms at the Judson Church. Moreover, I would like to emphasize that Brown is 'talking' here, as the piece is not called 'Accumulation with Speaking...'. Talking, in my view, is the equivalent of 'conversing' whereas 'speaking'' is rather a one-way activity, as in 'to make a speech'. Even if Brown is not directly conversing with her audience, she is, as I will demonstrate, indirectly interacting with them.

includes not only the study of forms and qualities of movement, but also the study of structures, methods, norms and rules specific to the dance and their interrelatedness (p.34).

Sanchez-Colberg has identified five strands to accommodate the whole range of those factors in a nexus, i.e. a web, that makes 'a dance a dance': *Body, Movement, Sound, Space and Process/Production.*

In <u>Accumulation with Talking plus Watermotor for Stephen</u>, Trisha Brown's talking is intricately intertwined with her dancing. Such is the analysis of the aspects language/text and movement - which seems primarily to hint at the strands sound and movement - with the analysis of the remaining strands. This is because dance does not happen in a vacuum; to secure the integrity of the mise-en-scène in the analysis, it is, as Patrice Pavis emphasises, necessary to preserve the 'totality of the staging':

As for the distinction between fixed signs and moveable signs (decor vs. actor, stable components vs. moveable ones, etc.), it is no longer relevant to contemporary practice (1993, p.15).

Pavis criticises a common practice of semiologists: he maintains that they follow the programme of linguists, searching for "the [semiotic] units necessary for a formal description of performance". He argues, however, that for a semiotics of performance, "it would not be any use to subdivide the continuum of performance into temporal micro-units". Rather,

it would be better to isolate an ensemble of signs forming a gestalt pattern, with overall significance instead of simply adding signs (minimal units) together (ibid.).

Pavis developed his theories for theatre performance and not for dance. Yet, he advocates a broad notion of semiology as concerned with the problem of discourse, including for example socio-semiotics and historical aspects,

without being intimidated any longer by the genre that is specifically theatre but encompassing all types of performance (ibid. p.20).

Connecting Pavis' theories with Pierre Guiraud's linguistic model of semiotic functions (1988), I will try to adapt his approach to Trisha Brown's performance. In order to do so, the strands concept, inasmuch as it shows homologies with these semiotic theories, could be regarded as a blueprint for a 'semiotics of dance'.

The scope of this essay does not allow a comprehensive investigation of all the strands; therefore I will look at them from a certain angle. In agreement with Pavis, I would argue that I have to set up my own code as an interpreter, a hermeneut, reading

a given aspect of the performance according to a freely selected code (ibid. p.17).

I have explained my hermeneutics above: I engage with this work primarily through a semiotic-structural consideration of the relationship between language/text and movement within the nexus of the strands.

Before I come to the analysis I wish to make some introductory remarks regarding the artists and the work at issue. First, I will explain Brown's 'accumulation principle', then I will describe the genesis of <u>Accumulation with Talking plus Watermotor for Stephen</u>, and eventually address Brown's relationship to talking and to music.

background to the artists
background to the work

Trisha Brown was born in 1936 in the state of Washington, USA. After participating in Graham technique and Louis Horst composition classes, she studied with José Limón and Merce Cunningham. In 1959, she went to California and started experimenting with improvisation and task-oriented choreography in the workshop of Anna Halprin, where she also met Simone Forti and Yvonne Rainer. After arriving in New York City in the early 1960s, she started to take Robert Dunn's choreography courses at the Merce Cunningham Studio which had been initiated by John Cage (see Brown 1975, pp.20/22). The course continued until the spring 1962, immediately followed by the first 'Concert of Dance' at the Judson Church. The concerts became a regular feature and the group, of which Trisha Brown together with Rainer, Forti, Steve Paxton, David Gordon, Lucinda Childs and others was a co-founder, began to call itself 'Judson Dance Theater' (see Dunn 1989, pp.10-13). The group disbanded in 1964 and Brown continued her work as an independent choreographer. In 1970, she founded her own company with which she has performed worldwide.

Stephen Petronio was the first male dancer of the Trisha Brown Company (1979 - 86). In 1984, Petronio founded the Stephen Petronio Company (Stephen Petronio Company 1997). Brown's performance of <u>Accumulation with Talking plus Watermotor for Stephen</u> at a Joyce Theater benefit-gala in New York City on April 9, 1996, was a homage to ten years of Petronio's work as an independent choreographer. Brown has always been very supportive of Petronio's choreographic career and can be regarded as his mentor. In this capacity, she was asked to perform at the gala.[3]

The title of the work I am analysing here is actually composed of three separate titles stemming from three different choreographies: <u>Accumulation</u> (1971), <u>Accumulation with Talking</u> (1973), <u>Accumulation with Talking plus Water Motor</u> (1979) culminating, eventually, in <u>Accumulation with Talking plus Water Motor for Stephen</u> (1996). As one can observe from this genesis, the title of the homage to Petronio is itself an accumulation. The original <u>Accumulation</u>, as Brown says while dancing[4] was four and a half minutes long to the Grateful Dead's 'Uncle John's Band'. She describes her principle, based on mathematical systems of repetition, as follows:

> *Movement two was added and one and two were repeated eight times. Then movement three was added and one, two, three were repeated, eventually bringing into play the entire body* (Brown, 1975, p. 26).

Banes adds that

> *As the piece progresses, succinct gestures - a twist of the pelvis, a bend of the knee, a turn of the head… a lift of the leg - are strung onto the end of the accumulation, and sometimes sandwiched into earlier sections of the progression* (1987, p. 82).

Thus applying the format of a structured improvisation, the original solo was performed in one place, using simple everyday gestures as a point of departure (see Blackwood, 1979). A later version of the same piece and principle was, as

Trsha Brown *Lois Greenfield*

Brown also mentions in her dance, fifty-five minutes long and in silence (Brown, 1996).

Already in 1973, Brown thought that

> she had mastered the problem of keeping the movement clear in the face of relentless repetition (Banes, 1987, p.82)

and, complicating her problem, started talking while dancing. In Accumulation with Talking, she made remarks about performing the dance that she was performing; she also integrated autobiographical remarks and individual addresses to the audience, depending on where she was showing her piece.

In 1978, Brown choreographed a two and a half minute solo for herself, called Water Motor. Banes describes this dance as

> a syncopated listing of gestures and positions, [evoking] images like the prow of a boat slicing the water, diving, falling; at times in seemingly impossible combinations...... Often, Brown's body looks as if it is gleefully going in two directions at once. Water Motor is a dance that pries open Brown's logical systems to make room for exquisite disorder. (ibid. p. 91).

Brown thus seemed to break away from the mathematical systems of her accumulation pieces, which happened more or less in one place, and to indulge in metaphorical movement, using all the space she needed to explore her motions. However, she did not regard Water Motor as a creation that was irreconcilable with her earlier work, namely with her accumulation pieces. Rather, she took their difference as a challenge and choreographed Accumulation with Talking plus Water Motor (1979), integrating 'logical systems' and 'exquisite disorder', according to Banes.

Brown's choreographic imagination, her way of working and her relationship to music were considerably moulded by the experiments of the Judson Church group. These group experiments were, as mentioned before, initiated by the ideas and the teaching of John Cage and Robert Dunn. Neither of them was a dancer or choreographer, both were composer-musicians. Cage, and later Dunn, however, taught choreography classes at the Merce Cunningham Studio (Dunn, 1989, p.10). Dunn promoted, as Marni Mahaffay - another participant at his course - said,

> Cage's precept that any sound is valid as part of music, that any movement is valid as part of a dance... And that continuum of sound and of movement extended, critically, to silence and its correlate, stillness... The possibilities came out limitless (quoted in Banes. 1983, p.8, my emphasis).

---

3 Oral communication by Robert Russo, Managing Director of the Stephen Petronio Company, July 1997.

4 The full transcript of Trisha Brown's talking is included in the appendix.

The Judson Dance Theater literally experimented with a 'democratic' use of (stage) space, of dancers (i.e. they worked with trained and untrained dancers), of body parts and movement (i.e. not neglecting any part of the body, and not relying on canonised dance techniques), and - with a non-hierarchical, democratic concept of music.

Trisha Brown's definition of music has been as all-inclusive as Cage's. At her choreographic outset, however, Brown was very reluctant and careful in her use of conventional music. Only by avoiding the 'tyranny of music' could she find her own movement style:

> I could not make movement to music without having the movement affected by the music. If I had worked with music, I would never have developed my movement vocabulary to include polyrhythmic structures in the body. You can't do the rhythmic structures and intricate moves if you have to be attentive to the beat (quoted in Sommer, 1993, p.6).

Neither wanting movement to narrate the tempos, dynamics or textures of music nor the music to dictate movement choices, Brown

> came to love the sound of movement - how you look at movement when you do not have music telling you what you are seeing (ibid.).

Brown's movement creates its own musicality:

> Rhythms and pulses are amplified by the sounds of dancers dancing - the symphony of breath, heartbeat and footfall (ibid.).

From this we can conclude that 'the sound of movement' as well as talking are legitimate ways for Brown of using sound in performance; she does not distinguish between those sounds and music in a more traditional sense.

strand analysis: body Trisha Brown's dance is, as I mentioned before, a solo performance. Her performing body is that of a female dancer. Brown's femininity is emphasised by her open, long hair and by the stylised costume she wears: it is an elegantly plain, light grey, long-sleeved, loose-fitting combination of overall and unitard that blurs the actual forms of her body. The costume emphasises the fluidity of her movement, particularly when she is dancing in the flamboyant watermotor-mode.[5] Yet, it does not attract the audience's attention when she moves in the calm accumulation-mode:[6] since the movement in this mode happens more or less in one place, the costume hangs loosely on her, letting her movement still look fluid but also unobtrusive. The costume thus has a defining role, contributing to movement qualities. It has not been designed for this particular performance; Brown has already worn it in earlier versions of Accumulation with Talking plus Watermotor (see photograph in Goldberg 1991, p.5).

The treatment of the body in this dance is complex: Brown

sometimes uses it as a reified mechanism, only to modify it in the next moment into a sensuous organism whose physicality is not denied. As I will show, it is also used as a social unit, portraying aspects of social order, as a political unit, portraying power structures, as a personal unit, referring to autobiographical matters, and as a gendered body. The treatment of the body in this piece is closely connected to Brown's movement, her choreographic process and the topic of abstraction and expression in her dance. I will return to this issue when I come to the discussion of the *movement* strand and in my conclusion.

Referring to what Guiraud calls the *emotive function*, and what could be described as the relation between the message (i.e. the performance) and the emitter (i.e. the performer), it is important to highlight Brown's *performance persona*; her influence as a performer is clearly stated: it is not any-body but Brown's body that dances this homage of a mentor to her protegé. It is difficult to imagine that this particular homage with its intricate interweaving of language/text and movement, its autobiographical accounts and references to her relationship with Stephen Petronio[7] could be performed by someone other than Brown. The audience is well aware of these circumstances.

---

[5] See Banes' aforementioned depiction of Brown's movement in Water Motor. I will define this mode and the accumulation-mode later within my comments on the movement strand.

[6] See my comments on Brown's Accumulation above.

[7] For a full transcript of Brown's talking, see appendix.

When Trisha Brown starts her dancing, she simultaneously says:

> *This is an improvisation.*

Thus, she is immediately setting up a code regarding the nature of her performance, and at the same time makes it clear to the audience that a performance is taking place as such. What we get to see, however, is a specific kind of improvisation, because it is structured according to the two dances Brown is interspicing: in an *'accumulation-mode'* and a *'watermotor-mode'*.

Movement in the *accumulation-mode* generally happens in one place (there is the odd step forward, backward or sideward, but Brown always returns from there to a parallel standing position) and is based on gesture. These gestures are cool, intelligent concatenations - their mathematical system has been explained above - of pedestrian everyday motions without any ostensible formal, conventional expressivity; they could be described as a list of abstract gestures. The signature gesture is the rotation of the right wrist, thumb extended. Goldberg suggests various meanings that the sign-referent relation of this gesture could evoke:

> *Brown replaced the finger with the thumb as the indexical piece of human anatomy. The incongruity of a pointing thumb evokes a plethora of connotations that seem relevant to the dance's polemics: thumbing your nose, thumbing a ride, thumbing to point out the particularly human evolutionary difference that distinguishes homo sapiens (Goldberg, 1991, p.7).*

So what are Brown's "dance polemics"? While Goldberg leaves this question open, I would argue with Carroll and Banes that

> each movement is a studied omission of the movement qualities found in ballet and modern dance (Carroll and Banes 1982, p.40),

and add that it is as well a studied admission of everyday movement into the dance canon, emphasising the non-hierarchical Cagean position that any movement is valid as part of a dance. On the meta-linguistic level, that is to say that those movements were anything but mere abstract bodily motions. "They were", as Carroll and Banes state,

> actions, reframings whose implicit disavowal of the traditional qualities [annot.: and hierarchies] of dance movement enabled them to be understood as polemical (p.40).

Brown's polemics also hint at a more general issue: can a task-oriented, reductionist 'movement per se' - approach lead to abstract gestures without any expressive or representational connotations? Or can dance just not help being expressive because the human body is intrinsically expressive? Carroll argues that what gets expressed in dance in the narrower sense of expression is either an emotion, or some other anthropomorphic quality, like wit, charm or sentimentality (see Carroll, 1979, pp.97/98). But, in his view, there is also a broader sense of expression, one that is very close to the notion of communication. He concludes that post-modern choreographers

> have drained expression from their choreography in the narrowest sense of expression... but certainly not in the broadest sense, that is, the expression of ideas (ibid. p.99)

and adds:

> Because of the historically-sedimented nature of each dance, it is hard to imagine how an avant-gardist could fail to be expressive in the discursive sense insofar as each deviation from tradition will imply (if only negative) some conception of dance (ibid. p.102).

While Brown says that during the performance of Accumulation, what went through her mind was,

> This is all there is (1975, p. 26)

asserting a reductionist intention, she nevertheless accepts that her dances are expressive in a discursive sense:

> ...I tried to make the body be a stick figure..., but it's impossible. I accept the inevitability of connotational spill-off. But I do not set up connotations (Goldberg, 1986, p.160).

It is out of this tension of a choreographic practice striving for

---

8 Gestures are identified by Argyle as one of the main non-verbal signs (1972, p.249).

reduction and abstraction on the one hand, and the realisation that dance is inevitably expressive on the other, that Brown's discursive polemic arises.

The same is valid for the *watermotor-mode* (see Banes's depiction of <u>Water Motor</u> above) which contains more outgoing movement without spatial restraints, virtuosically involving the whole body, extended limbs and a released spine.

Summarising, it could be stated that Brown's body is engaged in movement that is, in the *accumulation-mode*, treated as a reified mechanism, whereas in the *watermotor-mode*, her physicality is not denied. The body is used as a socio-political unit, polemically criticising traditional movement hierarchies and power structures in dance through the omission of movement qualities found in ballet and modern dance and the admission of non-hierarchical everyday movement. This discursive polemic results from the tension between an abstract conceptualisation of the dance and an inevitably expressive realisation of the movement.

Brown's movement is developed from multiple sources: release-based, virtuosic dancing (especially in <u>Water Motor</u>), pedestrian movement and gestures. The movement in the two modes is not integrated, but juxtaposed. Brown states:

> I put all these movements together without transitions. I do not promote the next movement with a preceding transition and, therefore, I do not build up to something. If I do build up, I might end up with another build up. I often return to a neutral standing position between moves; it is for me a way of measuring where I have been and where I am going.
> (1975, p.35).

This is precisely what Brown does when she finishes a movement sequence in *watermotor-mode*: she returns into a parallel standing position in order to start with movement in the *accumulation-mode*. Her statement hints also at the multiple temporal structure of this performance: there are various build ups in both modes. However, the development of the movement is not linear; as Brown states above, she concludes one build up with another build up, not really ending the previous sequence. The rhythm of the movement is organic, i.e. following the internal logic of the piece and its phrasing. Brown highlights this internal counting that does not seem to follow any ostensible external logic by saying numbers in irregular intervals, mocking at a metric, conventional musical counting:

> Three,... One. Several... Four... four, remember three... forget three...[9]

strand analysis: sound

I have illustrated Trisha Brown's relationship to music and talking above. In <u>Accumulation with Talking plus Watermotor for Stephen</u>, she uses a whole range of sounds, which she might also consider as music. There is coherent talking and silence, and we can also hear paralinguistic effects of her voice and sounds produced by her costume. Furthermore, mostly through laughter, the audience participates in the creation of sound.

Brown's talking is, as is her movement, a structured improvisation. For example, she fuses paradigmatic autobiographical glimpses[10] with syntagmatic comments regarding the respective occasion. In the piece at issue she refers to Stephen Petronio and a gala-audience, skillfully interweaving literary devices as, for example, an alliteration:

> This is a ga-la. La, la, la première fois - the first time I foisted my foibles on an audience, this dance was four and a half minutes long... The first time I met Stephen Petronio, he was six and a half feet tall, black of hair, backstage at another gala (see appendix).

It is interesting to observe that most of Brown's narration takes place in the *accumulation-mode*. When Brown moves in the *watermotor-mode*, she is only talking 'intrinsically' (i.e. about the dance or about what she is currently doing). One reason for this might be that it is easier for her to talk while she is in the calm *accumulation-mode*, which with its rigid mathematical

Trisha Brown *Lois Greenfield*

structure, is a rather mechanical, automatic activity. In this mode, she can concentrate better on saying more complex phrases. Another reason, however, might be that she does not want her audience to be distracted by flamboyant moves, but rather to focus on what she says. This is also a link to Brown's use of space, an issue I will refer to later. Furthermore, an interesting observation can be made when we compare Brown's usage of the *accumulation-* *and watermotor-modes* with the structure of recitative and aria in opera. As I have pointed out, most of her narration takes place in the calm *accumulation-mode*, which could therefore be seen as a kind of recitative, or 'Sprechgesang', a

---

[9] See appendix for the full transcript of Brown's talking.

[10] Like when she says, "My father died in between the making of this move and this move", a phrase she used similarly in her original version of <u>Accumulation with Talking</u> (Brown 1975, p.40).

> style of singing which is more closely related in pitch and rhythm to
> dramatic speech than to song (*Westrup and Harrison*, 1959, p.534).

Brown's elegant, lyrical watermotor-mode with its intrinsic
utterances, could then be compared to a song or an aria, which is

> opposed to the declamatory recitative... [intensifying] the dramatic
> situations (ibid. p.31).[11]

On the non-verbal aspects of Brown's speech, i.e. its
paralinguistic and prosodic features (see Argyle, p.251),
Brown's voice quality, pitch, stress and particularly her juncture
patterns (pauses and timing), all amplified by a small
microphone pinned at chest height on her costume, contribute
considerably to the effect that her intersplicing of dancing and
talking has on her audience:

> I know the timing for speaking in relation to moving that will make the
> audience laugh (quoted in Brunel, 1986/87, p.66).

Brown refers here to what Guiraud calls the injunctive function.
This function denotes the relation between the message (i.e. the
performance) and the receiver (here: the audience), which aims
at getting a response from the audience. Brown applies this
function very successfully as she stimulates her audience to
frequent laughter, which is sometimes stifled, sometimes loud.

On the meta-linguistic level (what Guiraud dubs metalinguistic
function; that is, the relation between the message (i.e. the
performance) and the code (here: a structured improvisation)
we can maintain what Carroll and Banes stated in regard to
movement: Brown's non-hierarchical integration of sound,
respectively talking, gives her work the character of a polemical
comment as it infers an

> implicit disavowal of the traditional qualities (p.40).

Sound is therefore treated in order to set moods (injunctive
function) and temporal structures as a cue for the duration of

sequences (in *watermotor-* or *accumulation-mode*). Movement and sound are integrated, reiterating the thematic content of the performance, and reinforcing the choreographic structures.

Trisha Brown is performing at the Joyce Theater in New York City, a conventional proscenium theatre. She does not use stage properties or décor. The lighting is a bright white wash that remains unchanged throughout the performance. Brown starts, finishes, and although she travels a lot, always returns to centre stage in the course of the performance. This makes her use of stage space conventional as well. Brown's mise-en-scène maintains the division between her as a performer and the audience as observers. The audience, nevertheless, participates in the performance as a whole. Pavis emphasises the necessity to follow the process of reception by a given public in situ, quoting Nadin who states that

> anyone watching a performance does not carry out semiotic analysis in the theoretic sense, although the processes through which he may see, hear and feel become the processes of evaluation and those are always processes of a semiotic nature (p.17).

In this light, I will have to look at the establishment of meaning through the participation of performer and audience. Guiraud points out that

> linguistic communication uses not only gestures but also space......
> thus the distance that we place between ourselves and the person we are talking to [annot.: respectively communicating with] (p.88).

This condition, which is described by E.T. Hall (1982) as proxemics, in itself constitutes signs.

First, I will examine the proxemic relationship between Brown and her audience. She maintains, as mentioned above, the division between herself and her audience, giving them no control over the onstage event. This distance, described by Hall as a "public distance" (pp.123 ff.), has the effect that

> [for an actor] the subtle shades of meaning conveyed by the normal voice are lost as are the details of facial expression and movement. Not only the voice but everything else must be exaggerated or amplified. Much of the nonverbal part of the communication shifts to gestures and body stance (ibid. p.125).

Hall depicts here a general performance problem which could be characterised as the 'loss of small detail'[12]. In regard to sound/voice, Brown makes up for this loss by using the aforementioned small microphone. In terms of gesture/movement, she neglects non-verbal signals like facial

---

[11] The observation of this structural homology becomes even more interesting when seen in context with Brown's 1986 choreography for the opera 'Carmen', directed by Lina Wertmüller, her choreographed versions of Monteverdi's opera 'L'Orfeu' (1999) and Sciarrino's opera 'Luci mie Traditrici' (2001).

[12] Apt title of a work by American choreographer William Forsythe

expressions in favour of gestures. Moreover, the fact that most of Brown's narration, as I pointed out before, takes place in the gestural *accumulation-mode*, implies that she takes these communicative difficulties caused by distance into account: she does not want her audience to be distracted by flamboyant moves (in *watermotor-mode*) that could blur her 'message' in the distance. Thus, she remains in the calm *accumulation-mode* while talking so that her audience can focus on what she says ñ verbally and non-verbally.

Another important feature of proxemics is the orientation of the performer towards the audience, i.e. the angle at which Brown performs in relation to the audience (see Argyle, p.247). She sees her accumulation pieces as 'object-like dances' and describes a section from <u>Primary Accumulation</u> (1972) as follows:

> The phrase is repeated until a 360 degree turn is achieved, revealing all
> sides of the dance/dancer in the last two minutes of the dance (1975, p.27).

This description is interesting, because Brown, in the piece at issue, is changing her orientation regularly throughout the performance when she returns to her neutral standing position in *accumulation-mode*, thus marking out a one and a quarter circle and emphasising the object-like character of the dance. This, again, hints at the abstract conceptualisation of this dance.

There is, however, another important proxemic feature in this performance: Brown dances, as the title of the dance implies, in honour of Stephen Petronio, and refers verbally to him, giving a short account of their relationship[13]. Thus, although Petronio is not on stage during the performance, he is still 'there' as the absent referent of this performance. This 'virtual' proxemic distance hints at Guiraud's referential function as the 'basis of all communication'. This function

> defines the relations between the message [the performance] and the object
> to which it refers [in this case: Petronio] (p.6).

Through the referential use of her verbal signs, Brown makes it clear why she is performing at this particular occasion. Here, it seems to be important to link what I said above in regard to Brown's performance persona to the 'audience persona', because the audience is not an ordinary audience: rather, it is an invited audience at a benefit-gala. It consists of highly influential people: politicians, lobbyists, journalists, corporate executives, admirers - and sponsors.

> A benefit is not just a performance with a party attached; it is a business
> operation (1990, p.54),

points out Mazo, emphasising the economical relevance of benefit-galas. A benefit-gala is an opportunity to gain publicity, to woo potential new sponsors, and to improve the budget, as U.S. dance companies rely heavily on their income from galas (see Mazo, p.54). Since Brown thus addresses an audience of benevolent cognoscenti, she can be sure that her diachronic references to Petronio are generally understood.

The structure of the choreographic process is, as I have demonstrated, improvisational, both in regard to sound and movement. The process is partly revealed, as Trisha Brown comments on her performance while moving, explaining intrinsic features of her dance:

> Unfortunately for me, I don't have the preparation for the next move...
> [she starts movement in watermotor-mode]. That was approximate.
> That was passion (see appendix).

Yet, she does not aim to disclose everything:

> I also use quirky, personal gestures, things that have specific meaning to
> me but probably appear abstract to others. I may perform an everyday
> gesture so that the audience does not know whether I have stopped dancing
> or not and, carrying that irony further, I seek to disrupt their expectations
> by setting up an action to travel left and then cut right at the last
> moment... (Brown, 1975, p.35).

This statement echoes my comments on abstraction and expression and hints at what Guiraud calls the phatic function. This function describes how signs affirm, maintain or halt a communication (see pp.7/8). As Brown continuously builds up movement sequences in order to conclude them with other build ups, she could stop her performance almost at anytime. Thus she has absolute control over the setting up and ending of the communication between her and the audience[14]. The phatic function, as Guiraud highlights, plays an important part at

> solemn occasions... in which the content of the communication is less
> important than the fact of being there (p.8).

This gala, celebrating the tenth anniversary of Petronio's independent work as a choreographer, can be regarded as a "solemn occasion" and the mere fact that Trisha Brown, worldwide acknowledged as an outstanding exponent of American contemporary dance, is present on stage, is important as such (e.g. as a recognition of the relevance of Petronio's work). However, Brown is not just 'present' but she is performing. This is how she 'means' with her dance: Brown transcends a phatic application of her verbal and non-verbal signs, making extensive use of the meta-linguistic, referential, injunctive and emotive functions of her communication.

The strands are, as I have demonstrated, intricately interwoven. Although the movement material is juxtaposed, the overall impression of the performance is not one of disintegration.

---

[13] See the last paragraph of the transcript (see appendix).

[14] This absolute control is emphasised when Brown, concluding her performance, looks into the wings and, by raising her left arm and saying "Now!" to the stage manager, is giving the signal to turn down the lights.

Neither of integration. I would rather argue that Brown's production is a synthesis on the basis of a contrapuntal use of the strands in the nexus, particularly regarding the dyad language/text and movement.

an 'intelligent dance'

In the course of this analysis, I have delineated certain homologies between Guiraud's model of semiotic functions and the structure of the strands concept. I have also demonstrated how the synchronic interplay of the strands is linked to diachronic references Trisha Brown makes considering her own biography and Stephen Petronio. The tension of abstract conceptualisation and expressive realisation gives rise to a polemic that also includes diachronic features: Carroll and Banes describe this polemic as an

> implicit disavowal of traditional qualities (p.40, my emphasis).

Pavis hints at another parallel set of structures between the strands concept and his semiotic model. Both concepts are concerned with the discourse (or the "totality") of staging, with a holistic approach to a performance text:

> Semiology is concerned with the discourse of staging, with the way in which the performance is marked out by the sequence of events, by the dialogue and the visual and musical elements. It investigates the organization of the 'performance text'; that is, the way in which it is structured and divided (1990),

The nexus of the strands could therefore be compared to what Pavis calls the 'score' or the 'spectacle text' (p.18) of a performance, fusing diachronic and synchronic perspectives. Pavis admits that

> the advent of structuralism has confirmed the tendency to dismiss research into the origins… of theatrical forms, in order to concentrate on the internal and synchronic functioning of the system of the performance (ibid.).

Therefore, he recommends a

> return to History in full force, in an attempt to go beyond the Saussurian opposition… between 'social system, independent of the individual' and 'individual act of will and intelligence' (ibid. p.26).

In this light we could see how Brown, as Banes affirms, is taking the issue of the "intelligent dancing body to new heights". Even without overt feminist rhetoric, the sheer complexity of Brown's task in <u>Accumulation with Talking plus Water Motor…</u>

> easily stakes out a space for women as intellectual artists on a par with men.

Thus, Brown's performance has also a historico-political dimension which, next to its synchronic functioning, cannot be denied. Her performance can be seen as a

> site of political transformation in the artworld itself (Banes, 1996, p.37).

dance and the performative

From this, it becomes clear that the performance at issue is more than a mere homage to Stephen Petronio. Through the investigation of the dyad language/text and movement, I have shown that Trisha Brown's intersplicing of verbal and non-verbal articulations is a process of humorous, virtuosic, intricate meaning making. The contrapuntal use of dances (in *accumulation-* and *watermotor-mode*) and diverse 'story-lines' (next to an homage to Stephen Petronio, autobiographical, political and self-referential accounts) gives the work an immensely rich texture and makes us perceive it as an 'intelligent dance'.

transcript of
Accumulation With Talking Plus Watermotor For Stephen

Choreography: Trisha Brown
Lighting Design: Ken Tabachnik and Spencer Brown
Costume: Nancy Graves

Danced by Trisha Brown in honour of Stephen Petronio
(The Joyce Theater, New York City, April 9, 1996)

(Curtain up)
"This is an improvisation. Three, you're looking at - 35 years of dance ideas. All of them trying to get out of my mouth at the same time. With a word I learned from Stephen Petronio in #6 (sounds). One. Several. Calm down. Go for precision. What happened? My God, I'm in another dance! (Sounds). Four. Like, a question in my mind is: What do you want? Form or content? Law and order - or erotics? My father died in between the making of this move and this move. Unfortunately for me, I don't have the preparation for the next move. That was approximate. That was passion. The sound of. What was that? I started talking and dancing at the same time. Four. Because I found I liked the fact - that I could not keep track of my dancing - while talking - and vice versa. This is a ga-la. La, la, la première fois - the first time I foisted my foibles on an audience, this dance was four and a half minutes long to the Grateful Dead's "Uncle John's Band". Those were the days, my dears. That was an old-fashioned breast thwack, complete with heart quench. The next time - four, remember three - I performed this dance, forget three, it was fifty-five minutes long and in silence. Did I say that before?
The first time I met Stephen Petronio, he was six and a half feet tall, black of hair, backstage at another gala. Soon after, I invited him to join the company. The verb should be "nabbed". And it's fairly difficult to be a choreographer in this country, when you are neither emerging nor established. It's a very long trail. Many don't make it. Keep going, Stephen. When I asked Merce Cunningham, how did he do it, he said: 'One step at a time'. Now!"
(Lights go down)

Brown, Trisha	Accumulation	Brown	1971
	Accumulation with Talking	Brown	1973
	Water Motor	Brown	1978
	Accumulation with Talking plus Watermotor	Brown	1979
	Accumulation with Talking plus Watermotor for Stephen	Brown	1996

Argyle, M. (1972). Non-verbal Communication in Human Social Interactions. In Robert A. (ed.) *Non-Verbal Communication.* (Cambridge: Cambridge University Press).

Banes, S. (1983). *Democracy's Body, Judson Dance Theater 1962-1964.* Ann Arbor, Michigan: UMI Research Press.

Banes, S. (1987). *Terpsichore in Sneakers.* Middletown, Connecticut: Wesleyan Paperback.

Banes, S. (1996). Feminism and American Postmodern Dance. *Ballet International/Tanz Aktuell,* June 1996.

Blackwood, M. (1979). *Making Dances: 7 Post-Modern Choreographers.* Video film with excerpts of works by and interviews with Trisha Brown and others. New York: Blackwood Films.

Brown, T. (1975). Trisha Brown, A Profile. In Trisha Brown, Lise Brunel, Babette Mangolte, Guy Delahaye (eds.) (1987) *L'atelier des choréographes - Trisha Brown.* Paris: Éditions Bougé.

Brown, T. (1996). *Accumulation With Talking Plus Watermotor For Stephen.* Video recording of the benefit-gala at the Joyce Theater, New York City, April 9, 1996. Stephen Petronio Company.

Brunel, L. (1986/87). Limitations and Expositions. Interviews Lise Brunel/Trisha Brown, May 1986 - March 1987. In Trisha Brown, Lise Brunel, Babette Mangolte, Guy Delahaye (eds.) (1987) *L'atelier des choréographes - Trisha Brown.* (Paris: Éditions Bougé).

Carroll, N. & Banes, S. (1982). Working and Dancing: A Response to Monroe Beardsley's 'What is Going On in a Dance?'. *Dance Research Journal,* Vol.15, No.1, Fall 1982.

Carrol, N. (1979). Post-Modern Dance and Expression. In Gordon Fancher and Gerald Myers (eds.) *Philosophical Essays on Dance* (1981). New York: Dance Horizons.

Dunn, R. E. (1989). Judson Days. *Contact Quarterly,* Vol.14, No.1, Winter 1989.

Goldberg, M. (1986). Trisha Brown - All of the Person's Person Arriving. Interviews by Marianne Goldberg, August 1983 - October 1985. *The Drama Review,* T 109, Vol.30, No.1, Spring 1986.

Goldberg, M. (1991) Trisha Brown's Accumulations. *Dance Theatre Journal,* Vol.9, No.2, Autumn 1991.

Guiraud, P. (1988). *Semiology.* London: Routledge.

Hall, E. T. (1982). *The Hidden Dimension.* New York: Anchor Books.

Morris, W. (1981). *The American Heritage Dictionary of the (ed.) English Language.* Keyword homage'. Boston: Houghton Mifflin.

Pavis, P. (1993). *Languages of the Stage.* New York: Performing Arts Journal Publications.

Sanchez-Colberg, A. (1992). *German Tanztheater: Traditions and Contradictions.* A Choreological Documentation of Tanztheater from its Roots in Ausdruckstanz to the Present. Unpublished PhD-thesis. London: Laban Centre/CNAA.

Sommer, S. (1993). The Sound of Movement. *Dance Ink,* Vol.4, No.1, Spring 1993.

Stephen Petronio Company (1997). *Unpublished public relations material.* New York: Stephen Petronio Company.

Westrup, J.A. & Harrison, F.LI. (eds.) (1959). *Collins Music Encyclopedia.* Keywords 'Recitative' and 'Aria'. London and Glasgow: Collins Publishers.

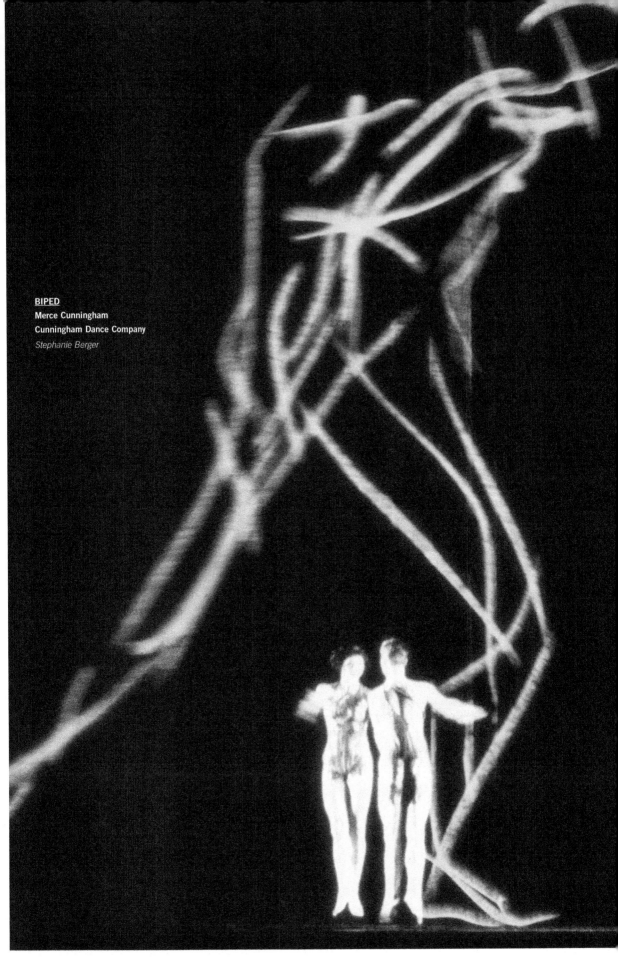

BIPED
Merce Cunningham
Cunningham Dance Company
Stephanie Berger

chapter 13
looking at dances: beyond communication to transaction
Valerie Preston-Dunlop

In October 2000, in London, I attended three performances, all of which were sold out and received standing ovations.

The first was Merce Cunningham's double bill, given at the Barbican Centre by his current company, which included his early work Summerspace(1958) and his new work BIPED (1999).

The second was Lloyd Newson's new physical theatre work can we afford this: the cost of living (2000) given with his company DV8 at the Queen Elizabeth Hall as part of the Dance Umbrella season.

The third was not a dance performance but the London premiere of a musical work The Fool by John Tavener, interpreted for theatre by Lucy Bailey and presented by "the gogmagogs" at the Queen Elizabeth Hall as part of the Tavener Festival Ikons of Light.

Tavener/Bailey, The Fool *Ivan Kyncl*

In this paper, the concepts of Roman Jacobson on communication and of Jean Jacques Nattiez on semiotic transaction in musical performance are presented, used and developed by reference to the priorities of the performative in dance as an embodied phenomenon in the three events cited above.

From the programme notes, it is clear that Cunningham did not intend to communicate anything directly to his audience but that he expected them to engage with the work in some way and to make whatever sense of it they required. He tells us that it contains ideas about unbounded stage space and extremes of time. On the other hand, Newson appeared to wish to communicate since his performers spoke directly to the spectators and his images referred to all manner of elements out there in the culture of 2000. His programme notes are enigmatic and ejaculatory but the concept of the body as a focus is reiterated.

Tavener's programme notes provide a title for each scene which tells the spectator that the topic is a perspective on the year of the Christian church. One can glean that this will be sung and played and acted. Provided are historical notes on the nature of the fool "as a timeless Orthodox religious figure." Tavener composed the score and Mother Theka wrote a brief text with a view that his idea would be, at least, approachable. Bailey's and "the gogmagogs" credits suggest innovation as a topic.

These three performances serve to inform my presentation of a position that to appreciate dance works, it is helpful to know something about communication and semiotic theories, but necessary in order to critique their value and to forefront a deeper interaction with the work than such theories can accomodate. Corporeal works demand their own kind of appreciation to which communication theory and semiotics can do no more than contribute.

Cunningham's work is not a message, message being the form in which the ideas of one set of people are transmitted to another set of people. A message is meaningful. To be efficient, it carries something that has to be said and has to be understood in as unconfusing a way as possible. A message is sent in order for the recipient to get the meaning. Clearly this concept is an absurd way to start looking at Cunningham's works since he makes no attempt to embody meanings at all.[1] However, some audience members will see meanings in his dances, they will imagine meanings, even believe that Cunningham has put "their" meanings in to the work. A theatre sets up expectations that meaning will be present somewhere since theatre operates in a situation conducive to message sending; namely, one set of people watching and listening to another set of people who are doing something knowing that they are being observed and listened to. Both parties are aware of the situation and one party, the performers, spend a great deal of effort getting the performance right, that is, in a state to be watched. The question is, is it created and rehearsed in order that the watching generates understanding (which is just the purpose of a lecture) or, is it created to achieve something else, something that is particular to art works, and more particularly, to works of corporeal theatre art?

When I give a lecture, in order to succeed in getting my

message across I use a medium, probably words, intonation, pace and pause, visual aids, gestures, in an organised and coherent manner conforming to codes of interpersonal exchange and language. Through my sound, my images and gestures, I refer to topics, events, or people which the audience recognise. If I refer to things they do not recognise, or use [a] language unfamiliar to them or a manner of presentation that does not conform to the norms, efficient communication breaks down.

Purposely, just such broken down "lectures" were given by the Dadaists in Zurich in 1916 in the Cabaret Voltaire in order to cause disorder and disarray and thereby confront convention. On one evening, poetry readings were advertised and read by three actors in three different languages: concurrently, accompanied by abusive gestures, in slow motion, reading the text backwards, one reader with a waste paper basket on her head, another with his back to the audience, a third who disappeared under the piano. The result was chaotic abuse and confusion from the audience who felt misled, did not understand, had their conventions and value systems confronted. Some people loved it, laughed and applauded, while others demanded a refund. The organisers, in particular Tristan Tzara, writing in his diary, considered the event a huge success because it succeeded in getting the audience to listen, to engage, to react, to interact, to question, to be annoyed (Richter, 1965). Tzara was presenting a performative art evening, one so designed to generate a negotiation between all parties, not an entertainment whereby one party does all the work and the other sits back. Nor was it in lecture form in order for its content to be fully understood. All the requirements of conventional communication were purposely disrupted at the Cabaret Voltaire. And yet something was very definitely aroused. An event was experienced.

For such an experience to occur, Tzara had put in place an almost identical situation to that required by conventional communication; namely, senders and receivers in a shared space and time with an event in a medium. But, instead of conforming to conventions and culturally agreed codes, he played with conventions, disrupted them and formed them in new ways.

ruptures of communication

KARAWANE

jolifanto bambla ô falli bambla

grossiga m'pfa habla horem

égiga goramen

higo bloiko russula huju

hollaka hollala

anlogo bung

blago bung

blago bung

bosso fataka

ü üü ü

schampa wulla wussa ólobo

hej tatta gôrem

eschige zunbada

wulubu ssubudu uluw ssubudu

tumba ba- umf

kusagauma

ba - umf

(1917)
Hugo Ball

Hugo Ball. Lautgedicht. Zürich. 1917

---

[1] That is an over simplistic statement. In his interview with Jeremy Isaacs (Loader, 1986) Cunningham states that he hopes that his work reflects contemporary culture and in that general way has the potential for meaning. But this is very different from a specific meaning embodied in a specific work.

At the next performance of the Cabaret Voltaire the poems were jibberish; they were sound poems, perfomed by Hugo Ball dressed in an extraordinary cardboard garment. The event demanded that the form of the actor's recitation be listened to, not the meaning, for the meaning was not there while the sonorous rhythms were. The audience were invited to suspend their interest in meaning and concentrate their focus on engaging with the extraordinariness of the forms being offered them. This was no message but a transactional performative event.

engagement

Each of these Dada performances demanded a different way of looking and listening, neither of which is the way required for efficient communication. And yet communication of some sort did take place. It is "of some sort" that requires attention since the art form itself (or anti-art form in the Dada case) dictates what "of some sort" might be. The three London performances cited above each require their own kind of appreciation, for each work has its own sort of [non]communication and invites a particular kind of engagement. Engaging is an active process of attending, allowing the work to draw you into its [heightened] world to experience that world directly, phenomenally. A mix of attending phenomenally and generating meaning seems to be the way of getting at the "communication of some sort" in works of performance.

Each of the works given in London contain vestiges of the Dada experiments since all three are innovative and confrontational works. How do we recognise innovation? What does innovation look, sound and feel like ? We recognise that something is new because we know what "old" looks like. "Old", in a dance theatre sense, refers to ways of doing things that are established as norms, even rules, of presenting works. That includes the codes of dance whereby we accept that certain things will be as they are, like blocked ballet shoes, tutus, auditorium behaviour, dancers' age and physique, lighting. These coded elements carry, not only themselves, but a deeper reference to the subculture from which they come. In the language of communication theory, innovation is the outcome of rupturing the metalinguistic function of creating, sending and receiving messages so that a hiatus occurs. The culture ostensibly referred to is not recognised, because newness is never there to be recognised but rather to be added to the existing base.

innovation

Knowing what "old" is depends on education and experience. It is one thing to "know" the dance codes of your immediate era and location: it is quite another to "know" both eastern and western dance codes, balletic and contemporary codes, 20th century and 19th century codes, and, more specifically, the codes created and used by individual artists. What is innovative for you may be already known by me and packed away in what I expect to see, and vice versa.

what was it in each work that struck me as innovative?

Cunningham's programme, starting as it did with one of his early works, invited comparison between it and <u>BIPED</u>. By the time he made <u>Summerspace</u>, Cunningham had already established the kind of nexus between the strands of the dance medium that he preferred, a co-existing nexus.[2] This principle of (non)connection between Morton Feldman's sound score and Cunningham's movement is in place. Rauschenberg's pointillist costumes and decor seem to integrate with the inherent lyricisms of the material. It was in <u>Rainforest</u> (1968) that Andy Warhol's helium-filled silver pillows co-existed with the dancers creating the kind of arbitrary connections that a bus, a dog and a blue sky have in the street. Cunningham's manner of generating movement material through chance methods was already established, as was his organising of it rhythmically through allowing the innate rhythm of the action material to come through and be harnessed by dictates of phrase duration. Accurate duration takes on a functional importance for Cunningham when structuring an ensemble work around co-existing movement material. In their day these ways of working were innovative, in that previously the integration of all the elements to support and underline each other was the norm. In 2000 these ways are established as a norm against which the innovations in <u>BIPED</u> can be appreciated.[3]

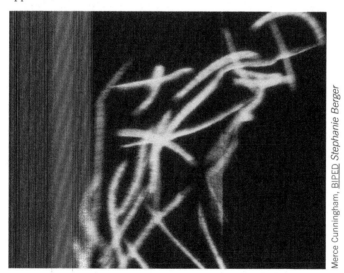

Merce Cunningham, <u>BIPED</u> *Stephanie Berger*

poietic information

The manner in which Cunningham regularly collaborated with his dancers is not changed in <u>BIPED</u> but extended. He generates the material himself through chance-based procedures. The

---

[2] He reiterates co-existence as his method in his interview for TV (Loader, 1986) but it was introduced much earlier in <u>Dance Perspectives</u> 34, 1968, ed. S.J. Cohen.

[3] Even after 40 plus years this way of working is "new" for people brought up with traditional ballet or mainstream modern dance.

material is then learned and danced by the company (rather than leading the dancers to generate the material themselves). What is new in BIPED is the tool used by Cunningham for that generation, namely a computer embodiment of dancers dancing that can be manipulated digitally to give two sets of moving figures: ground-based actual dancers and virtual figures who can travel in cyberspace.[4] Knowing about his computer generation is poietic information, that is, information on the processes employed in the making and rehearsing of the work.[5] The spectator may recognise computer use in the product itself but to know the full extent of Cunningham's use of technology, and his purpose, is only available to the public if they read their programme thoroughly, or especially, if they participate in the attendant seminars or have watched relevant dance on television. In BIPED the movement is not only created by "the new animation technology of motion capture" it is manipulated by digital means, enabling him to be more ruthless and radical in his search for movement that has no prior existence. He cannot have his corporeal dancers doing what cyberspace figures do: melt and merge, fly away and return, somersault and disintegrate. However, he can, having kept their feet on the ground and their bodies in one piece, pursue bodily fragmentation to its limits. In BIPED, that is what is new in the grounded movement material: the depth of its fragmentation and the process used to get at it.

Merce Cunningham, BIPED *Stephanie Berger*

dehumanisation

What does fragmentation do to human movement? Ultimately, it dehumanises it. Cunningham's dancers' move their limbs, head, torso as independent co-existing body parts. In this dance, they move their heads more independently of the rest of the body than ever before. Faces are uptipped; they turn, lean, twist, jump, land, with heads tilted backwards, an incredibly difficult and disorienting feat. Computer objects can do that with ease but people cannot. The natural kinetic rhythms of action and recovery are ruptured by computer manipulation.

The dancers' fragmented movement dictates disintegrated rhythms which add to the image of reification. As a former dancer, my engagement includes empathetic feeling of what it must be like to dance that material, and it was not a comfortable feeling, nor a humane one. At the end of <u>BIPED</u> the dancers looked (to me) drained.

Cunningham's well established method of collaboration with his designers through co-existence of the visual with the kinetic, continues here. What is new is the nature of the design element which is cyber spatial. The "set" includes both virtual vertical forms and occasional floating digital figures projected on to an invisible scrim. The rear virtual "wall" of the stage is black through which the actual dancers emerge. Cunningham has achieved in his designs what earth-bound dancers cannot achieve. Technology enables the co-existence of the virtual with the actual, the cyber with the terrestrial.

cyber and terrestrial space

How can we engage with his abstract, dehumanised work? Not everyone did, as discussion in the foyer revealed, but judging from the applause many could. Firstly, there is the *aesthetic* dimension.[6] This piece inspires an aesthetic response. It sets up its agenda by forefronting its medium(a) and retains that coherently and positively. It purports to carry nothing: it is itself, not a sign for something else. Its arbitrary spatial patterning appeals to the eye of anyone familiar with the abstract visual arts while at the same time bringing that eye up to date, through the cohabiting of digital bodies and phenomenal persons.[7] The uncompromising movement is softened by its co-existing sound - Gavin Bryer's score directed live from the orchestra pit by Takehisa Kosugi. The sparse density of the music enables it to occupy the same space as the dancers without impinging upon them. Its sonority and texture is softer than the dance. For me it was a simple matter to engage with it, my ear welcomed it. The music contributed to my ability to respond aesthetically to the work as a whole, to engage with "each single instant as it came along", as well as to the imageful cyber space designs of digital artists Shelley Eshkar and Paul Kaiser and shining costumes of Susanne Gallo.

aesthetic

Secondly, there is the *injunctive* element. What does the performance arouse? Possibly because the up-to-dateness of the choreography is achieved by an octogenarian, there is an element of awe, of admiration. There is no place for laughter, for tears, for argument or disgust, but a place for surprise that this creation, created to the limits of the dancers, could be made and could be danced. And a place for sheer appreciation of Cunningham's structuring skill and coherence. A few people

injunctive

---

[4] See Atlas, C. and Lockyer, B. (2000). <u>Merce Cunningham: A Lifetime in Dance</u>.

[5] Nattiez, J.J. (1990, p.17), developing the introduction of "poietics" by Jean Molino.

[6] Jacobson's understanding of the six functions in communication, of which the aesthetic is one, is discussed further later in this essay.

[7] For pure cyber space dance see Sarah Rubidge's essay in Part 2.

were aroused to criticise the austerity of the movement and the duration of the work. Too long, I heard. What did Cunningham want the performance to arouse? Just what he always has: enough attention to engage with the dancers moving in that space and time with that sound for 45 minutes and make of it just that, or more, if you wish.

performative The *performative* element[8] is more problematic in <u>BIPED</u>. What can these dancers add to what they are asked to do? Mainly, they add integrity of bodily performance, sheer stamina and grit, but the material itself makes them land heavily and sometimes appear clumsy. Cunningham gives no opportunity for a soft landing, for a rebound, no leeway for fluidity anywhere. Dancers' capacity for interpretation and personalisation of the material is out of place in a Cunningham work and here subtlety of interpretation is not required or given. Several people were heard to voice their disappointment in the company as performers, but my belief is that such movement requires inanimate performance and got it. To my eye one dancer stood out, her lithe suppleness not entirely hidden by the material, her personality not entirely negated by the work. But did Cunningham want personality and litheness? Or did I want it ?

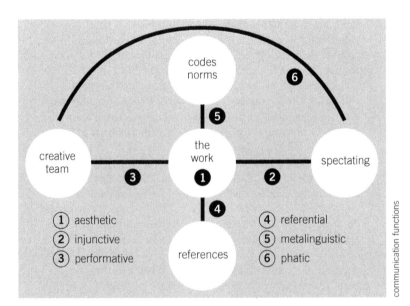

references communication functions

communication functions

referential The *referential* element is, to all intents and purposes, absent in <u>BIPED</u>. But is it ? Does it really refer to nothing but itself? Cunningham's ensemble treatment of the company and the democratic use of space act as a metaphor for his preference for a non-elitist social structure. His co-existence structure of elements refers to his belief that art and life co-exist on equal terms and haphazardly overlap and, by chance, occasionally integrate. The computer-generated flying figures and set are not inert forms. They refer to the present and future domination of the human body and person, by technology. The dance might be taken as a celebration of technology over the humane or as a

warning of things to come; that is, if you are drawn to take the
performance beyond itself.

metalinguistic

The *metalinguistic* element - that is, the matter of Cunningham's
manipulation of codes and norms - has already been discussed
which leaves, according to Jacobson,[9] the *phatic* element. This
element sets up the possibility of communication, putting in
place access to the virtual world of the work and of maintaining
its world [or disrupting it] for the duration of the performance.
Cunningham is quite traditional in this. The work begins as the
house lights go down, it continues uninterrupted for its
intended period and stops. All transitions are taken care of, all
exits and entrances smoothly dealt with, no surprises of lights
going on and off `a la Forsythe, no coming in and out of the
virtual cyber world - just a seamless kaleidoscope of differences.

These six functions of communication, articulated as elements
to be adhered to in message sending, but in art used as
elements to question and disrupt, have perversely assisted me in
considering the ways in which I might engage with a work that
has no aspirations to communicate. Certainly, unless one is
prepared to interact pro-actively with Cunningham's work,
rather than wait to be communicated with by him, the
performance may pall, and comparison with other ways of
dancing messages might creep into your consciousness. Of the
six functions, he is relying on the aesthetic markedly [and
markedly assisted in this by his composer], plus his enormous
metalinguistic innovations and the modernity of the work's
references. The injunctive response he leaves up to the spectator,
the performative function is constrained, and the phatic is
traditional. The question must be: can the level of and nature of
his innovation and the contemporary nature of his references
hold a 2001 audience's aesthetic attention for 45 minutes? And
does it matter if for most people BIPED did with acclaim, and
for some others it could not?

Jacobson's seminal model of communication is quoted and
given a context of earlier models and later developments in
Fiske (1990) and is critiqued and adapted for musicology in
Nattiez (1990). It is the basis for Guiraud's discourse on
linguistic communication (1975). It does not need to be said
that it is implausible to take a model designed for linguistics,
even one adapted for musicology, and expect it to be valid for a
very different means of interpersonal engagement, dance. Dance
is not a language, it does not have a grammar. When the term
'language' is applied to dance by dance people (Mary Wigman
in her book The Language of Dance, Ann Hutchinson Guest in
her teaching method The Language of Dance) it functions as a
metaphor, not a factual statement. Some dancers feel as if they
were "speaking" but they are not, and they know that they are

Jacobson, Molino,
Nattiez and
a choreological
perspective

---

8 This function is termed 'the emotive' function in linguistic theory but that is problematic in dance since emotions are often
primary matters referred to and not something added by the dancer's commitment. The latter may not be emotive at all.
Whether 'performative' is more appropriate is open to discussion.

9 Jacobson's model for communication, quoted and given context in Fiske, (1990, p.35 et seq).

not for they quite specifically say that what is being "said" is unsayable in words and only danceable. The term "grammar of dance" is used again metaphorically[10] to point to the structures in time and space that hold a work together but in fact no such thing exists and, if anything, several quasi-grammars [structures] can be thought to exist for the various genres of dance, and even for individual choreographer's oeuvres.

Nattiez's translation of Roman Jacobson reads:

	Context	
	Message	
Addresser	**Contact**	**Addressee**
	Code	

As Jacobson explained the diagram, "the addresser sends a message to the addressee. To be operative the message requires a context referred to......, must be siezable by the addressee, and either verbal or capable of being verbalised; a code fully, or at least partially, common to the addresser and the addressee (or in other words to the encoder and decoder of the message); and finally a contact, a physical channel and psychological connection between the addresser and the addressee, enabling both of them to enter into and stay in communication" (Jacobson, 1963, p. 213 -14) (in Nattiez, 1990, p.18).

Jean Molino's proposal for semiology of the arts, developing Peirces's original work, critiques the even simpler schema on which Jacobson bases his position.

"Producer"·············> **Message** ·················> **Receiver**

We might suppose that Molino... was merely re-covering a classic schema for "communication". This is not at all the case. For this traditional schema we need to substitute the following diagram, one that makes no sense except when connected to the theory of the interpretant:

| **Poietic process** | **Esthesic process** |
| **"Producer"**·············> **Trace** <················· **Receiver** |

Here the arrow on the right - and this makes all the difference - has been reversed (Nattiez, 1990, pp. 16-17).

Molino, considering not prose but poetry, proposed that, far from understanding a message, the addressee of a poem constructs his own meaning. That is what occurs when the codes in which the message is embodied are not entirely, or at all, shared, he asserts. Since in the arts innovation is a code breaking activity, especially in the avant-garde arts, the construction of meaning is what is undertaken in making sense, of poetry, of music and of dance. Molino goes on to show that the interpretant (interpretation) of a work alters every time it is seen since the second viewing is influenced by the first interpretant, and that that process is on-going and never complete.[11] This never ending process of meaning construction is termed by Molino an esthesic process and produces an *esthesic layer of meaning* with each (reading of a poem) viewing of a work. Molino continues by identifying a layer of meaning that is evident in the processes of making, evident in "the rules of the game" laid down by the artist as he makes. These "rules" are evident in the making of abstract as well as referential works and are meaningful in the sense that the intention and manner of structuring can be seen to be present. These processes Molino terms "poietic processes" and provide a *layer of poietic meanings* in the work. Molino completes his tripartition by discussing the layer of meaning that is in "the trace". The trace is defined as:

> *the material reality of the work (its live production, its score, its printed text) that is, the physical traces that result from the poietic process.* (ibid. p.12).

The trace is a level of meaning that is accessible to us because it is actual, embodied in the material of the work and available to us through our senses, while the poietic levels have to be searched for, or require prior knowledge of the making processes. The esthesic level is dependent on the lived experience of "receivers".

What has to be asked is: does the concept of three semiotic levels - the poietic, the trace and the esthesic - have any value for dance? Referring back to Cunningham's <u>BIPED</u>, my position is that it might add considerably to an engagement with it while disrupting and enlarging Jacobson's perspective. It can be argued that having access to the poietic signs of Cunningham's methods contributes to an appreciation of his work, while the signs in the fabric of the performance (the trace) are a broad cultural comment and may be missed. The esthesic level of BIPED is multi-interpretational, open to each viewer to make of it what he/she will, and these interpretants add a layer to the recognition that his work is a performative negotiating work (and not a form of communication).

poietic, the trace, esthesis layers and dance

These ideas will only be helpful to dance if we combine them with the choreological perspective discussed in Part 1 of this text, in particular with the tripartite perspective of making, performing and appreciating as processes. Nattiez presumes a reductive position since he is writing primarily for classical musicians and their way of working traditionally includes the composer as maker, alone, writing the score, the instrumentalists or singers as performers of the score, and the concert goer and/or musicologist as appreciator. He associates the poietic with the composer as person rather than with the process of composing (or making). In dance, the making process is undertaken by both choreographer and performer, as already discussed, and in some current events by the spectator also.[12]

---

[10] Jean Johnson Jones, notator, quoted in Preston-Dunlop, V. (1995).

[11] The term "interpretant" is "a mental concept produced both by the sign and by the user's experience of the object" referred to. (Fiske, p.42) A sign stands for something, to somebody, (eg the word DOG) and that sign (DOG) is shown\said to a second person and creates in that person a similar imagined sign or a more developed one (their idea of DOG). The second person's "mental concept" of DOG is an interpretant sign.

[12] A striking example of the spectator becoming the work was in the Tate Modern, where people looking at Louise Bourgeois's installation "Toi et Moi: I do I undo I redo" in the main turbine hall were invited to climb its staircase to a look out. They are watched by gallery visitors standing on the main viewing platform, who in turn are watched by the people from the look out.

Jacobson's model is directed to understanding the content of 'the trace'.[13] He does not apply the functions more broadly to the poietic making processes and the esthesic interpretants. His concept of the (emotive) performative function is the added layer that the (speaker) performer gives to what has to be (said) performed at the moment of the event. However, in dance, particularly postmodern dance, performers may also be the generators of the material. They may not add anything to the material since they *are* the material. Jacobson's concept of the (speaker's) performer's addition holds good in traditional dance where given steps, as written in the movement score, are interpreted by the dancer. In a main stream ballet company in Britain, such as The Royal Ballet or Birmingham Royal Ballet, the choreologist's score written in dance notation is regarded as the work, the text of the performance. The *corps de ballet* are asked to add nothing to it beyond unified articulation while a soloist offers a dramatic interpretation of it.

Jacobson's model was conceived as illuminating primarily verbal language as a communicator. Pierre Guiraud is broader, in that, although he regards Jacobson's concepts as compatible with both communication and semiotics, he regards verbal language as a special case and semiotics primarily as

> *the study of non-linguistic sign systems* (Guiraud, 1975, p.1).

critique of communication theory for dance

Hence Guiraud's writing opens up beyond verbal language the kinds of embodiment that he sees as mediating communication and sign systems - the paralinguistic aspects of social interaction, for example head nods, hand shakes. His examples are not wide enough for the kinds of materials embodying signs of a work of dance theatre: theatre codes, lighting, shoe tapping, movement systems, etc.

For dance, we need also, and fundamentally, to look and listen to the work phenomenally; to live it and not to look and listen only for meaning in it. Indeed the term 'the plane of intersection of phenomenology and semiotics' as the experiential place where a dance performance is, illuminates the multi-engagement with a work from spontaneous, irrational, personal, corporeal absorption to intellectual searching for significance, concurrently, that audiences bring to an event.

Is the esthesic level in music analogous to the esthesic in dance? In music it begins with the musician's interpretation of the composer-generated score and concludes with the concert goer's constructed interpretant - two distinct occasions and two distinct sets of people involved. In dance it begins much earlier, in the period of making, since the three processes of making, performing and appreciating are almost concurrent in the dance studio. The dancers may interpret the choreographer's instructions or watch each other or make sense of what they are in the process of refining, or generate the material themselves, all in one rehearsal. The processes may be concurrent again during a dance performance.

Molino/Nattiez's ideas about signification remain further problematic unless we remember that the medium of dance is multistranded. It is the notes in music that are discussed by Nattiez as the medium of music while for dance it is, as stated, at least the performer, the movement, the sound and the space, and their nexus. It is in any sub-strand of that entire nexus that a sign is created. Molino/Nattiez's ideas can contribute but not suffice for we have to remember that dance is not about understanding, primarily, but about engaging with the work phenomenally and searching for meaning, maybe.[14]

engaging with Tavener's The Fool (2000)

With Molino/Nattiez concepts in mind, tempered by choreological essentials, I turn to John Tavener's work. I chose The Fool for this discussion because it is a border- crossing work, Tavener's music being, through Bailey, a multistranded event. I witnessed the première which was attended by Tavener.

Tavener/Bailey, The Fool Ivan Kyncl

[13] A longer discussion is required than can be undertaken here on what "the trace" is in dance. As originally conceived by Molino, the trace was the published written poem, therefore embodied as marks on paper. The concept continued in that vein by Nattiez to be the musical score as written by the composer, but Nattiez was challenged by the practice of jazz music, folk singing et al for which a score is not apposite. What was "the trace" for a jazz trio improvisation? Since dance has such varied genres, for some, ballet in particular, the concept of the written score is appropriate but for others such as a tanztheater work, a video dance, it is clearly inappropriate. From a choreological perspective, a working definition of the trace might be: the embodiment of that mix of the nexus of the strands of the dance medium deemed to be essential in each performance of the work. See Rubidge's essay in Part 2 for a further discussion.

[14] In October 2000 I saw the new Corder work performed at the Royal Opera House. There was no purpose in searching for meaning there but rather in celebrating with the company their joy in classicism.

My poietic knowledge was limited to experience of Tavener's choral music primarily as a listener but somewhat as an amateur singer. In company with millions of others I had seen and heard his elegiac <u>Song for Athene</u>, sung as the draped coffin of Princess Diana was slowly transported down the aisle of Westminster Abbey, to pause on the threshold as the sound crescendoed its lament of mourning. I had sung Taverner's choral setting, "simple yet penetrating," of William Blake's 1789 poem <u>The Lamb</u> "that beautifully conveys the tenderness of divine love expressed through every living thing."[15] I had attended the première of his vast cori spezzati composition <u>Apocalypse</u> at a BBC Promenade concert in 1994, a work for huge forces performed in the Royal Albert Hall. Blake, whose mystic <u>Songs of Innocence</u> had inspired Tavener, was both painter, engraver, poet and visionary. The Tate Britain's Blake exhibition (2000 -01) evoked for me the depth of his spiritual conviction as well as presenting his idiosyncratic imagery. Tavener's feeling for Blake, his love of Christian Orthodox liturgy, biblical and Islamic texts inspire the simple but profound musical statements of intense choral harmony which appear in his prolific output. His work is not heady spirituality but physical in its uncompromising embodiment of human feeling. It is easy to see why he is attracted to the corporeal way of directing that Lucy Bailey brings to the production of <u>The Fool</u>.

The programme tells us that the event is

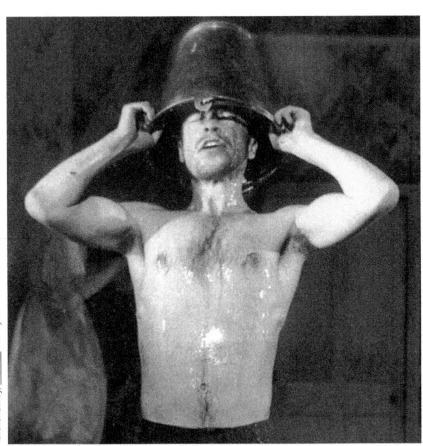

Tavener/Bailey, <u>The Fool</u> *Ivan Kyncl*

a contemporary parable for salvation and deals with the meaning of life
and death through the portrait of a 'Fool for Christ' (Stewart, 2000).

The participants are the Fool, who is a singer/cellist, seven
string players, and The Pegasus Choir, mostly off-stage. It takes
place in a white box set with perspective designed by Bunny
Christie and lit by Chris Davey.

I, and others, were immediately struck by innovation in the
musicians' behaviour, the string playing "gogmagogs". They
rupture the norm for musicians. They do not sit to play from
music scores on stands but are moving performers, almost
dancers who play. Scanning their biographical notes it is clear
that there is a poietic level to be found, for several have studied
with the Théâtre de Complicité[16] and several are members of
jazz, pop and rock bands as well as of contemporary music
groups. They are entering the event with the phenomenal
engagement that such experiences prepared them for. These
players, when still, are alert and alive in designed grouped
stillnesses, framing the main protagonist, the Fool, with whom
they are juxtaposed, not integrated.

engaging with the work

> *It is only through mockery, indecency, vulgarity, folly, vulnerability and in*
> *an almost indescribable anguish which tears him to pieces, can we*
> *understand the depth of 'the Fool for Christ's Sake' (ibid.).*

So writes John Tavener in the programme note. The Fool enacts
and sings all of those things, sometimes raucous and wild,
sometimes collapsing and inebriated. The gogmagogs, in white,
act as voyeurs of his anguish, detached but ever present
themselves. Who are these people, one asks oneself,
constructing and deconstructing various scenarios for these
angelic(?) figures. The strangeness of the figures with their
mesmerising string-played music, their contrast with the vulgar
Fool, the short pithy scenes drew me in. The weird world of
The Fool is so constructed and entered into by all participants
that I, and, it seemed, all the other spectators with me, engaged
with the piece and started to live it. Let understanding go hang
or at any rate wait its due time.

What signs could I recognise to help me appreciate more deeply
what I was seeing? What is in the trace, the strands of the
medium of the performance available to perception? In the
white space is a bedstead, on which a prone Fool lies in the
opening scene. Around the bed are various, almost invisible
levels on which the players are designed, including one halfway
up the wall, from which a player appears to be suspended. Each
short scene begins from, and ends with, a blackout during
which the players shift their positions in the set into a new
grouping in relation to the Fool. They are integrated with him
in terms of focus but not in behaviour or voice or movement

signs ?

---

[15] Richard Steinitz in the sleeve notes for the CD of Tavener's Innocence, (1995).

[16] The theatre company who concentrate on the physicality of the performance, movement being a main medium of their theatrical exploration.

quality. Fools, in their heydey of the sixteenth century, I read, were solitary figures, apart, part hermit, part vagabond.

The programme tells me scene 1 was "Good Friday (Death of Christ)." I say "was" because I had no idea what it was until after the event. I recognised no images of the Good Friday I know: no visible crucifix, no weeping mother, no robbers beside Jesus, no tomb, no Stations of the Cross intrinsic to Catholicism. But then Tavener is a convert to Greek Orthodoxy, with a vehement hostility to papal Catholicism. I read what Mother Theka, the octagenarian Abbess of an Orthodox Monastery, had to say about the text she has written for the piece with her long-time collaborator:

> The minimal text for The Fool is written as if words are no longer important and completely incidental to the real matter at hand (ibid.).

I comforted myself that I was on target to have given up trying to understand the words, the work. I simply li(o)ved it. Latterly, Mother Theka's writing:

> has become more sparse, with huge concepts contained in three or four words (ibid.).

Tavener too writes sparsely, uncompromisingly and repetitively, his harmonic sonorities readily recognisable, full of labile tensions and extremes of pitch that one knows confidently he will resolve. His music is idiosyncratic and profound to the organisers of his festival Ikons of Light.

communicating transacting ?

The piece moves from scene to scene shifting the spacing in the [relatively] small area of the "set with bed". The Fool falls, the Fool sleeps, the Fool takes off his shirt, the Fool carries his 'cello. Subtle mood changes, pace changes, foci are all that there are for you to hang on to if you must try to understand. Like BIPED, this piece engrosses by its metalinguistic function; it breaks every expectation (the off stage choir burst in at "Christmas" in party mood, only to freeze mid-voice, carry on partying and freeze again) and by its aesthetic function. Lucy Bailey's eye for the physical expression of geometry, for dynamic physicality, is combined with an exquisite editing and restraining hand so that the whole event is in sympathy with the white on whiteness of the set. It has in abundance what BIPED eschewed: the performative layer, functioning through the intention and integrity added by the musicians to what they have to play, through their training, their treatment by Bailey, and her and her co-director Nell Catchpole's desire

> to release the physical expression of the classical musician (ibid.).

Is the work injunctive? It will arouse a response from several perspectives not least through its tension between tradition and the new. For example: a committed Christian may be surprised - even outraged - by the Fool's treatment of the church's festivals, while a musician may be enchanted by the freedom of movement of the string players or worried by the border crossing nature of the genre. No one can be [was] unmoved.

Structurally, in terms of the use of juxtaposition rather than integration of performer, text, and all aspects of the medium, the work seems to succeed in saying:

> The fool challenges the world by flagrant inversion of accepted moral and spiritual values (ibid.).

It allows one, after the event, to consider one's moral and spiritual values and thereby to construct a meaningful relationship with the work as an added layer to the phenomenal experience of living the work. I found that the phenomenon was all-pervading and any esthesic interpretant that I might have constructed had to wait. Looking back, searching for poietic references, plenty could have been found even from my (limited) knowledge of Tavener's harmonic structures, through my own experience of Blake's Rosicrucian spirituality and Tavener's earlier uses of Christian liturgy. But these seemed irrelevant. It was Bailey's production that inspired my interpretant. For me, it was redolent of the same kind of corporeal veracity I had seen in Theatre de Complicité productions. As a dancer with a Central European training, I entered viscerally into the event. I felt it. My interpretant was less conceptual than kinaesthetic. I understood the work through what Laban would term a bodily perspective. Signs, after all, are "perceivable by our senses" as Guiraud reminds his reader, and the sense that I shared with the performers was not visual, marginally aural, but essentially haptic.

Needless to say, other spectators' esthesic response would be as individually coloured as mine.

a partial analysis of and personal esthesic response to Newson's <u>can we afford this, the cost of living</u> (2000)

Newson does not regard himself as a choreographer but as a director. We know from the programme's text that the work had been devised by the company under his direction. From acquaintance with Newson's earlier work, one can be fairly sure that a message is something that interests him. He writes of his "need to connect meaning to movement" and clarifies:

> To make movement is one thing - to make movement that is about something is a greater challenge for me and what leads DV8's process. (in Beedham, 2000, p.11).

Strange Fish (1993) looked at the tragedy of perceived social incompetence. The company name, DV8, clues a newcomer into Newson's concerns. From Dead Dreams of Monochrome Men (1988), he has done more than expose what society sees as deviance; he has set forth his own position of inclusiveness and offered the spectator the lived experience of people who feel [are] socially excluded or harrassed. Will he continue that concern here? Newson tells us in the same article written during the rehearsal period:

> The current title (can we afford this) sums up the themes of the piece......
> The whole issue of values and expense is central to the work. It is about the
> loss of innocence, trust and ideals. How to hide our (my) disillusionment -
> we smile play the game and pretend that things are all right (ibid.).

This clue to his concerns offers poietic information. The reader cannot be sure that all the ideas will be processed to appear in the performance itself - in Nattiez's terms, "in the material trace". Some may remain unembodied, unmaterialised in the complex medium of a theatre work, or be so hidden that they cannot be recognised, or edited out during the rehearsal process.

A work of performing art is regarded as a symbolic form. Nattiez writes

> a symbolic form of art is not some "intermediary" in a process of
> "communication" that transmits the meaning intended by the author

but is instead

> the result of a complex process of creation (the poietic process) which has
> to do with the form as well as the content of the work

and also

> the point of departure for a complex process of reception (the esthesic
> process) that reconstructs a "message"(1990, p.17).

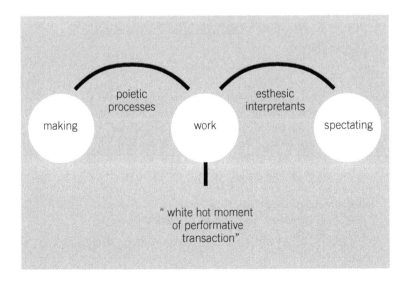

While Nattiez's ideas of a symbolic work might serve well for music, a work of physical theatre such as Newson's confounds it as too limited a view, for the work contains not only material trace that is connotive and thereby open to esthesic reconstruction, but images that are denotive and thereby referential signs intended to communicate directly. The undoubted success of Newson's productions may lie in how this complexity allows the spectator to function as both receiver of Newson's injunctive trace and concurrently creators of interpretants through their engagement of themselves with it.

the valueful event

The first thing that Newson does in the event is to insist on commencing the connection between stage and auditorium exactly when he said he would. The evening's work is scheduled to begin at 7.45, the public in the foyer are warned that it will, a large clock ticks away on stage and on the dot of 7.45 the show begins. The connecting channels between artists and spectators are opened up, on time, and latecomers will wait. Is this a counter blast to William Forsythe's now famous play with the phatic function at Covent Garden? He deliberately began <u>Steptext</u> before the Royal Opera House spectators were fully seated and before the behind scenes crew had left the stage, so generating consternation and confusion in the auditorium. Newson's device had the effect of congratulating the seated and embarrassing the late comers, while asserting who was in charge. It was a combined phatic and injunctive act.

One of the "values" named by Newson in this work concerns bodies and what it is like to be one that does not conform to society's norm. Newson's cast is a mix of what might commonly be called the "beautiful" and the "unbeautiful". Newson is focusing on a current debate on how society pressures itself to desire a particular kind of body, and how the influential powers in our consumer world attempt to dictate what "beautiful" might be. Hence, obesity, physical disability and age are at home in his cast with the ballet-trained body, the dextrous body, the tough and the delicate, the hirsute and the bald. His message accumulates, in my reading, as: none of these corporeal conditions is more or less valuable than any other and that living is in any case a costly business, having all manner of "costs" for each individual. The words of the last song sung by the cast are "You are so beautiful".

using the injunctive

This work is injunctive. It gets half its message over by an "in your face" presentation of all manner of bodies. It is David Toole who epitomises the issue, and Toole who is the shock factor for a lot of people. Newson expertly helps people through the inevitable curiosity about David's body by having a fellow performer quiz him about the parts of himself that are apparently not there so that we can all get on with the further layers of Newson's message / material trace. Before that, and still working with the injunctive, the spectator now knows what happens to unfettered male genitalia during a pas de basque and a battement six as danced by another cast member, the warning THIS PRODUCTION MAY CONTAIN SCENES AND LANGUAGE OF AN ADULT NATURE...... having been enacted.

Pursuing values of equality beyond difference, this time in the dancing itself, the aesthetic qualities of his work have their time. Starting from ballet expertly performed, Newson offers a delicious transition from that genre to contemporary dance. He, with his cast, have deconstructed the form of ballet and, bit by bit, transform a "pas" into a piece of "material". What is the difference? If one is a "pas" and the other "material", so what? Newson presents the ludicrous barrier between the two, put there by people's perception, not by the movement itself.

He proceeds to elicit from each cast member material that he or she is extremely dextrous at performing. The performative layer is used for us to engage with the gifts, talents and personality of each member, their skills being in direct conflict with society's view of their potential because of the current hang up on the 'body beautiful' concept. The material ranges from juggling, to virtuosic "keen as mustard" dancing, to dancing on your hands, with Byron Perry, Paul Capsis and David Toole to Diana Payne Myers telling us that she had several young lovers at her 72 years of age. Choose your skill. As Newson writes, "DV8's work is about individuals."

referring and metaphors

Alongside Newson's use of the injunctive, the performative, the aesthetic, is his need of reference since everything that is danced and said acts as a metaphor for his theme: values? whose? at what expense? The title Newson finally decided upon affects what references spectators might pick up. What does he have in mind by "cost"? Literally finance and its endless problems? Or human cost? Emotional cost? As those thoughts mill around in my head - after the show not during it - my esthesic response to the work mills too and then settles as an interpretant.

The set is an impressive installation constructed by Steel The Scene, used primarily as a means of containing and connecting each scene so that the phatic channel remains open between spectators and performers throughout. The way the highly raked back of the installation lowers and rises is intriguing as well as providing an unusual means of exit and entrance. The work was originally planned as site-specific, in the funfair Luna Park in Sydney during the year the Olympics were held there. Newson tells us that the original title as the work began was Funnyland and "it became Wasted" and later can we afford this. But Luna Park pulled out. What does that piece of poietic knowledge offer the spectator? My mind takes in the values of the superb bodies of Olympic athletes; the word 'wasted'; the use Newson has made in the past of extensive hydraulically operated sets and water; the dynamic potential of the funfair in Sydney and the static potential of the Queen Elizabeth Hall. The cost of having to change gear mid-project is considerable.

Jacobson's sixth communicative function, the metalinguistic, is subtly used throughout the event. What rules and norms is Newson celebrating or rupturing in this production? For some people, the whole theme of bodies unbeautiful / beautiful in a performance with dance is norm-breaking. It is not a new topic: other works have celebrated disability as ability through Candoco Company's telling repertoire. Maguy Marin's well known dance for plump dancers dressed in blown up costumes was a look at extremes of physicality and there is nothing new these days in male nudity. So aggressive or astounding newness was not present, for me, but it clearly was for many spectators.

Lloyd Newson, can we afford this: the cost of living © 2000 Jane Joyce

This is a border-nudging event. Performers speak directly to the audience in an event in which classical dance is danced beautifully. These two things rarely go together. Physiques of all sorts, skills of all sorts, juxtapose. The work shifts between movement materials from diverse genres. The separateness of the "grammars" of dance is addressed and the separation erased. Newson shows his mastery of movement manipulation eliciting new movement material unique to each dancer, not necessarily new to the domain of physical theatre. These he structures together as a chain of original events exploring a common theme. In that respect there was a similarity of structure with that preferred by Pina Bausch in her tanztheater works; an episodic way of addressing her theme focally from several points of view. Looking at the ages of the audience members at QEH and their diversity, I suspect that many will not be familiar with Bausch so that the structural episodic method here may well be received as innovative and exciting while for others, it would seem familiar and reassuring.

response

My esthesic response to <u>can we afford this, the cost of living</u> shifted, starting with my first during-the-show interpretants based on the immediate mix of phenomenal, body-mediated and semiotic engagement with the work. On the way home I had time to let that merge with my personal experience of its themes, bodies, values, costs, Newson's previous works, my own experience of putting work on, my acquaintance with Bausch's work, with other events at the QEH and more. As Nattiez expected, my interpretants changed and shifted, each one building on or refuting the first. Weeks later I read the Dance Theatre Journal article written by Newson and DV8 performer Rob Tannion referred to above. My thoughts of the work shifted again as poietic information and trace experience engaged.

Esthesic, in Molino / Nattiez terms, refers to signs. Was it my shifting interpretation of the signs in the work that remained with me? Is that it? Yes but, much more vivid are the flavours of the work as a whole, the physical feel of the evening, the visual impact of the stage, the artistry of the performers felt in my own body - a mesh of feelings phenomenal and semiotic.

Lloyd Newson, <u>can we afford this: the cost of living</u>

dance and music works cited and bibliography

Cunningham, Merce	Summer Space	Cunningham Dance Company	1958
	Rainforest	Cunningham Dance Company	1968
	BIPED	Cunningham Dance Company	1999
Forsythe, William	Steptext	Royal Ballet	1999
Newson, Lloyd	Dead Dreams of Monochrome Men	DV8 Physical Theatre	1988
	Strange Fish	DV8 Physical Theatre	1993
	Can we afford this: the cost of living	DV8 Physical Theatre	2000
Tavener, John and Bailey, Lucy	The Fool	the gogmagogs	2000
Tavener, John	The Lamb		1982
	Song for Athene		1993
	Apocolypse		1994

Atlas, Charles (director) with Lockyer, Bob (executive producer) (2000). *Merce Cunningham: A Lifetime in Dance.* (in the series *Summer Dance*) (a collaborative programme by BBC and Thirteen/WNET). London: British Broadcasting Corporation.

Beedham, E. (ed) (2000). Perfection and Pretense. *Dance Theatre Journal,* Vol,16, No. 3.

Cohen, S.J. (1968). *Dance Perspectives,* 34.

Fiske, J. (1990). *Introduction to Communication Studies.* London: Routledge.

Guiraud, P. (1975). *Semiology.* London: RKP.

Jacobson, R. (1963). *Essais de linguistique générale.* Paris: Minuit.

Loader, K. (executive director) (1986). *Face to Face with Jeremy Isaacs: Merce Cunningham.* London: British Broadcasting Corporation.

Nattiez, J.J. (1990). *Music and Discourse.* Princeton: Princeton University Press.

Preston-Dunlop.V. (ed) (1995). *Dance Words.* London: Harwood Academic.

Richter, H. (1965). *Dada Art and Anti-Art.* Oxford: Oxford University Press.

Steinitz, R. (1995). Sleeve notes to CD of *Tavener's Innocence.*

Stewart. A. (2000). Programme notes for *"Ikons of Light: The Inspiration of John Tavener".*

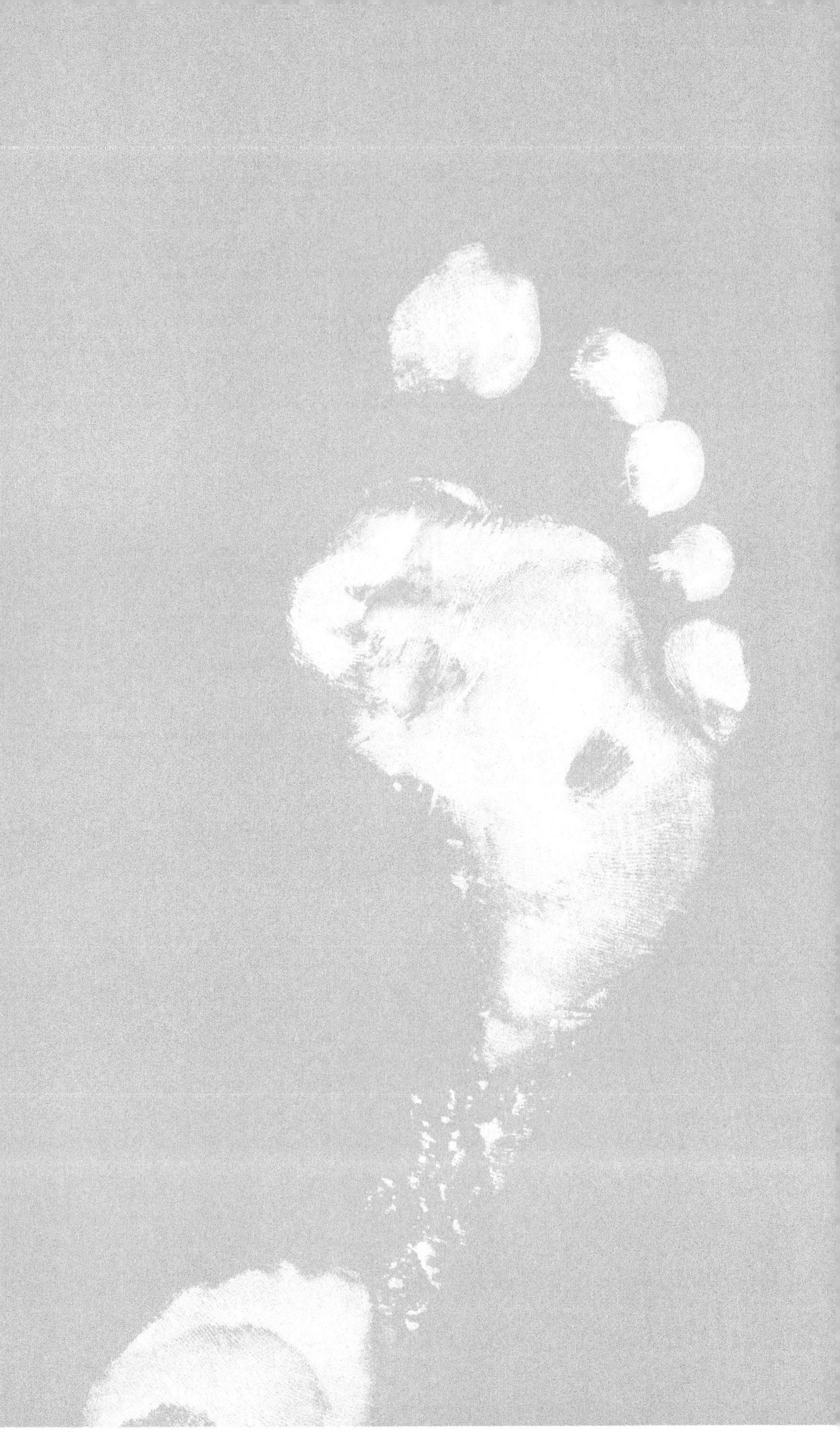

permission for the use of the following visual images is gratefully acknowledged:

William Forsythe for cover image of Frankfurt Ballett in <u>Artifact</u>, *photo. Dieter Schwer*, and <u>Quintett</u>, *photo. Dominik Mentzos*

Courtesy Cunningham Dance Foundation for Merce Cunninghams' <u>BIPED</u>, *photo. Stephanie Berger*

The Gogmagogs for Lucy Bailey's production of John Tavener 's <u>The Fool</u>, *photo. Ivan Kyncl*

Dansgroep Krisztina de Châtel for the company in de Châtel's <u>Paletta</u>, *photo. Ben Van Duin*

DV8 Physical Theatre for Lloyd Newson's <u>can we afford this: the cost of living</u>, *photo. Jane Joyce, Jimmy Pozarik and Michael Rayner*

Tanztheater Wuppertal for images of Pina Bausch's <u>1980</u> and <u>Café Müller</u>, *photo. Gert Weigelt*

Swedish Royal Ballet for Ulysses Dove's <u>Dancing on the Front Porch of Heaven</u>, *photo. Mats Bäcker*

Transitions Dance Company for Stuart Hopps' <u>Dr Dollie's Follies</u>, *photo. Chris Nash;* for Lea Anderson's <u>Les Six Belles</u> and <u>Factor 6</u>, *photo. Toni Nandi, Fred Whisker;* for Hervé Jourdet's <u>Crabs</u>, *photo. Chris Nash;* for Barak Marshall's <u>Susan and the Saints and the Neighbours</u>, *photo. Toni Nandi;* for <u>Iris Fung Chi Sun</u>, *photo. Fred Whisker;* for Hélène Blackburn's <u>Black Embrace</u>, *photo. Chris Nash*

Lea Anderson for <u>The Cholmondeleys, the Featherstonehaughs and the Victims of Death in Smithereens</u>, *photo. Anderson*

Ana Sanchez-Colberg for images of Theatre enCorps in <u>Futur/Perfekt</u>, *photo. Max Thielmann, Paul Houghton and Liam Muir.*

For drawing from The Classic Ballet by Lincoln Kirstein and Muriel Stuart, copyright 1952 by Lincoln Kirstein. Used by permission of Adolf A. Knopf, a division of Random House, Inc.

Eakins Press Foundation for Baron Adolf Meyer's photograph of Nijinsky in <u>L'Après-midi d'un Faune</u>

Trisha Brown Dance Company for M/s Brown in <u>Watermotor</u>, *photo. Lois Greenfield*

Dance Notation Bureau for excerpt from Labanotation score by Els Grelinger of Charles Weidman's <u>Lynchtown</u>; excerpt from score of Lester Horton's <u>The Beloved</u>

V&A Picture Library/Theatre Museum for Robert Cohan's <u>Cell</u>, *photo. Anthony Crickmay*

John C. and Anastasia Lyra for <u>Xedia Polis</u>, *photo. Takis Anagnostopoulos*

Paula Salosaari for drawing

Toni Nandi for Valerie Preston-Dunlop's re-creations of Laban's <u>Kammertanz</u> repertoire

Thames and Hudson Ltd for Hugo Ball's poem <u>Karawane</u> from Richter's <u>DADA : Art and Anti-art</u>

Rosemary Butcher for Butcher's <u>The Site</u>

Scapino Ballet Rotterdam for images from Ed Wubbe's <u>Kathleen</u>, *photo. Hans Gerritsen*

New York Public Library for Martha Graham's <u>Errand into the Maze</u>, *photo. anon*

Leslie E Spatt for the Royal Ballet in Forsythe's <u>Steptext</u>; for Dutch National Ballet's mounting of Kurt Jooss' <u>The Green Table</u>; for Forsythe's <u>Artifact</u>.

Ann Hutchinson-Guest and Anna Markard for excerpt from the Labanotation score of <u>The Green Table</u>

Ann Hutchinson-Guest and Claudia Jeschke for excerpt from the Labanotation score of <u>L'Après-midi d'un Faune</u>.

Laban Collection, Laban Centre London for excerpt from Adda Heynssen's <u>Machine Rhythmns</u>; for Mary Wigman's <u>Hexentanz</u>; for <u>Kammertanzbühne</u> Laban in <u>Die Grünen Clowns</u>; for Tanzbünhne Laban in <u>Gaukelei</u>; for Dusseldorf Stadt Oper in Miloss's <u>Gaukelei</u>; for Folkwangbühne Essen in Jooss's <u>Gaukelei</u>.

Ross Cameron for lighting plan for Thompson and Baker's <u>Intaglio</u>.

Dale Thompson for her <u>Intaglio</u>, *photo. Tony Nandi.*

Dorothy Madden for Madden's <u>Zero Six</u>, *photo. anon.*

Associated Press for <u>Cambodian Casualty</u>.

Ballett Freiburg Pretty Ugly for Amanda Miller's <u>Kunst der Fuge</u>.

Chris Nash for London Contemporary Dance Theatre in Christopher Bruce's <u>Waiting</u>.

A.C.Cooper Ltd photographers for Sophie Fedorovitch's model for Ashton's <u>Symphonic Variations</u>.

KD Producrions for Adventures in Motion Pictures' <u>Swan Lake</u>, chor. Matthew Bourne.

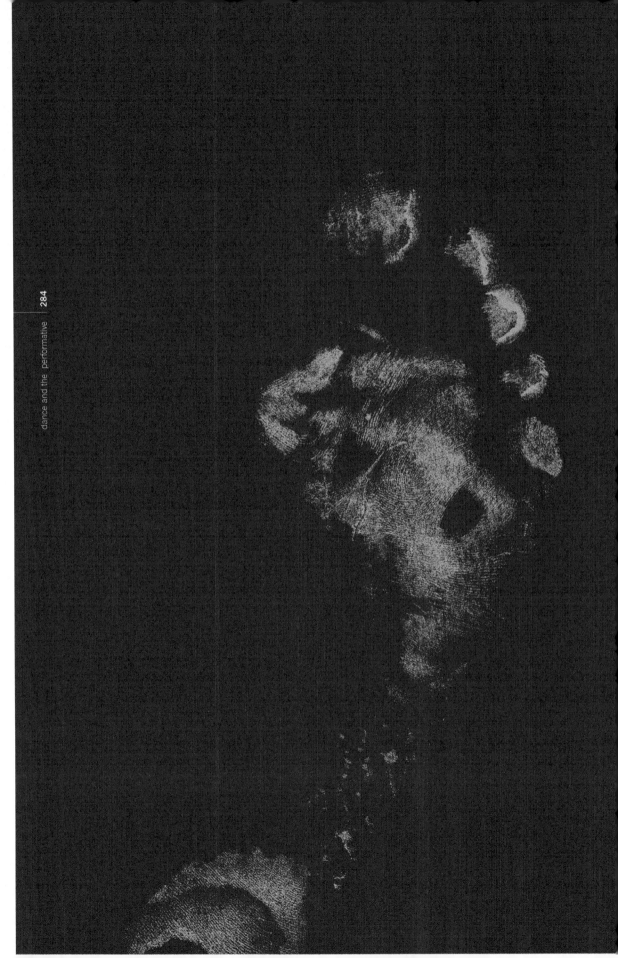

list of illustrations

The Beloved Lester Horton

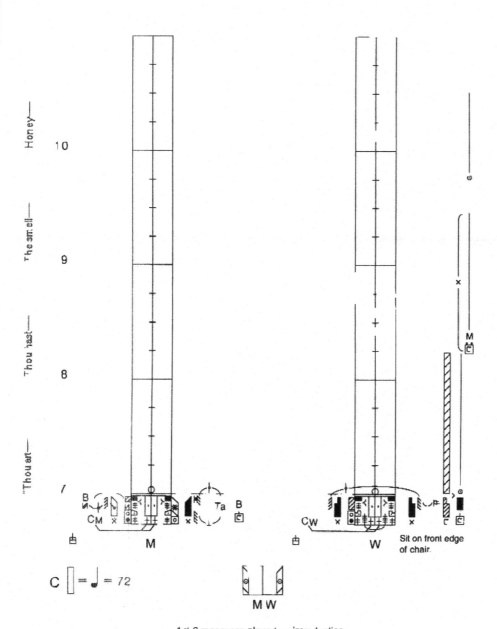

1st 6 measures played as introduction

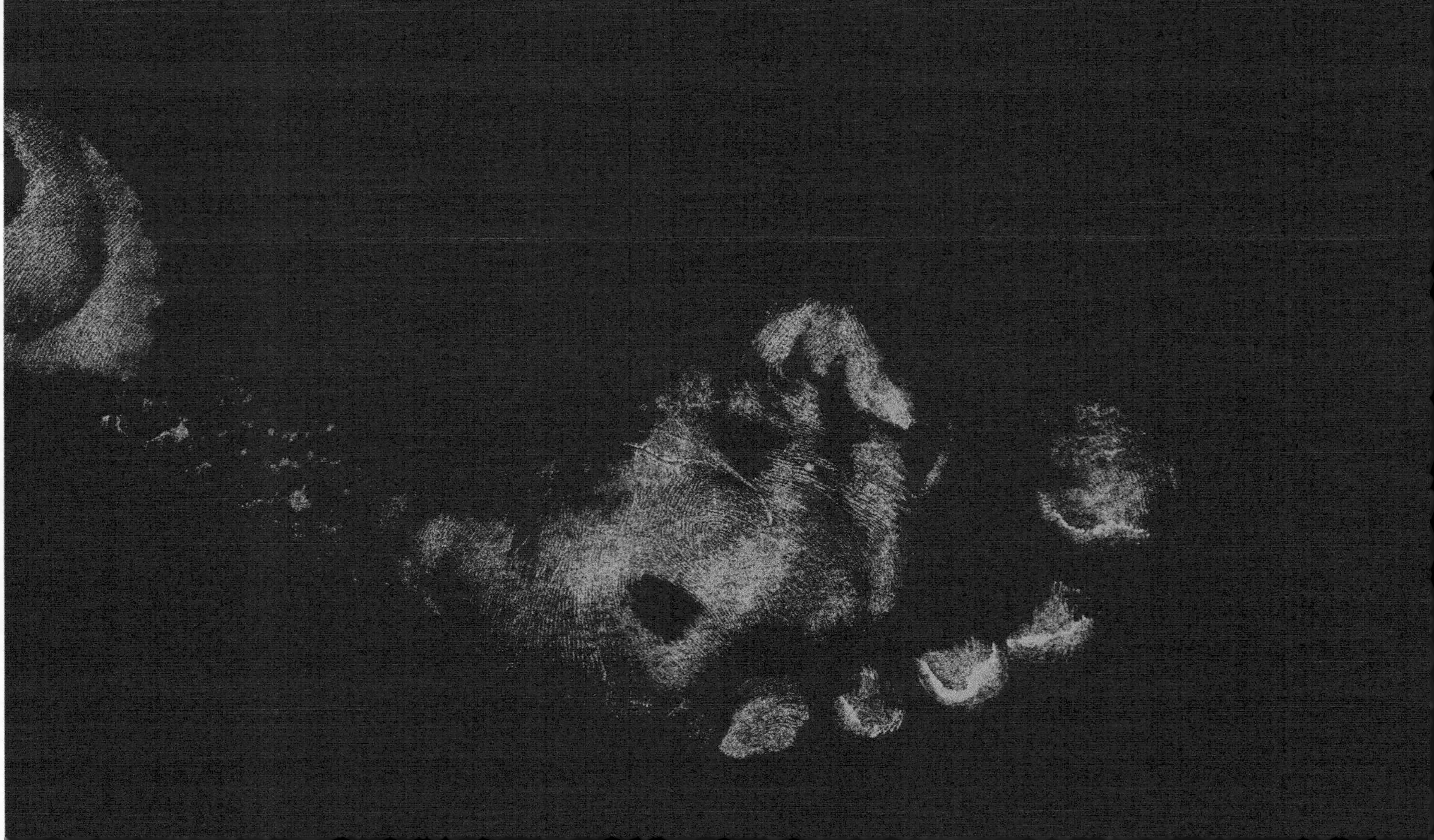

subject index

name index

dance and the performative

name index

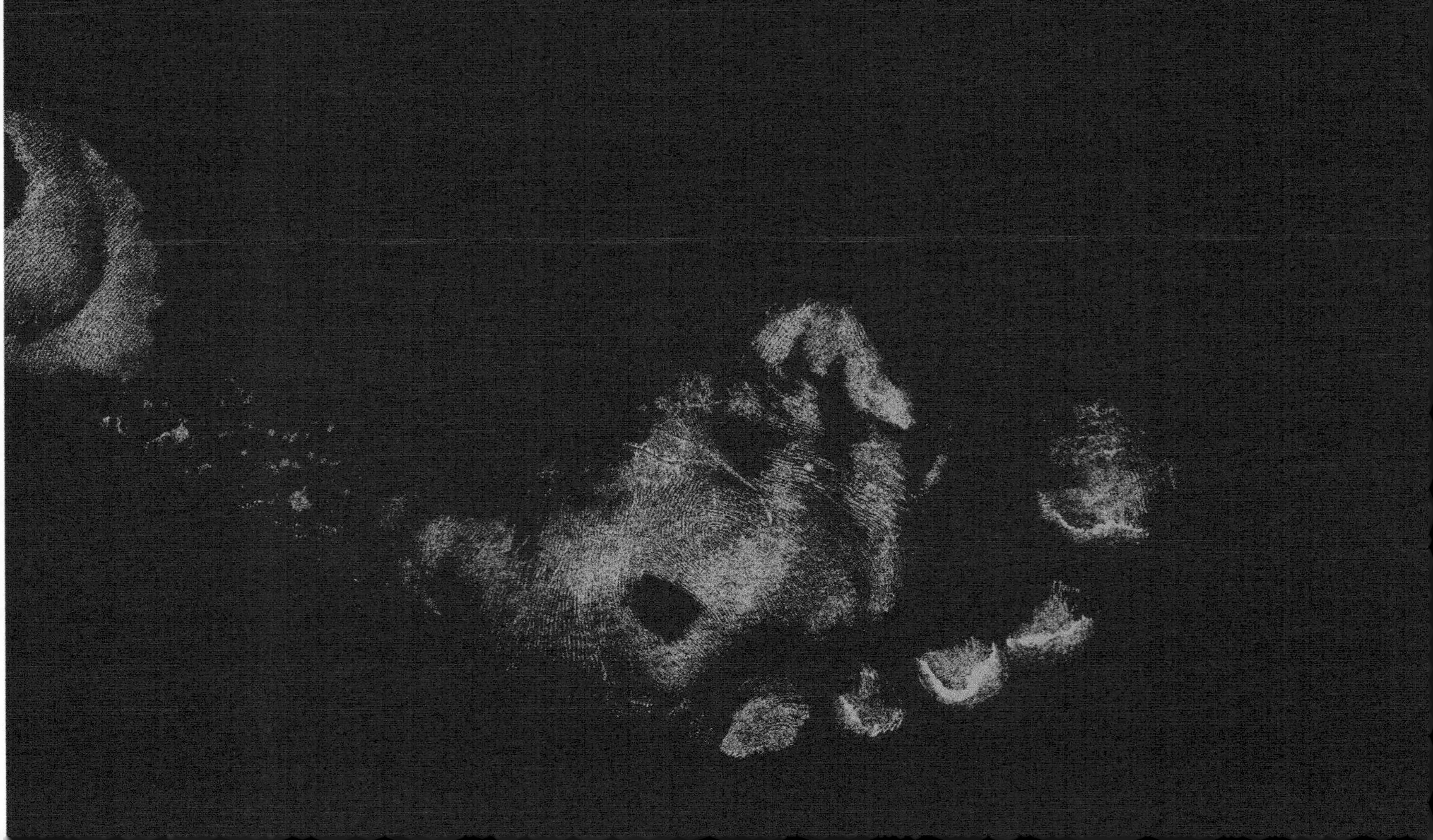

Valerie Preston-Dunlop, MA, PhD commenced her dance training under Rudolf Laban, continuing at the School of Russian Ballet in London and at the Folkwanghochschule in Essen under Kurt Jooss and Albrecht Knust. After performing with British Dance Theatre Preston-Dunlop enjoyed an influential career in dance education. She shifted her practice back into dance as a theatre art through her practical postgraduate research in choreutics and choreography. She is a practical dance scholar, currently consultant for postgraduate studies and research at Laban Centre London. She pioneered the development of Choreological Studies, the practical theory for dance as a performing and performative art. She is a teacher, lecturer, jury member and mentor to young dance artists, researchers and teachers, working internationally, most recently in the dance departments of Keio and Kinki Universities in Japan and Bologna University, Italy. She contributes regularly to Dance Theatre Journal. Her recent major publications are Looking at Dances: A Choreological Perspective on Choreography, (Verve Publishing, 1998) and Rudolf Laban: An Extraordinary Life (Dance Books, 1998), winner of the 1999 de la Torre Bueno prize and the video Recreations of Laban Dances 1923-28.

Ana Sanchez-Colberg, MFA, PhD trained in classical ballet in her native Puerto Rico before turning to contemporary dance. After completing a BA(Hons) in Theatre at the University of Pennsylvania she pursued a Master of Fine Arts (Choreography) at Temple University in Philadelphia. Under the tutelage of Helmut Gottschild (assistant to Mary Wigman in Berlin until 1969) she trained in Wigman, Jooss and tanztheater techniques. During this time Sánchez-Colberg was a member of the Terry Beck Troupe, a Philadelphia-based dance theatre company and Movement Coordinator for Intuitons, a physical theatre company. In 1986, under the auspices of a fellowship from the Institute of Culture of Puerto Rico, she came to England to pursue further dance training and to follow a Ph D programme at Laban Centre London, which she completed in 1992. She established Theatre enCorps in 1989 and has since toured extensively nationally and internationally. Ms Sánchez-Colberg was the recipient of a Bonnie Bird Choreography Award in 1995. She has worked with various international companies including Ballet Concierto de Puerto Rico, the Balletts des Staatstheater Cottbus and Foreign Bodies Dance Company and contributes regularly to dance publications such as Performance Research , Total Theatre Magazine, Animated and Dance Theatre Journal. Ms Sánchez-Colberg currently lectures in Choreography, Theatre Workshop and Choreological Studies at Laban Centre London.

Sarah Rubidge, PhD is an AHRB Research Fellow in the Creative and Performing Arts at University College Chichester. A dance artist who is currently exploring the dialogue between performance and technology, she recently completed a practice-based PhD. at Laban Centre London. Sarah is particularly interested in sustaining a close link between the philosophical ideas in which she is interested and her artisitc work.

Paula Salosaari, MA, PhD has recently completed her Ph.D. degree "Multiple Embodimentin Classical Ballet" at The Theatre Academy in Helsinki, Finland. She currently teaches ballet at Laban Centre London and gives regular courses in dance analyses and ballet at The Theatre Academy, Department of Dance and Theatre Pedagogy.

Frank Werner, MA, born and raised in Germany he lived in Lisbon, received his MA in Dance Studies at the Laban Centre London, and moved to New York City, where he worked in an international performing arts agency and as Development Associate of Stephen Petronio Company, next to becoming correspondent of ballet-tanz. Based currently in Berlin, he publishes in Dance Theatre Journal and elsewhere, and has been consulting with the Goethe Institute and other institutions on both sides of the Atlantic.

Lightning Source UK Ltd.
Milton Keynes UK
UKOW05f1436030816

279863UK00001B/25/P